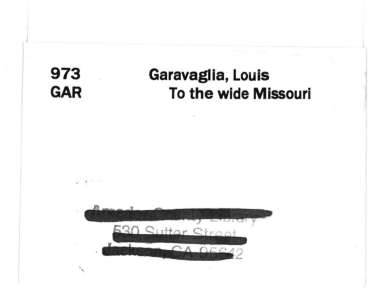

Built in 1813, the Casselman River Bridge in Garrett County, Maryland, was the longest single-span stone arch in the United States at the time. Critics thought the bridge would collapse when the wooden supports used during its construction were removed. Instead, the bridge carried traffic from Conestoga wagons to 12-cylinder Packards along the National Road until late 1933, when this photograph was taken. The bucolic scene above would have been familiar to travelers heading west for more than a century. The bridge is now the centerpiece of Maryland's Casselman River Bridge State Park. (*Historical American Building Survey/Library of Congress*)

TO THE
WIDE MISSOURI

TRAVELING

IN AMERICA DURING THE FIRST DECADES
OF WESTWARD EXPANSION

LOUIS A. GARAVAGLIA

WESTHOLME
Yardley

Westholme Publishing, LLC
904 Edgewood Road
Yardley, Pennsylvania 19067
Visit our Web site at www.westholmepublishing.com

First Printing January 2011
10 9 8 7 6 5 4 3 2 1

ISBN: 978-1-59416-120-9

Printed in the United States of America.

To my parents,
Audrey G. Underdown and the late Louis A. Garavaglia Jr.
For all they gave me.

Contents

List of Maps

PROLOGUE

IN THE UNITED STATES OF 1800, a man on horseback heading for the western country could travel forty miles a day without undue effort. But even leading a pack horse, he could take little with him. On the other hand, a covered wagon drawn by a four-horse team could carry a good deal, but could travel, on average, no more than fifteen miles a day. A three-hundred-mile journey, then, would take nearly three weeks. This rate of fifteen miles a day applied not only to wagons, but to keelboats making their way upriver. Moreover, pushing a keelboat upstream required endless, back-twisting work.

Within forty years, however, the time and effort needed for travel would decrease radically, and, in so doing, would lure thousands upon thousands of people to the West who might not have journeyed there otherwise.

Above, "View from Bushongo Tavern 5 miles from York Town on the Baltimore Road" by James Trenchard (1788). (*Library of Congress*)

Part One

1803-1819

PERHAPS ALEXIS DE TOCQUEVILLE said it best. After a visit to the United States in 1831, he noted that:

> [Americans] have been told that fortune is to be found somewhere toward the west, and they hasten [west] to seek it. . . . Ohio was only founded fifty years ago, most of its inhabitants were not born there, its capital is not thirty years old, and an immense stretch of unclaimed wilderness still covers its territory; nevertheless, the population of Ohio has already started to move west. . . . To start with, emigration was a necessity, [but] now it is a sort of gamble, and they enjoy the sensations as much as the profit. Sometimes man advances so quickly that the wilderness closes in again behind him. The forest has only bent beneath his feet and springs up again when he has passed. Traveling through the new states of the West, one often finds abandoned houses in the middle of the forest.[1]

As John Bradbury wrote in 1817, after sojourns in various states and territories between 1809 and 1811:

> Nothing so strongly indicates the superiority of the western country, as the vast emigrations to it from the eastern and southern states. In passing through the upper parts of Virginia, I observed a great number of farms that had been abandoned, on many of which good houses had been erected, and fine apple and peach orchards had been planted. On enquiring the reason, I was always informed that the owners had gone to the western country. From the New England States the emigrations are still more numerous. They mostly cross the Hudson River betwixt Albany and Newburg, and must pass through Cayuga in their way to Pittsburgh. I was informed by an inhabitant of Cayuga, in April, 1816, that more than fifteen thousand wagons had passed over the bridge at that place within the last eighteen months, containing emigrants to the western country.[2]

In November 1816 an Ohio newspaper, the Columbus *Monitor,* made the same observation:

> Only a few days since, a party of about thirty hardy, enterprising men, from New England, left this place, equipped each with a rifle and two traps, on an expedition to the upper parts of the Missouri... Before this period expires the banks of the Missouri will exhibit extensive settlements—even now the settlement at Boon's Lick, upwards of 500 miles up this river, is said to be increasing with an unusual rapidity. . . . and at Zanesville, in this state, not long since, 50 family waggons crossed the ford of the river in one day.[3]

A resident of Missouri confirmed the news account, saying simply that: "It is *astonishing* in what numbers the people are flocking to this country from every state, and of every description." Henry Schoolcraft, himself in Missouri in 1818, noted that "Emigration is now flowing into this region with unexampled rapidity; already do settlements extend to the mouth of the Osage and Mine rivers."[4]

The first phase of westward migration, in the twelve years following Thomas Jefferson's purchase of the seemingly boundless Louisiana Territory in 1803, was the more noteworthy because the Ohio and Mississippi valleys were continually hearing of wars or rumors of wars. By mid-1807, such events as the Aaron Burr conspiracy—a scheme to take over a large tract of land in the West and secede from the United States—and the boarding of the U.S.S. *Chesapeake* by a British warship off Norfolk, Virginia, had raised tensions on the frontier to the point that the *Mississippi Herald* actually proclaimed "WAR!!" At the same time, a young traveler riding along Zane's Trace west of St. Clairsville wrote that he had "met in straggling parties above fifty horsemen with rifles, who had been in Morristown at a militia muster, for the purpose of volunteering, or of being drafted to serve against Britain, in case of a war with that country, now much talked of." When the war actually started in 1812, it scorched any number of places westbound emigrants might pass, such as Buffalo in western New York and the fledgling villages on the Upper Mississippi.[5]

Nevertheless, the settlers kept coming. And when they came, most of them traveled not by land, but by water.

(Overleaf) *Map of the United States, Exhibiting the Post-Roads, the Situations, connexions, & distances of the Post-Offices, Stage Roads, Counties, & Principal Rivers* by Abraham Bradley (1809). Bradley, a long-term assistant postmaster general, produced several editions of his map between 1796 and 1812. His maps were well known because they hung for years in most of the country's larger post offices; in addition, copies were sold by the U.S. Post Office "folded and cased for the Pocket, for the convenience of Travellers." Ohio (March 1, 1803) is the most recent state admitted to the Union on this map. Note the territory labeled for the Wyandots, sometimes called Hurons, along the northern border of Ohio. Illinois, Indiana, Louisiana, Maine, and Mississippi would enter the Union between 1812 and 1820. Increasing settlements can be seen in Illinois and Indiana all along the Ohio River. The extent of the recently acquired Louisiana Purchase is shown in the inset. (*Courtesy of the David Rumsey Map Collection, www.davidrumsey.com*)

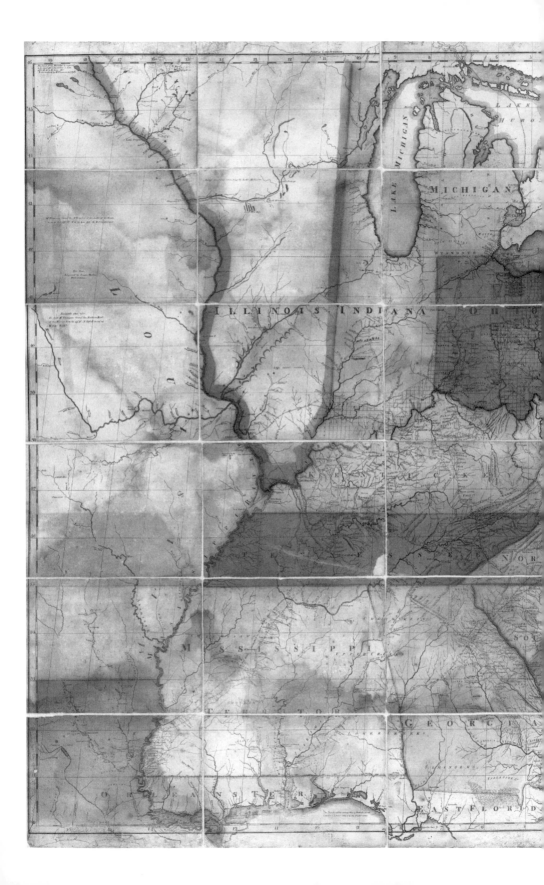

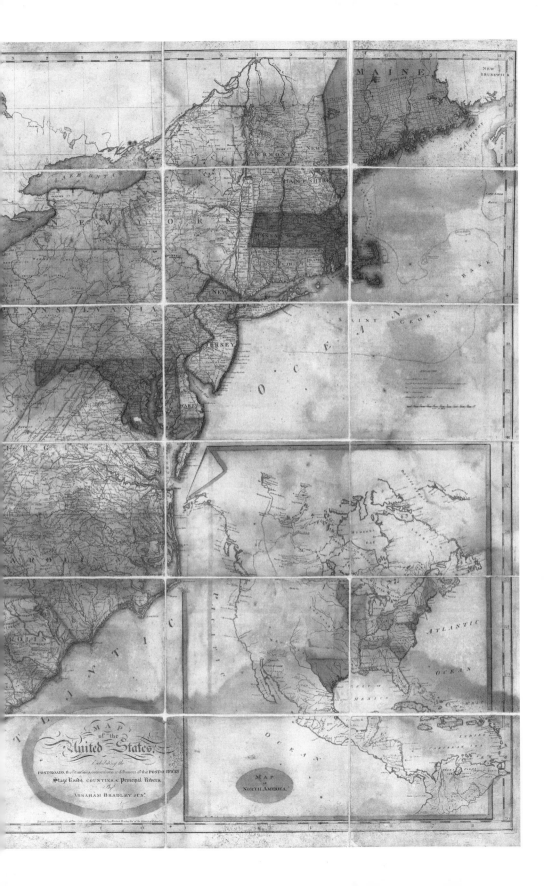

A keelboat using both sail and manpower to move upstream in the Mississippi River. Keel boats were a common cargo vessel along the Ohio, Mississippi, and Missouri Rivers during the first decades of westward expansion. (*Library of Congress*)

I

WATERWAYS

From time immemorial, the rivers were there. The Mississippi, the Ohio, the Missouri, and their major tributaries–the Tennessee, the Arkansas, the Red–extended across the center of the continent like glassy, winding trails, which indeed they turned out to be. Providentially, all of them except the Mississippi lay roughly on east-west courses. And west was the direction that excited the most interest.

During the early days of settlement, waterways and trails guided the emigrant west, as they had the explorer and woodsman who preceded him. Rivers provided the preferred avenues of travel, but no single river or creek led from one side of the Appalachian Mountains to the other. The Appalachians, more often called the Alleghenies at the time (although the Allegheny range was only one of several making up the Appalachian chain), extended for more than two thousand miles from northeast to southwest, and thus greatly hindered or actually blocked access to the Mississippi Valley. So the westbound explorer, standing on the eastern slope of the mountains near the source of an east-flowing creek, had to find a land route–a trail–over the crest to another creek flowing west. As with any mountain stream, following this creek downhill would lead to a larger waterway, and a larger. So in 1808, when Secretary of the Treasury Albert Gallatin laid before Congress his landmark *Report on Roads and Canals*, a good part of the document dealt with the roadways needed to connect the east-flowing rivers with those flowing to the west.[1]

Specifically, the report suggested building, "Four artificial roads from the four great Western rivers, the Allegany, Monongahela, Kanhawa, and Tennessee, to the nearest corresponding Atlantic rivers, the Susquehanna or Juniata, the Potomac, [the] James river, and either the Santee or Savannah."

Gallatin's "four great Western rivers" were all tributaries of only one river: the mighty Ohio. As French explorers had learned more than a century earlier, the Ohio was almost ideal as a route from the Appalachians to the Mississippi Valley. With good reason, French maps of the late 1600s labeled it La Belle Riviere–the Beautiful River. Formed at the juncture of two major waterways in western Pennsylvania–the Allegheny to the north and the Monongahela to the south–the Ohio flowed generally west-south-west for nearly a thousand miles until it emptied into the Mississippi. Although it had its snags and sandbars, it was, for most of its length, friendly to voyagers. Gallatin's report made special mention of that fact:

> As early as the year 1793, a schooner, built on the Monongahela, between Brownsville and Pittsburgh, reached New Orleans by that extraordinary inland navigation [of the Ohio and the Mississippi]. . . . This first essay stimulated the spirit of enterprise so conspicuous in the American character, and numerous vessels, of one hundred to three hundred and fifty tons burden, are now annually built at several shipyards on the Ohio, even as high up as Pittsburgh, and [bring] down to New Orleans the produce of the upper country.

Besides the Ohio, there was another waterway from the east to the Mississippi: the chain of Great Lakes. It sidestepped the Appalachians instead of crossing them, and so was much more roundabout, lying well to the north. From Lake Ontario the voyager made his way around Niagara Falls and across Lake Erie to its western shore, then north, past Detroit, through Lake St. Clair, and into Lake Huron. Pressing farther north brought him close to the top of the Michigan peninsula, and at that point he had a choice: to continue north around Sault Ste. Marie into Lake Superior, or to swing west through the Straits of Mackinac into Lake Michigan. From the western shores of either lake, various rivers and portages (overland trails connecting one waterway with another) would bring him to the Mississippi. The river-and-portage systems most heavily used for this purpose, the Illinois and the Fox-Wisconsin, both ran southwest from Lake Michigan.

The Great Lakes and their tributaries formed another of Gallatin's extraordinary inland navigations:

> From the eastern extremity of Lake Ontario, an inland navigation for vessels of more than one hundred tons burthen, is continued for more than one thousand miles, through Lakes Erie, St. Clair, and Huron, to the western and southern extremities of Lake Michigan, without any other interruption than that of the fall and rapids of Niagara, between Lake Erie and Lake Ontario. . . . Lake Superior, the largest of those inland seas, communicates with the northern extremity of Lake Huron, by the river and rapids of St. Mary's. The fall of these is not ascertained, but it is said that a small canal has been opened around the most difficult part by the Northwest Fur Company.[2]

Once on the Mississippi, the explorer could find numerous tributaries leading west. Of these, the most important was the Missouri–the route Lewis and Clark followed during their epic journey to the northern Rockies of Montana in 1804–05. But there were other waterways worth noting as well, such as the Arkansas, which rose in the Rocky Mountains of Colorado, and the Red, rising in northern Texas.

To reach these far-western rivers, the emigrant's first task was to get into the Mississippi Valley, and for that, no better route offered itself than La Belle Riviere–the Ohio. Only one spot was a constant threat: the rapids, called the Falls of the Ohio, opposite Louisville, Kentucky. Plans had already been laid to solve that problem, by means of a canal; and although years would pass before it materialized, the early voyager could usually find skilled pilots at the site to guide him through. Another benefit for travelers on the Ohio lay in the settlements or military posts along its banks, which could offer supplies or assistance when needed. Most of these settlements had been founded before 1800: Steubenville, Wheeling, Marietta, Limestone (later Maysville), Cincinnati,

Louisville, Yellow Banks (later Owensboro), and Fort Massac. During their historic journey down the Ohio in the summer and fall of 1803, Lewis and Clark had stopped at some of these ports and jotted down notes about them in their journals.[3]

A fortunate circumstance for voyagers on the Ohio was the appearance in 1801 of a little book entitled *The Navigator*, which would go through at least ten editions and sell thousands of copies. Written and published by Zadok Cramer of Pittsburgh, it was a guide to negotiating the Ohio; it pointed out landmarks, suggested places to anchor, and warned of danger spots:

> Mill Creek Island, one quarter of a mile long. . . . Channel right side–the first chute is at the upper end of the island; here keep close to the right shore; when half way through, pull for the island, and keep close to it for 150 yards. . . .
>
> In the bend half a mile below Big Sandy, on the right shore, is a dangerous ledge of rocks, and a little farther down on the left shore is another ledge equally dangerous; to avoid both, keep as near the middle of the river as you can. . . .
>
> Salt Lick creek, left shore. . . . The best water here is in the middle of the river, both beaches being very rocky; but there is a good Landing place in an eddy 400 yards above the creek, and also at the mouth of the creek. . . .
>
> [However, as] frequent landing is attended with considerable loss of time and some hazard, you should contrive to land as seldom as possible; you need not even lie by at night, provided you trust to the current, and keep a good look out; if you have moon light so much the better.[4]

The two major ports for embarkation on the Ohio were Pittsburgh and Wheeling. But Pittsburgh, lying at the junction of the Allegheny and Monongahela rivers, had a major advantage: it was the easternmost of the two. Wheeling was farther downriver, and about fifty-five miles southwest by land; so Pittsburgh, as the first encountered, catered to untold numbers of westbound voyagers. To emigrants, in fact, all roads seemed to lead there. Thomas Ashe, who visited Pittsburgh in 1806, noted:

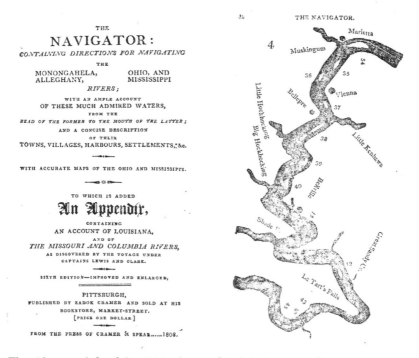

The title page, left, of the 1808 edition of Zadok Cramer's *The Navigator* and an example of the line drawings that accompanied Cramer's instructions for traveling the waterways from Pittsburgh to the Mississippi.

The spot on which this town stands is so commanding (in the military phrase) that it has been emphatically called the key to the western country; and its natural situation is peculiarly grand and striking. Blest as it is with numerous advantages, there is nothing surprising in its having increased rapidly within the last few years. . . . To this place most of the goods conveyed in waggons over the [Allegheny] mountains in spring and autumn, and destined for the Kentucky and Louisiana trade, are brought, to be ready for embarkation. Many valuable manufactories have been lately established here; among which are those of glass, nails, hats, and tobacco. . . . Ship-building is practised to a considerable extent in and near this town, and several vessels of from 10 to 350 tons are now on the stocks. They are frequently loaded here with flour, hemp, glass, and provisions; and then descend with the stream to the sea, a distance of 2300 miles.[5]

As Fortescue Cuming, a widely traveled young Englishman, described the place in 1807–08, it was an almost ceaseless source of noise and smoke:

> Either as a trading or a manufacturing town, I think Pittsburgh for situation, is not excelled in the United States, and that it bids fair to become the emporium of the centre of the federal union. There are 24 taverns . . . two breweries, where are made excellent beer and porter, equal to any in the United States; an air furnace, where all sorts of hollow iron utensils are cast; four nail factories, at one of which, one hundred tons of cut and hammered nails are made annually; seven coppersmiths . . . one brass foundry, six saddlers and harness-makers; two gun-smiths . . . one bell-maker . . . three wheel-wrights . . . eight boat, barge, and ship builders; one pump-maker . . . two rope-makers . . . seventeen blacksmiths; one machinist and whitesmith; one cutler and tool-maker . . . four lumber-yards; [and] one copper-plate printing press.

Added to these were glass works, brickyards, tailors, shoemakers, watchmakers, barbers, butchers, bakers, candle makers, and "four schoolmistresses." Furthermore, Cuming noted, "The situation of Pittsburgh is unrivalled with respect to water communication, with a great extent and variety of country; and would also be so in beauty was it not hemmed in too closely by high and steep hills. [But the hills] admit between them fine vistas up the Allegheny and Monongahela, and down the Ohio."

Sadly, however, the town itself had a drab appearance because of its extensive use of coal, "as fine coal as any in the world, in such plenty, so easily wrought, and so near the town, that it is delivered in wagons drawn by four horses, at the doors of the inhabitants, at the rate of five cents per bushel. . . . This great consumption of a coal abounding in sulphur, and its smoke condensing into a vast quantity of lampblack, gives the outside of the houses a dirty and disagreeable appearance."[6]

Despite its dingy appearance, Pittsburgh was a welcome sight to most emigrants, because after the overland trek to get there, they were now within easy reach of the Ohio.

In giving instructions for descending the river, Cramer's *Navigator* also provided descriptions of major tributaries and near-by settlements. Such descriptions could be very useful to travelers who planned to stop short of the Mississippi. For example, a voyager might float down the Ohio only as far as the mouth of the Muskingum, and from there work his way upstream to a settlement such as Zanesville; or he might travel as far as the mouth of the Cumberland, and then push upriver to Nashville. As Cramer noted, the Ohio

> receives in its course many large and navigable streams, the principal of which are; On the right, Big Beaver, Muskingum, Sciota, Little and Great Miami, and the Wabash. On the left, Little and Great Kanhawa, Sandy, Licking, Kentucky, Green, Cumberland, and Tennessee.
>
> Big Beaver creek, right side, (M.D.) 29-1/4 [i.e., measured distance below Pittsburgh, 29 1/4 miles] . . . a large stream, 60 yards wide at its mouth, affording water enough in swells, for keel boats to Youngstown.

Roughly thirty miles below the Big Beaver (by Cramer's somewhat-long reckoning) was "Crockton's run and mill, right side; Black Horse tavern, left side." Fortescue Cuming, descending the Ohio in a twenty-foot skiff, tied up there: "[W]e stopped at Wm. Croxton's tavern, the sign of the Black Horse, on the Virginia side, and got a bowl of excellent cider-oil. . . . [Croxton] complained of a tooth-ache, from the torture of which I relieved him, by burning the nerve with a hot knitting-needle, which however did not prevent him from charging us for our cider." [7]

About thirty-five miles below the tavern, on a high bank, sat Wheeling. When Christian Schultz anchored there in 1807 and went ashore, he found "Considerable boat building." He added, "if I may judge from the stock of one man, *bear raising* must be either an employment of profit or pleasure, as he had no less than five of these monsters, all nearly full grown, chained to as many posts in the front of his house; and according to his own expression, 'would rather lose his child than one of them.'"[8]

Below Wheeling, Cramer's next major tributaries were the

Muskingum River, (that is Elk's eye,) right side; (M.D.) 172. This is a fine gentle river, 250 yards wide at its mouth, and navigable without any obstructions to the Three Legs, 110 miles up, with large bateaux. . . . Marietta is finely situated [here], having about 90 houses on the upper and 30 on the opposite bank, where Fort Harmar formerly stood. . . . Zanesville, the seat of justice for Muskingum co. is seated on the E. side of the Muskingum river, 50 miles by land above Marietta. . . .

Great Kanhawa river, left side, (M.D.) 283. This is a considerable river of Virginia, 500 yards wide at its mouth, and might be taken for the Ohio, especially when ascending that river. It has gentle navigable water for 10 miles; thence for 60 miles to the falls the water is rapid and difficult of navigation. . . . Point Pleasant, a small town situated at the confluence of the Great Kanhawa with the Ohio [and] commanding a handsome view of that river . . . is a place of considerable embarkation for those descending the Ohio from the western parts of Virginia. . . .

Great Sandy, or Tottery R[iver]., left side, (M.D.) 341-1/4 . . . the dividing line between the states of Virginia and Kentucky. . . . navigable with batteaux to the Ouasioto mountain. It is a long river [and] has few branches.

Just below the Big Sandy Creek, on the Ohio side, Cramer took note of the "French Grant," a tract of twenty thousand acres extending for eight miles along the river, granted by Congress to French settlers who had been dispossessed of their homes at Gallipolis, sixty miles upriver, due to a title dispute. Thomas Ashe stopped at this spot in 1806: "I was very much alarmed on approaching a house, at the door of which a large cub-bear was hugging a child between his paws, and rolling and tumbling with it on the ground. The mother perceiving my apprehensions,

exclaimed "O! Monsieur, ne craignez rien, ils sont bons amis"–
[Don't worry, they are good friends].[9]

The Big Sciota river, (M.D.) 390, was next in Cramer's directions:

> This is a large and gentle river of the state of Ohio, bordered
> with rich flats, meadows, or prairies. . . . Chillicothe, which
> signifies town in the Indian dialect, is most beautifully situat-
> ed on the banks of the Scioto, about forty five miles by land,
> and nearly seventy following the meanders of the river, [north
> of] the Ohio, which it joins between Portsmouth and
> Alexandria–In all that distance, the river has a gentle current,
> and unimpeded navigation for large keels and other craft of
> four feet draught of water.[10]

Near Salt Lick Creek, about twenty miles below the Big Scioto,
Christian Schultz learned a big lesson about river travel:

> [I]n one of my former letters, I described the navigation of the
> Ohio to be perfectly safe, yet experience has shewn me it is at
> least necessary to keep a constant look out. We were about
> three miles below Salt Lick Creek when our boat drifted very
> gently against a pointed log or snag, which was barely cov-
> ered with water. The boat was under such moderate way, that
> we had not the least idea that she was injured, as she wheeled
> around and continued her course. I soon, however, perceived
> the water rising fast over the timbers, and at the same time
> heard a rippling noise, which I at first supposed was occa-
> sioned by the current, but was soon convinced that it pro-
> ceeded from the leaking of the boat. I removed some of the
> baggage, and perceiving the water gushing in with great vio-
> lence, thrust an old great coat into the hole, and directed my
> men to make for the shore, where we unloaded and drew the
> boat out of the water. On examination we found one of the
> planks stove through; but by means of a thin piece of board
> and a few nails, we soon covered the fracture, and paved it
> over with some of the rich mud of the Ohio, which, on this
> occasion, answered all the purposes of tar, without the trou-
> ble of boiling.

After the Big Sciota, Cramer records another major tributary:

Licking river, left side, (M.D.) 524-3/4. This is a considerable
stream of Kentucky, navigable for about 70 miles. . . .
Newport, a small town pleasantly situated just above the junction of Licking with the Ohio river . . . has an Arsenal, or place
of deposit, a magazine of public arms, ammunition & c. . . .
Cincinnati is handsomely situated on a first and second bank
of the Ohio, opposite Licking river–It is a flourishing town
[and] contains about 400 houses.

Anchored in the Ohio just below the arsenal, Christian Schultz
saw "two gun boats belonging to the United States, waiting for a
fresh[et] to take them over the falls; they were built at Marietta,
and are about the size of large Albany sloops."

Below Cincinnati, Cramer describes two more rivers empyting
into the Ohio:

G[reat] Miami (or Mineami) R., right side (M.D.) 551. . . . [It]
has a very stony channel, a swift stream, but no falls; is 200
yards wide at its mouth; at the Piccawee towns, 75 miles up,
it is contracted to the breadth of 30 yards; it is nevertheless
navigable for loaded canoes 50 miles above these towns. The
portage from its western branch into the Miami [Maumee] of
lake Erie, is five miles; that from its eastern branch into
Sandusky river, is nine miles. . . .

Kentucky river, (M.D.) 627-3/4. . . . [N]avigable during the
seasons of high water for loaded boats about 200 miles; it is
90 yards wide at its mouth and also at Boonsborough, 80
miles above. . . . Frankfort, the seat of government for the state
of Kentucky, is situated on the east side of [this] river, about
60 miles from its mouth. It contains about 100 houses.

Not far below the Kentucky's mouth, Schultz commented on

what are here called floating mills; they are of a very simple
construction, and consequently the more valuable in a country so destitute of mill-seats as this. The mill is supported by
two large canoes, with the wheel between them; this is

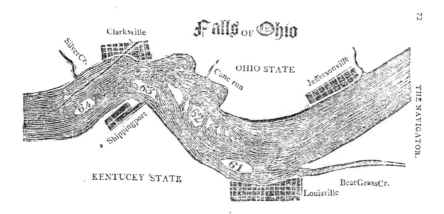

The illustration from Cramer's *Navigator* of the Falls of Ohio, a particularly dangerous point in the journey downriver due to the varying depths and rapids of the Ohio here.

> moored wherever they can find the strongest current nearest to the shore, by the force of which alone the mill is put into operation. . . . they are literally floated up and down the stream, wherever the customer calls, [so] instead of the farmer's going to mill, the mill comes to him.

About eighty miles below the Kentucky, at the bustling city of Louisville, were the Falls of the Ohio–actually rapids, with a drop of twenty-two feet over a distance of two miles. Christian Schultz noted:

> When the river is high, I am told, there is not the least appearance of any fall, except that the current is somewhat swifter at this place than ordinary; but when low, as at present, nearly two thirds of the breadth of the river may be walked over without wetting your ancle. There are three different passages or shoots over these falls, all depending, however, on the state of the water. . . . Two fine large ships, of two hundred and fifty and three hundred tons burthen, were lying upon the falls as we descended the river, having attempted to pass without a sufficient rise of the water; they had their keels knocked out, and were otherwise considerably damaged.

Just below the falls, Schultz learned another lesson about life on the river:

> You must never, on any account, advance money to your boatmen. One of my hands, being arrested by a constable for a debt of eight or ten dollars, at the moment we were leaving the shore, I paid the money without the least hesitation, thinking to deduct it from his wages. After descending a mile or two, I observed a fine stream of spring-water on the shore, and expressing a desire to have a keg filled with it, this fellow was ready in an instant; we accordingly landed him, and, after waiting near an hour, and receiving no answer to our repeated calls, I sent our pilot after him; but the fellow had left the keg at the spring, and escaped to the woods.

Below the Great Miami and Kentucky rivers, Cramer's next major tributary was the "Green river, left shore, (M.D.) 925-1/2. This is a large water of Kentucky, and is navigable with a gentle current for about 150 miles." And below the Green lay the

> Wabash river, and island No. 32, (M.D.) 1022-3/4 . . . a large navigable river of the Indiana Territory, formed by the junction of several branches, one rising within 9 miles of the Miami of lake Erie, another near the head of St. Joseph's river. On the former branch the town of Vincennes, the capital of the territory, is beautifully situated. . . . Vincennes is a thriving place, has a printing office, several mercantile stores, a post office, and about 100 houses.

Some forty miles below the Wabash, and a few miles below Shawneetown in the Illinois territory, was a spot that drew comment from most of those who passed it: Cave in the Rock. Going ashore to inspect it, Schultz noted:

> In some few places you may learn the names of former visitors, which they have left inscribed on the rock. I could not help observing what a very convenient situation this would be for a hermit, or for a convent of monks, as it is large enough to accommodate several hundreds of them. From an examination of the cave, I have no doubt that it has been the

dwelling of some person or persons, as the marks of the smoke, and likewise some wooden hooks affixed to the walls, sufficiently prove. Formerly, perhaps, it was inhabited by Indians; but since, with more probability, by a gang of that banditti, headed by [Sam] Mason and others, who a few years ago infested this part of the country, and committed a great number of robberies and murders.[11]

Cramer's last two major tributaries were the

Cumberland or Shawanee river, M.D. 1113. This river rises in the Cumberland mountains, on the confines of Virginia. . . It is 300 yards wide at its mouth, and is navigable for large barges up to Nashville, and for smaller crafts to the division line between that state and Kentucky. . . .

Tennessee or Cherokee river and island, No. 97, channel right side, M.D. 1131. This is the largest river that empties into the Ohio, is navigable up to the Muscle Shoals, a distance of 250 miles from its mouth, for vessels of considerable burden; from thence boats of 40 tons burden can ascend to the mouth of [the Holston], thence up that river to Long Island, from which place to the mouth of [the] Tennessee is reckoned 1000 miles. The passage of this river through the Cumberland mountains is esteemed a great curiosity; ten miles above it is 1200 yards wide, yet at the mountains it is contracted to the breadth of 70 yards. . . . The Muscle Shoals are 20 miles long and three broad, and are formed by a great number of small islands, which very much interrupt the passage except in high floods.

Finally, the "Mouth of the Ohio river, (M.D.) 1188. You now enter the noble stream of Mississippi, where you will find the velocity of your boat considerably increased by the additional body of water you swim in, and the prospect of the country much altered from that on the Ohio."

Cramer's measured distance for the total length of the river was later proved excessive by some two hundred miles. But his book was nonetheless a valuable guide, endorsed by any number of voy-

agers. While floating downriver, a "Traveller to the West" counted
one sunken flatboat after another, then wrote:

> On coming down the Ohio, I passed not less than 50 arks, or
> family boats, stranded or sunk and abandoned. Indeed from
> the experience I had, I think it wonderful so many escape.
> Nine out of ten are wholly unapprized of the difficulties of the
> new navigation, especially at low water, from shoals, mistak-
> ing the channel by the numerous islands, but more particular-
> ly from the logs and snags which sometimes warn you, and at
> others are just below the surface of the water, or in currents
> where they cannot be well avoided. In a small skiff, such a one
> as I had on the Allegany, which was sufficiently large to hold
> three persons, there is nothing to be apprehended. But most
> of those who descend this river, wish to save as much expense
> as possible, and neither hire a pilot or purchase a "Navigator,"
> (an excellent guide in 19 cases out of twenty) which may
> always be had at Pittsburg.[12]

Christian Schultz, who had his own copy of the *Navigator*
aboard, mentioned this technique:

> The Ohio, particularly in the spring, is subject to be covered
> with fogs, which sometimes remain suspended over the river
> for three or four hours after sun-rise, during which it is very
> difficult to know which is the nearest shore, unless previous-
> ly acquainted with the old Indian mode of ascertaining this
> point. . . . The Ohio, throughout its whole course, (with very
> few exceptions,) is subject to a very strong echo; and the
> method to ascertain the proximity of either shore, is to strike
> the boat with a club or an axe, and the echo will be first heard
> from the nearest shore. But when in a situation where no
> echo is returned, or where the water is too deep to be sound-
> ed with a pole, or when not provided with a line, take a tin
> cup, and dip up water [away] from you on each side of the
> boat, and the resistance of the current, upon one of the trials,
> will soon satisfy you which way it is setting.[13]

A flatboat moving cattle and passengers along the Ohio River in the early nineteenth century. (*Library of Congress*)

No doubt hundreds of other copies of the *Navigator* came down the Ohio, not only because of the book's reputation, but also because of the sheer numbers of emigrants on the waterway. In mid-1819, some ten years after Cramer and Schultz wrote their passages, John Woods and his party descended the Ohio. Somewhere below Gallipolis,

> We passed an ark sunk in the river. . . . After dark we anchored on the Virginia side, with a store-boat and a light ark that contained a rather numerous family of English from the neighbourhood of Manchester going, like ourselves, to look for a home in the western country. The master of the store-boat was also a fellow-countryman; he had been settled a short time at Marietta, but now purposed going further westward. He had freighted his boat with store-goods and fruit, to pay his expenses down the Ohio. He intended settling in the neighbourhood of Cincinnati, or of going down to the State of Indiana. He said that, in April last, near a thousand boats of different descriptions passed Marietta going westward; most of them with emigrants.[14]

As Cramer's book mentioned, voyagers entering "the noble stream of Mississippi . . . will find the velocity of your boat considerably increased by the additional body of water you swim in." So, once in the Mississippi, those emigrants bound for St. Louis now had to turn north and, for more than 180 miles, force their craft upstream against a strong current to get there. Whether it was a skiff, keelboat, or barge, pushing it upriver could be a back-wrenching, muscle-straining job. Amos Stoddard's *Sketches of Louisiana*, published in 1812, stated that boats "calculated for a number of oars" could indeed ascend the Mississippi, but only if the crews knew their business:

> Keel boats, however strongly manned, cannot possibly ascend to any great distance in the middle of the current; in some places, indeed, they cannot make head against it. They are obliged not only to ply along the shore, where the water is less rapid, and where counter currents or eddies frequently prevail, but they also find it necessary to keep on the side opposite to the bends. Hence they cross the river at the lower extremity of every bend, which can seldom be done without falling down with the current about half a mile. . . Boats usually ascend from fourteen to twenty miles in a day. The labor of propelling them is excessive; it requires great exertion to move them against the current; and boatmen find it necessary to rest every hour, or at least at every traverse.[15]

Small wonder, then, that the boatmen earned the phrase so often applied to them: "half-horse, half-alligator, and a little touch of the snapping-turtle."

Timothy Flint began his acquaintance with the Mississippi and its boatmen in 1816. At New Madrid, near the confluence of the Mississippi and the Ohio, Flint saw boats

> arriving in fleets. The boisterous gaiety of the hands, the congratulations, the moving picture of life on board the boats, in the numerous animals, large and small, which they carry, their different loads, the evidence of the increasing agriculture of the country above, and more than all, the immense distances which they have already come, and those which they

JONES & STRICKLAND,
Ship-wrights & BoatBuilders.

INFORM the public that they are now engaged in this business, and carry it on at the mouth of Suke's run, adjoining the French Yard, where orders for any kind of KEEL-BOATS, BARGES, SKIFTS, &c. will be punctually attended to, and executed, in a manner that shall be neat and strong, and on the most reasonable terms. Having stuff on hand, and of the best kind, they will be enabled to fill orders with dispatch. From their long experience in ship and boat building, they feel confident that they will be able to give entire satisfaction to those who may favour them with their orders.

Application may be made to either of us at our yard, or to GEORGE ROBINSON, Merchant, Pittsburgh.

N. B. A Keel Boat, set for the Mississippi trade, for sale, apply as above.

Pittsburgh, July 20th, 1807.

Wanted Immediately,

A fit person to take charge of a Keel Boat—also four good Oarsmen, to go to Natchez. The boat will be lightly loaded, and comfortably fitted out. Liberal wages will be given. Apply to
ANTHONY BEELEN.
Pittsburgh, July 5, 1808.

FOR SALE,

AN ORLEANS BOAT, now lying at the mouth of the Scioto river, oppofite the Ware-Houfe. The Boat is New and was built at Pittfburgh: She is made ftout and ftrong, her timbers are planked with an inch and an half good plank—fhe is every way made ftrong and firm. together with two Side Oars and a Stearing Oar, with a good Brick Chimney—fhe is 40 by 12.— Whoever wifhes to purchafe faid Boat will pleafe to inquire at the office of the Supporter.
December 15, 1810.

P. Haldeman & Co.

HAVE for Sale on Commission,
12 Pipes Holland Gin,
A few kegs Nails, at reduced prices,
Whiskey, Flour, Tobacco & Country Linen,
—ALSO—
Several Keel Boats, which they will sell on reasonable terms, or load to any port, on the Mississippi or Ohio above the Mouth.
March 22th.—48tf-

For New-Orleans.
The Barge FREEDOM.
Geo. Carr, master, will sail on the 10th April next, for passage, having excellent accommodations apply to the master on board, or to Oliver C. Johnson.
March 30th, 1819.—48

For Pittsburgh,
Or any Port on the Ohio.
THE fast-sailing KEEL-BOAT
GOVERNOR CLARK,
Oliver C. Johnson, master, will sail on the 10th of April next. Having two-thirds of her cargo engaged, for balance of freight, or passage, apply to the master on board.
March 30th, 1819.   48

Newspapers of the time were full of advertisements and classifieds for river-related goods and services. On the left, a boatbuilding notice, *Pittsburgh Gazette*, July 1807; a want ad for a keelboat captain, *Pittsburgh Gazette*, July 1808; an Orleans [Flat] boat for sale, *Chillicothe* (Ohio) *Supporter*, December 1810. Above, notices in the *Missouri Gazette*, April 1819.

have still to go, afforded to me copious sources of meditation. You can name no point from the numerous rivers of the Ohio and the Mississippi, from which some of these boats have not come. . . . [T]he hands travel about from boat to boat, make inquiries, and acquaintances, and form alliances to yield

mutual assistance to each other, on their descent from this to
New Orleans. . . . About midnight the uproar is all hushed.

The fleet [will unite] once more at Natchez, or New
Orleans, and, although they live on the same river, they may,
perhaps, never meet each other again on the earth.

Flint, like so many others, was headed not to New Orleans but
upstream to St. Louis. From the mouth of the Ohio, he and his
crew, manning an eighty-five-foot keelboat, first made their way
north by staying close to the bank and using oars, poles, or

a process, which, in the technics of the boatmen, is called
"bush-whacking." It consists, by commencing at the bow, to
seize a handful of bushes, or a single branch, and to pull upon
them and walk toward the stern, as the boat ascends. The
crew follow each other in this way in succession to the stern,
and walk round to the bow, on the opposite side. The banks
slope so rapidly, that the "setting pole" is not long enough, in
the general way, for use on the opposite side, and they commonly put two hands to the oars.

Flint's upstream voyage, pleasant enough at first, soon became
otherwise:

No employment can be imagined more laborious, and few
more dangerous, than this of propelling a boat against the
current of such a river. . . . At one time you come to a place
in the current, so swift that no force of oars and poles can
urge the boat through it. You then have to apply, what is
commonly called here a "cordelle," which is a long rope fas-
tened at one end to the boat, thrown ashore, and seized by a
sufficient number of hands to drag or track the boat up the
stream.[16]

Skiffs, keelboats, and the big many-oared barges, as well as
dugout canoes and pirogues, all had pointed bows and so could
travel upstream when necessary–whether rowed, poled, cordelled,
or bushwhacked. Not so the flatboat, a large, rectangular vessel
variously called the ark, Kentucky boat, broadhorn, or family boat,
and suited only for downstream travel. James Hall described it as

a mere raft, with sides and a roof; but it is more roomy and convenient than the keel, if well built and tight, as indeed they mostly are. An immense oar is placed on the roof on each side near the bow, (which has given these boats the nick-name of "broad horns,") and another at the stern. They are used only to direct the course of the flat, which is allowed to float with the current, and thus she pursues her voyage, like man on his earthly pilgrimage, to that undiscovered country from whose bourne no traveller of her species ever returns; for, being calculated to [drift only with] the current, she is useless after she has reached her destination, except as so much lumber.[17]

So, as a downstream craft, a flatboat could begin its journey at Pittsburgh, float all the way down the Ohio to the Mississippi, and all the way down the Mississippi—past Memphis, Vicksburg, Natchez, and Baton Rouge, past the mouths of the Arkansas and the Red—to the great terminus of river travel, New Orleans. Amos Stoddard called the place "the great mart of all the wealth of the western world." Christian Schultz, who got there in 1808, said of it:

The Levee in front is crowded with large vessels from every part of the world. They generally lie three deep, in a line extending from near the centre of the town to one quarter of a mile below. The same distance at the upper end is always lined with one or two hundred Kentucky and New-Orleans boats. . . . Not withstanding New-Orleans is, and I fear must ever remain, an unhealthy situation, yet I do not hesitate to express as my opinion, that it will at some future period not only rival all the great commercial cities of the United States, but even of the world. . . .

[She is placed] by nature at the mouth of the noblest of rivers, running north two thousand five hundred miles; [with] another arm extending to the north-west the same distance; a third to the north-east twelve hundred miles; while a fourth, below the two last, extends westwardly nearly fifteen hundred more. These again receive in their courses many navigable streams, which in any other country would be denominated rivers of the first magnitude. Thus she receives the produce of a thousand soils and climates, which have no outlet except by her port.[18]

The rivers that led there, despite their dangers, could exert a powerful attraction. As Timothy Flint said of the Ohio:

> Almost every boat, while it lies in the harbor, has one or more fiddles scraping continually aboard, to which you often see the boatmen dancing. There is no wonder that the way of life which the boatmen lead, in turn extremely indolent, and extremely laborious . . . should always have seductions that prove irresistible to the young people that live near the banks of the river. The boats float by their dwellings on beautiful spring mornings. . . . The boatmen are dancing to the violin on the deck of their boat. They scatter their wit among the girls on the shore who come down to the water's edge to see the pageant pass. The boat glides on until it disappears behind a point of wood. At this moment perhaps, the bugle, with which all the boats are provided, strikes up its note in the distance over the water. These scenes, and these notes, echoing from the bluffs of the beautiful Ohio, have a charm for the imagination, which, although I have heard a thousand times repeated . . . is even to me always new, and always delightful.[19]

AGAIN, EITHER THE OHIO RIVER or the Great Lakes routes would bring the traveler to the Mississippi. Both routes had their blockages: on the Great Lakes, obstacles included Niagara Falls and the various portages needed; on the Ohio, the hindrances included the falls at Louisville and periodic low water. For a man on foot or horseback, traveling light, these obstacles posed no great problem. But they posed problems indeed for freighters, or for families moving their household goods.

Recognizing this fact, Gallatin's report devoted many paragraphs to facilitating the passage on these waters, principally by means of canals. A few such canals had been built, and more were in progress, while numerous others were proposed. Most of those completed or in progress were short, measuring only a few miles in length, but one exception, a well-built canal of moderate length that Gallatin cited as an example, was the Middlesex Canal of Massachusetts. Started in 1793 and finished ten years later, it was twenty-seven miles long, had twenty locks "of solid masonry and excellent workmanship", and–to the benefit of Boston merchants– diverted traffic on New Hampshire's Merrimack River into Boston instead of allowing it to flow to its natural destination at Newburyport.

Showing commendable analysis and equally commendable foresight, Gallatin outlined a number of practical canal routes by which a boat on the Atlantic shore could, without once crossing dry land, follow a course through the center of the continent all the way to the Mississippi. However, more than fifteen years would pass before the first of these canals became a reality. And, as events would prove, many of the others never materialized, or reached completion too late to have much of an impact on westward migration.[20]

ROADWAYS

DESPITE THEIR ADVANTAGES, and despite the general desire to travel by water, canals "of excellent workmanship" had a big drawback: their cost. The price for the Middlesex Canal had amounted to some $550,000, or more than $20,000 per mile. This was far greater than the cost of cutting a simple roadway through the woods, which, Gallatin estimated, could be as little as $500 a mile. Of course, for "artificial roads of the best construction . . . exclusively of bridges over large rivers," the cost could jump to $7,000 per mile, but even this was substantially less than the per-mile cost of a solidly built canal.[1]

As secretary of the treasury, Gallatin had good reason to know the cost of roads and bridges: at the time he wrote his report, the federal government had already decided to enter the road-building business. In 1802, after years of debate about legalities and funding, Congress had authorized a "National Road." A prime mover behind this idea was George Washington, who, in his later years, had shown increasing concern about the need to draw eastern and western settlements closer together. In fact, he and Gallatin had met in 1784, in a cabin not far from the Ohio River, and discussed the matter. And, appropriately, it was Gallatin who finally ended the congressional debates about funding the project. His plan, presented to Congress in February 1802, proposed that states selling plots of federal land within their borders set aside a percentage of the proceeds and allocate it to road construction. Congress passed such an act two months later.

As generally conceived, this National Road was to start in a major eastern city and lead to some point on the upper Ohio River. But which of the eastern cities would win the honor? Not surprisingly, its location became a focal point for numerous arguments and political machinations; Philadelphia, Baltimore, Washington, and Richmond all had their advocates. Finally, in December 1805, the Senate committee overseeing the project recommended a route from Cumberland, Maryland, to either Steubenville or Wheeling on the Ohio. A road (not in the best of shape) already lay between Cumberland and Baltimore; so the new turnpike, when completed, would link Baltimore with the Ohio River—or, when regarded as a wheels-and-water route, would link Baltimore with the Mississippi.[2]

The plan would also meet one of Gallatin's specific requirements. Since Cumberland was generally regarded as the highest navigable point on the Potomac, the road—reaching from there to the Ohio—would connect a "great Western river . . . with the nearest corresponding Atlantic river."

Nearly two years of surveys followed, one of them carried out by a three-man commission appointed by Thomas Jefferson. In a report filed in December 1806, the commissioners noted that their survey had presented "a work of greater magnitude, and a task much more arduous, than was conceived before entering upon it." The next three years saw a series of delays, one of which resulted from Pennsylvania's demand, eventually agreed to, that the road pass through (and thereby benefit) two of its towns, even though they lay north of the most desirable pathway. Then, late in 1810, notices to contractors titled "United States Western Road" began appearing in the newspapers. To avoid misunderstanding, these notices, or requests for proposals, went into great detail about the work required. Finally, in 1811, construction of the National Road actually started.[3]

For those folk unwilling to wait—and there were thousands of them—any number of westbound roads were in place by 1808, the year of Gallatin's report. Some of them were newly cut, but others were merely widened versions of centuries-old Indian trails. Whether old or new, these roads were often rough and rutted, washed out by floods, or littered with stumps and other debris, but they nevertheless formed access routes through the great Eastern forests. A good many of them were the post roads used by mail carriers, and so specified by Congress in its *Act to Establish the Post-Office and Post-Roads* of 1794.

Most such roads were shown on one of the best-known maps of the period, Abraham Bradley's *Map of the United States, Exhibiting the Post-Roads, the Situations, connexions, & distances of the Post-Offices, Stage Roads, Counties, & Principal Rivers.* Bradley's maps, which went through at least four editions between 1796 and 1812, were well known because they hung in most of the country's larger post offices. Furthermore, the U.S. Post Office was selling these maps, "folded and cased for the Pocket, for the convenience of Travellers," as early as 1797.[4]

As drawn by Bradley, the northernmost of the major roads, in New York state, ran west from the Hudson River along the valley of the Mohawk, then continued west below Lake Ontario, through Geneva and Batavia, to the eastern end of Lake Erie; from that point it paralleled Erie's south shore into northern Ohio. State officials, taking considerable latitude with the term, referred to it on occasion as the Great Western Turnpike, but some stretches fell far short of any turnpike standard, especially those crossing the swampy ground below Lake Ontario.[5]

Not far south of the New York road was another, one that qualified for part of its length as a full-fledged turnpike, and, appropriately, was often called the Lancaster Pike. A Pennsylvania traveler of the 1790s described it as "a masterpiece of its kind; it is paved with stone the whole way and overlaid with gravel, so that it is never obstructed during the most severe season." From Philadelphia the pike ran sixty miles west to its namesake village of Lancaster; then, losing its turnpike status, it continued generally west through central Pennsylvania to Harrisburg, Shippensburg, Chambersburg, Bedford, Greensburg, and finally to the forks of the Ohio at Pittsburgh. A variant of this route, called the Glade Road, veered slightly south at Bedford and passed through Somerset, but still brought its traffic to Pittsburgh. Reaching Pittsburgh, "the key to the western country," was no simple task, however, because the road between Chambersburg and Pittsburgh went through rough country–a "multitude of steep hills or ridges," as one traveler described it. Timothy Flint left a more graphic account:

> We passed [the Allegheny] hills on the common route from Philadelphia to Pittsburgh. . . . The grandeur of these mountains, so impressive when their blue outline just touches the horizon in the distance, diminishes when you approach their summits, [because of] the difficulty and danger of crossing them. I have no wish, however, to fatigue you with the recital of our exertions in lifting the carriage up precipitous ascents, washed by the rains, and the still greater exertions necessary to let it down again. We passed hundreds of Pittsburg wagons, in the crossing. Many of them had broken axles and wheels, and in more than one place it was pointed out to us, that teams had plunged down the precipices and had perished.[6]

FOR THOSE HEADED SOUTHWEST TO Virginia instead of due west toward Pittsburgh, another road starting in Pennsylvania would take them there. Known as the "Great Philadelphia Waggon Road" as early as the 1750s, this route followed the turnpike from Philadelphia to Lancaster, then turned gradually southwest, through York and Gettysburg, to Hagerstown, Maryland, and continued its southwesterly course through Winchester, Virginia, near the head of the Shenandoah Valley. Still following the Valley southwest, it passed through such Virginia hamlets as Staunton and Lexington before crossing the James River above Fincastle, where it swung south to Rocky Mount and dropped into North Carolina.[7]

(Overleaf) *A Map of the most Inhabited part of Virginia containing the whole province of Maryland with part of Pensilvania New Jersey and North Carolina.* Drawn by Joshua Fry & Peter Jefferson in 1751 (detail). This map is considered to be the most accurate of Virginia and portions of the adjacent colonies in the eighteenth century. Of particular note is the clearly drawn route of the Great Wagon Road from Philadelphia to Frederick Town (Winchester), Virginia. Peter Jefferson was Thomas Jefferson's father. (*Library of Congress*)

South of the Pennsylvania road leading to Pittsburgh lay another east-west route–or, more accurately, a pair of routes, within fifty miles of each other. These two roads were actually westbound extensions of clusters of roads near the Eastern Shore that converged to form them. The upper road of the pair, another full-fledged turnpike, "built in the most thorough and substantial manner, to resist the weight and wear of . . . enormous wagons," started outside Baltimore and went generally west through the Maryland countryside to Frederick. From there the road, now progressively rougher, swung northwest to Hagerstown (where the Philadelphia Wagon Road coming down from York crossed it), and from there proceeded, in a winding, westerly way, to Cumberland. From Cumberland the road ran almost due west through Maryland into Morgantown, Virginia.

The lower road of the pair began on the Potomac near Alexandria and wandered generally northwest, through a gap in the Appalachians, to the Shenandoah, crossing that river and continuing to Winchester (where the Philadelphia Wagon Road intersected it). At Winchester the road assumed a more westerly direction, running west-northwest to a crossing of the Potomac's south branch at Romney. From there it passed through a corner of western Maryland, coming within twenty-five miles of the upper road before it dipped west-southwest into Clarksburg, Virginia. There the two roads finally met, the upper route having turned southwest at Morgantown along the headwaters of the Monongahela. From Clarksburg the now-unified road ran almost straight west to the Ohio River, near Marietta. On the far bank, in Ohio territory, another pathway continued west through a new settlement named Athens to the thriving little metropolis of Chillicothe, sitting in south-central Ohio on the Scioto River. There it met another, older road coming in from the northeast, a road known since the late 1790s as Zane's Trace.[8]

ABOUT NINETY MILES UP THE OHIO from Marietta lay the town of Wheeling, one of whose major landholders was Col. Ebenezer Zane, a veteran of the Revolutionary War and a man open to opportunities. In 1794, when Congress published its list of post roads, the list included a route running from Wheeling southwest across Ohio to Limestone (later Maysville), Kentucky, to serve the new settlements there. At that time, however, no such road actually existed, and it was decided that "until the Postmaster General shall have made provision for the regular transportation of the mail from Wheeling to Limestone, the present post-road from Abington to Danville, in Kentucky, shall be continued." In 1796, Zane persuaded Congress that he was the man best able to blaze the needed trail, and so he did. Sometimes tracking existing paths, Zane's trace went almost due west from Wheeling to the Muskingum River; then, at the future site of Zanesville, it turned southwest and continued to Chillicothe. Crossing the Scioto there, the road again followed a southwesterly direction and met the Ohio River once more, some 220 miles after leaving it, opposite Maysville, Kentucky. Maysville, called by one contemporary "the oldest and most accustomed Landing Place on the Ohio," was a logical terminus, because from there another road ran inland toward Lexington.

At first Zane's Trace was hardly wider than a footpath, giving rise to the saying that a fat horse could barely squeeze through it. But its completion was nonetheless a feat, because it offered a recognizable route through hilly, heavily-wooded country that appeared to be well-nigh impassable otherwise. After achieving statehood in 1803, Ohio allocated funds for its improvement—and none too soon, because travel on it became very heavy indeed. By November 1805 the *Chillicothe Gazette* could report, "The emigration to the state of Ohio, the present season, far exceeds all reasonable bounds of calculation. We are inform'd by a gentleman who arrived in town last evening from Wheeling, that he passed not less than eighty wagons with families, from various quarters of the atlantic states, bound to different parts of this state." In the 1814 edition of his widely read work *The Navigator*, Zadok Cramer said, "The great leading road from Pittsburgh to Kentucky, goes through Zanesville, which generally keeps it alive with movers and travellers."[9]

Other roads soon grew out of Zane's. One of them cut west from his trace just below Chillicothe and led to Cincinnati. A northbound traveler on the trace came to the intersection of the two in 1807: "I passed a finger post on the left, a mile from Bainbridge, pointing to the westward and directing [me] to Cincinnatti seventy-three miles [away]."[10]

At Maysville, on the Kentucky side of the Ohio, was another road that in one sense was an extension of Zane's Trace, though it actually predated it. An 1806 traveler described it as "the main road [to] Lexington and other interior towns." Leaving Maysville, this "main road" dropped southwest through Paris to Lexington and then swung northwest to Frankfort, the state capital. (The Maysville-Lexington Road would get national attention in 1830, when Andrew Jackson vetoed a bill to improve it.)[11]

This whole long route, from Philadelphia to Wheeling and thence along Zane's Trace to Maysville and continuing to Lexington, was described by Thomas Ashe in 1806 as mainly "mountainous and swampy, notwithstanding which a mail coach is established on it, from Philadelphia to Lexington in Kentuckey, through Pittsburg, Wheeling, and Chitocothe [Chillicothe], a distance of upwards of seven hundred miles, to be performed by contract in fifteen days. Small inns are to be found every ten, or twelve miles of the route."[12]

THERE WAS ANOTHER ROUTE INTO KENTUCKY besides Zane's Trace, one far to the south of it, blazed by the legendary Daniel Boone in the 1770s and known as the Wilderness Road. Formed from the juncture of various trails in southwestern Virginia and northeastern Tennessee, this road led west along the Cumberland Mountains to a gap—the Cumberland Gap—that allowed it to turn north and enter Kentucky from the southeast. Once through the gap, the road crossed the headwaters of the Cumberland River and traveled generally northwest, through Flat Lick and Barberville, then continued north by northwest until it reached a fork. At that point, the right or eastern fork headed almost straight north to the settlement of Boonesborough, on the Kentucky River, while the left fork proceeded northwest, through Crab Orchard, to Danville and Harrodsburg. From those two points, other roads reached north or west. The road from Harrodsburg continued north to Frankfort, lying on the Kentucky River many miles downstream from Boonesborough. A road from Danville proceeded west through Bardstown to Elizabethtown and, branching out, continued west to various points on the Ohio River.

(Within a few years the northern branch, turning west at Frankfort and passing through Yellow Banks to Henderson, would extend thirty more miles to reach the juncture of the Ohio and the Wabash opposite Shawneetown, in the Illinois Territory.)[13]

At Frankfort, the extension of the Wilderness Road coming up from Harrodsburg met the extension of Zane's Trace coming down from Maysville. And in Frankfort began one of the lengthiest of all westbound roads, one reaching all the way to the old French settlements on the Mississippi. Eventually known as the Great Western Mail Route, it was a harbinger of things to come. Leaving Frankfort, the road ran west through Shelbyville to a crossing of the Ohio near Louisville, then west again, across the width of southern Indiana, to the old town of Vincennes, on the banks of the Wabash. Once across the Wabash it trended west-southwest across southern Illinois, finally reaching the Mississippi at the hundred-year-old French settlement of Kaskaskia.

From Kaskaskia another road ran north, along the east bank of the Mississippi, to Cahokia, opposite St. Louis. In St. Louis yet another road made its way about twenty miles west and, crossing the mighty Missouri River, ended at the village of St. Charles.[14]

A shorter path west started some sixty miles south of the Cumberland Gap. Emigrants passing through Knoxville or other settlements in eastern Tennessee could, if they chose, avoid the northern detour to the gap and instead travel west on an existing road that reached the Cumberland River at Fort Blount, then followed its north bank in a hook-shaped route through Dixon's Springs and Gallatin to Nashville. From Nashville the road ran almost due west to the Duck River, a tributary of the Tennessee, which in turn spilled into the Ohio.

The waters of the Ohio were also within reach of Richmond, capital of the then-vast dominion of Virginia, and vigorous trade rival of Baltimore and Philadelphia to the north. Richmond's route to the river, however, was long and roundabout. From the city, a turnpike ran west-northwest through Columbia and Charlottesville to Staunton, in the Shenandoah Valley. From Staunton (where it crossed the Philadelphia Wagon Road), the pike threaded its way through the Appalachians, generally west-southwest, to Bath Court House (later Warm Springs), then south-west to a point near White Sulphur Springs, where it turned west, passed through Lewisburg, and then, gradually, swung northwest until it met the Kanawha River near Gauley Bridge and followed it through Charleston to the Ohio River at Gallipolis.[15]

An early traveler noted that one stretch of this road, between Charlottesville and Staunton, was "made by cutting to a depth of three or four feet into the side of the mountain, and throwing the earth so as to produce a level. . . . In some places, to the inexperienced, it has an awfully dangerous appearance, running up the side of a steep mountain, and having no parapet wall. . . . Before you reach Staunton, the Blue Ridge is crossed, through Rock-fish Gap, which affords splendid views of the great valley."[16]

FOR THOSE AROUND RICHMOND WHO WANTED the most direct access to the Mississippi, and preferred to avoid the meanderings of the Ohio, another road, lying between the James and the Appomattox rivers, led west through Cumberland Court House and Lynchburg to the Philadelphia Wagon Road near Fincastle. At that point the route turned west-southwest, passing through Christianburg and Abingdon, to enter northeast Tennessee at Blountsville. From there a road continued along the Holston River to Knoxville, where it met the road leading to Nashville.[17]

Nashville was perhaps better known as the eastern, or northern, terminus of another route that led west: the Natchez Trace. The trace, however, was another lengthy path to the Mississippi: from Nashville it traveled more than four hundred miles southwest before reaching the town on the river that gave it its name. Actually, the trace was more of a west-to-east route than the reverse. Its original purpose was to provide a land route back to Tennessee for the "Kaintucks" who had taken flatboats down the Mississippi to Natchez or New Orleans. It was far easier to walk back north than to try forcing a flatboat upstream, against the Mississippi's current. In 1805, a Kentucky congressman described the route as "the road from Natchez to Nashville . . . on which all our people must pass who return by land after carrying down to Orleans and Natchez the produce [from] Tennessee, Kentucky, Ohio, and the western parts of Virginia and Pennsylvania; [a road] where many of them are robbed, some murdered, and all have to suffer hunger and want of the comforts of life in a wilderness."[18]

Gradually, however, individuals began using it to travel west as well as east, because soon enough, a road starting on the bank of the Mississippi opposite Natchez (shown on Bradley's 1809 map) led farther west—more than a hundred miles west across Louisiana, in fact, to Natchitoches, on the Red River. (Another road, coming in from the west and approaching the Red River not far above Natchitoches, was marked "Road from St. Fe" on the map.)

Some of the emigrants farther north, passing through Cumberland Gap, chose to keep to the west instead of traveling up to Boonesborough or Danville, and found a ready alternative by first crossing the headwaters of the Cumberland River and then following a trail along its northernmost bend until it merged with another route swinging down in a wide, southwestern arc from Danville and Stanford toward Bowling Green. Once past Bowling Green the road continued west to Eddyville, not far from the confluence of the Ohio and Mississippi rivers. Crossing the Ohio north of Eddyville, the road ran west along its bank past Fort Massac to the Mississippi and, once across the Big River, it hooked southwest to New Madrid.

(Overleaf) *United States of America Compiled from the latest & best Authorities* by John Melish (1818, detail). John Melish (1771–1822) was a prolific writer and draftsman of travelers's guides and maps during the early republic. Born in Scotland, he settled in Philadelphia in 1811. His maps are noted for their accuracy and his books were designed to encourage immigration from Europe to America. When this map was published in July 1818, Indiana and Mississippi had achieved statehood; Illinois would be admitted to the Union five months later. Note that Lake Michigan has been drawn too far east, creating an odd notch where Chicago is shown above Indiana. (*Courtesy of the David Rumsey Map Collection, www.davidrumsey.com*)

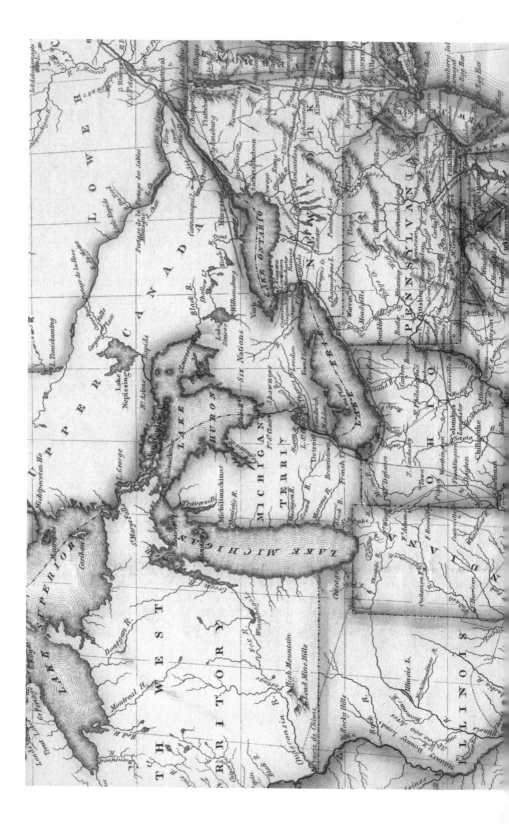

Those in the Deep South lured by the west could simply travel by water along the Gulf of Mexico shore from Tallahassee and Pensacola, Mobile, or other ports to New Orleans. But there was also a road available, starting from a merger of other roads between Milledgeville and Athens, Georgia, at least one of which originated in South Carolina. From Athens the route swept southwest in a broad arc through Coweta and Point Comfort to Fort Stoddart, at the junction of the Alabama and Tombigbee rivers some thirty miles north of Mobile. Once across, it took a short northward jog, then turned west and held that course until it met the Natchez Trace at the Mississippi River.[19]

Not all routes, when first designated as post roads, could handle coach or wagon traffic. Zane's Trace, for example, was blazed in 1796, but it was not really ready for wheels for another ten years. Similarly, the Natchez Trace, declared a post road in 1800, was still partially inaccessible to wheeled vehicles five years later. Late in 1806, in fact, the postmaster general required that it be "cleared of all tree logs and brush, twelve feet in width, and made passable for a wagon. All streams not over forty feet wide are to be bridged, and the banks of other streams are to be shelved or sloped down so that they may be passable for a wagon."[20]

When first cut, narrow trails could allow only the passage of horseback mail–in other words, post riders. And post riders might continue to follow such routes even when wide enough to accommodate any wagon. Unlike emigrant wagons, which could be found almost anywhere, post coaches (carrying mail under government contract) plied the roads only when it was a paying proposition. Too little traffic meant little or no stagecoach service, and in such areas post riders continued to carry the mail. William Blane (a traveler from England who wrote under the pseudonym "An English Gentleman") met one such rider:

> In passing a small belt of wood near a watercourse, I met the mail, that is to say, a man on horseback, who drove before him another horse, on which were fastened the leathern bags containing the letters. These bags were very large, and being packed upon a high wooden saddle, made a curious appearance. When I first saw the horse coming round a turn in the

road, I thought some animal was fixed upon its back. It is in this way that the mail is carried twice a week from Kentucky to Vincennes, and from Vincennes to St. Louis.[21]

SOME OF THE HIGHWAYS SHOWN on the Bradley maps came close to meeting Gallatin's requirements for roads connecting the "great Western rivers . . . to the nearest corresponding Atlantic rivers." Actually, the westward extension of Pennsylvania's Lancaster Pike formed a solid bond between the Susquehanna, just east of York, and the Ohio at Pittsburgh, but it was a long way between the two. (A northern loop of this pike, swinging up through Huntingdon and Armagh, did shorten this distance, linking "the Juniata branch of the Susquehannah" near Huntingdon with the Conemaugh, an indirect tributary of the Allegheny, near Armagh. Moreover, it was not as mountainous as the direct route from Philadelphia to Pittsburgh. But until the 1830s, its importance as an emigrant's route was secondary.)

A shorter link between eastern and western waters was the extension of the Baltimore-Frederick Turnpike through Hagerstown; at Cumberland, on the North Branch of the Potomac, it ran to Morgantown, on the upper Monongahela. (This was probably the link that Gallatin had in mind when he mentioned a road between the Monongahela and the Potomac.) Another connection, somewhat longer, was the road starting from Richmond and meeting the James River at Lynchburg; from that point, continuing west toward Fincastle and then bending southwest, it intersected the New River, a major tributary of the Kanawha, at Ingles' Ferry (later Radford), just west of Christianburg.

The true turnpikes–the few that existed before 1808–could reflect great credit on their builders. Gallatin's report spoke of the Lancaster Pike as

the first extensive turnpike that was completed in the United States, [and] the first link of the great Western communication from Philadelphia. . . . [E]xclusively of the side or summer roads [shoulders,] twenty four feet of the bed of the road are covered with a stratum of pounded stones, eighteen inches thick in the middle . . . and decreasing each way to twelve inches. The valley hills are the most elevated and steep on the road; but the angle of ascent no where exceeds four degrees. Stone bridges have been erected across all the intervening streams.

The Baltimore-Frederick Pike was just as sound. As on the Lancaster Pike, the "greatest angle [of ascent] which has been taken on this road in passing any hill, has not exceeded four degrees." In addition to gentle slopes, the pike boasted a durable surface:

> Depth of stone from ten to twelve inches, broken to pass through a three inch ring. . . . The most approved covering on the surface of the road is clean, washed sand or gravel from the creeks or rivers. Where the stones are broken to pass through a three inch ring, this kind of a covering makes a road very little inferior, in point of evenness on the surface, to the best gravel, and seems . . . to be the proper cement for a stoned turnpike road . . . vastly superior in point of durability, when made of the best kind of stone, to the best gravel road.[22]

OF THE "ENORMOUS WAGONS" that crunched over these early pikes, a majority were made in eastern Pennsylvania. York, in fact, was as famous for its Conestoga wagons as neighboring Lancaster was for its so-called Kentucky rifles. The U.S. census of 1810 showed more than 8,500 wagons made in Pennsylvania, compared with 2,200 in Massachusetts, and fewer in other places. The Conestogas, more often called "Pitt wagons" or "road wagons" in their heyday, usually had beds thirteen to fourteen feet long and three and a half feet wide, built with a noticeable dip between the axles to keep the loads from shifting during treks over the Allegheny ridges. The rear wheels could be as much as six feet in diameter, although a five-and-a-half-foot wheel was more common, with front wheels about three and a half feet. Woods such as poplar might be used for nonstressed parts, but wheels, axles, tongues, and the like were almost invariably made of white oak, the same wood preferred for artillery carriages. The five- or six-horse teams that pulled these wagons were often fitted with bell collars, which made a distinctive musical sound as they moved. One traveler passed "large wagons with five stout horses. Every horse had on its collar a set of bells, consisting of five different tones, which made a very singular music."[23]

Traveling through western Pennsylvania on horseback in 1816, David Thomas noted:

> In New-York, the two-horse Dutch waggon is fashionable [and] in the lower parts of Maryland and Virginia, the light three-horse team is common; while in this country, the heavy Lancaster waggon, drawn by five or six horses, which vie in stature with the elephant, is continually before us. The extreme slowness of these overland sloops, often attracted our notice; but heavy teams in all countries, perhaps, move slowly . . . [and slow or not,] no general, at the head of an army, feels better than the Pennsylvanian whip-cracker.[24]

Where the wagon's wheels were concerned, broad versus narrow became a topic much discussed. As a Virginia paper commented in 1810 in a piece headlined "Turnpikes":

> [I]n these roads the Pennsylvania five horse waggons must not be used, more especially if they run on narrow wheels. It is a rule in England that a four horse waggon must have six inch [wide] wheels. The Turnpike system cannot thrive and spread far as long as 5 & 6 horse teams are suffered to grind to the very bottom of the hardest road—no toll they can pay compensates for the injury. . . . The Secretary of the Treasury, in his report on public Roads and Canals, remarks:—"That the general adoption of broad wheels for the transportation of heavy loads is necessary to the full enjoyment of the advantages expected from the most substantial artificial roads."[25]

The "most substantial artificial roads"–true turnpikes–were indeed necessary to stand up under the wear and tear posed by five- or six-horse bell teams and five-ton wagons, not to mention the hundreds of lighter emigrant wagons that might use them. The big problem was that most of the nation's roads fell far short of turnpike standards. Gradually the terms "turnpike" or "turnpiking" came to mean solidly built roadways covered with two or more layers of broken stone, but this was not the case until about 1820. As the Virginia paper of 1810 noted:

> Thomas Cooper, now a judge in Pennsylvania, has made a tour to Niagara, through the Gennessee country, [and] remarks that the New York Turnpikes, like those of New England, are merely made by clearing out the stumps, ditching on each side of the road, and elevating it in the middle by means of the dirt thus thrown out of the ditches. Hence the people are enabled to make so many more Turnpikes than in Pennsylvania–whose roads are [regarded as] too expensive. He calculates that the cost of a New York road is not more than $1200 [per mile]–whereas the Lancaster Turnpike must have cost $8000.[26]
> (Almost–its actual cost was about $7,500 per mile.)

Wherever they were, or wherever they led, most of the common roads were so rough as to inhibit travelers who might want to use them. Small wonder, then, that some people chose to walk hundreds of miles to their destinations rather than deal with the wear and tear that such roads inflicted on wagons and draft animals. These pedestrians would ship their baggage separately, or just take along the minimum needed to survive: a rifle or musket, a knife or hatchet, a knapsack, and a bedroll.

A graphic example of how bad a road could be came from Christian Schultz, who, in August 1807, made his way west along a well-known water-land-water route: west on Lake Erie to Presque Isle, Pennsylvania, then south on a fourteen-mile portage road to Waterford, near the head of French Creek, then down French Creek to the Allegheny River, and down the Allegheny to Pittsburgh. He first commented that "Lake Erie is perhaps the most dangerous to navigate of all the lakes, affording no harbours, and almost one continued craggy, iron-bound shore." Then, arriving at Presque Isle, he had the experience of the portage road:

Conestoga Wagon by Newbold Hough Trotter (1883). Conestoga Wagons were among the chief wheeled transportation for westward migration for more than half a century. (*State Museum of Pennsylvania, photographed by Ad Meskens*)

[A] turnpike road over this route will soon be completed, [but while] I have travelled many hundred miles both in our old and new countries, and seen both rough and disagreeable roads, yet I never saw a bad road before this. What think you of starting at sunrise, at this season of the year, when the days are longest, and making it dark night before you could whip and spur through fourteen miles of mud and mire? A great part of which is up to your knees while sitting on the saddle. No doubt you have seen people treading clay for making brick; had you seen me at the time of my arrival at this place, you would have sworn that man and horse were both brick makers, for both were literally covered at least one-half inch thick with mud from head to foot . . . nor did I see any thing of the waggon until the next day, when it made its appearance with an additional yoke of oxen. The crippled condition of the waggon convinced me that it had seen hard times; and, upon inquiry, I found the whole waggon and cargo (by one wheel running over the stump of a tree) had been overset in a deep mud hole. . . . I ordered my things down to the stream, and rolling up my sleeves to the elbows, endeavoured to make the best of so bad a bargain.[27]

In the spring of the same year, Samuel Williams and his family decided to move west from Virginia "and commenced making arrangements for the voyage. We say for the voyage; for such was the wretched condition of the roads, especially down the Kanawha River, that no one would think of encountering the perils of traveling on them with loaded wagons where navigable waters led to the place of destination." Things didn't change much in the next few years. Business reasons brought Williams back to the East, but in 1815, he moved west again, this time from Washington, DC, to Ohio:

> Having adjusted his affairs preparatory to removing again to the west, Mr. W. placed his 'plunder'—as household goods were usually [called]—in a common road wagon, with a coarse linen cover drawn over bows, and . . . took the route through Winchester, Va., Cumberland, Md., Union and Brownsville, Penn. The National Road was at that time completed only a few miles west of Cumberland. And in many places across these rugged and precipitous mountains the old road was sadly out of repair. It was, moreover, in many places much obstructed by the work done on the new one, a considerable portion of which was located on or near it. Excepting these few miles of national highway, their whole journey from Washington to Brownsville was over unimproved roads, neither graded nor thrown up, and obstructed with stones and rocks, and often cut up by wagon ruts, and washed into gutters by rains, making the travel very difficult, and sometimes even hazardous. . . . [So,] plodding along in a heavy wagon, without springs, over wretched roads, and toiling hard from morning till night, to accomplish fifteen or twenty miles of weary travel [we finally reached] Brownsville—in olden time called Redstone—on the right bank of the Monongahela River, [whereupon] our weary travelers gladly transferred themselves from their unpleasant and ever-jolting wagon to an open freight boat, on which they embarked for Pittsburgh.[28]

As the Columbus *Ohio Monitor* stated the case late in 1816:

The subject of Roads, we have scarcely permitted to rest, since we commenced our publication. We have expatiated upon the subject in different shapes. The badness of the roads, the inadequacy of the system, the consequent disadvantages, have been discussed in communications, and in our editorial remarks, more, perhaps, than any other theme.[29]

Another Ohio publication, the *Cincinnati Directory* of 1819, said:

In no part of the United States are good roads more wanted [than in western Ohio]. During the winter months the ways are so soft and the mud so deep, that travelling, especially with loaded wagons, is very laborious, tedious and disagreeable. In a country so populous, rich and beautiful, such vile and dis-agreeable roads are degrading to the taste, public spirit, and enterprize of the inhabitants. They might be much improved with very little labour; but among the many improvements for which our young community is distinguished, the roads appear to have been most unpardonably neglected.[30]

James Hall offered a clever little tale about the situation:

A weary way-farer, who journeyed through Ohio a few years ago, illustrated his remarks about the badness of the roads, by relating the following curious fact. He was floundering through the mire . . . sometimes wading to the saddle-girth in water, sometimes clambering over logs, and occasionally plunged in a quagmire. While carefully picking his way [past] a spot more miry than the rest, he espied a man's hat, a very creditable beaver, lying with the crown upwards in the mud, and as he approached, was not a little startled to see it move. . . . [O]ur traveller's flesh began to creep at beholding a hat move without the agency of a head, [but,] determined to pen-etrate the mystery, the solitary rider checked his nag, and extending his long whip, fairly upset the hat–when, lo! beneath it appeared a man's head, [from] which our inquisi-tive traveler heard himself saluted with "Hullo, stranger! Who told you to knock my hat off?" The person thus addressed was so utterly astonished as not to be able for a moment to understand that the apparition was no other than a fellow-creature up to the neck in the mire; but he no sooner came to this conclusion than he promptly apologized for the indecorum of which he had been guilty, and tendered his services to the gentleman in the mud puddle. "I will alight," said he, "and endeavour to draw you forth." "Oh, never mind," said the other, "I'm in rather a bad fix, it is true, but I have an excellent horse under me, who has carried me through many a worse place than this—we shall get along."[31]

Emmanuel Howitt's description was less humorous and nearly as graphic:

We got our horse and waggon up the hill with much difficulty, for the wagon as well as our boxes, was very much broken and shivered by the rocks and stumps over which we had travelled. . . . A young man overtook us this evening, who had been with some rye to be ground at a mill 28 miles distant. His wagon light as ours, and a load not half the weight, drawn by two horses abreast, was broken down upon the rocks . . . and it was wonderful to see with what facility he supplied his loss, by cutting down a fine young white oak, and shaping it into a new axle.[32]

The recurring complaints about stumps often resulted from a stipulation found in any number of contracts, which allowed the road builder to leave stumps in place provided they were no more than twelve to fifteen inches above the ground. Obviously, such a provision practically guaranteed wagon damage. And while roadside repairs might work for wagons, rough roads were even harder on the animals that did the pulling. As Howitt lamented, "Terrible roads still; and the bridges over the small streams nothing more than poles laid across; those over the large ones, of framed timber and covered with 2-inch plank,—which soon wears through, and endangers the horses' legs."

William Amphlett warned that the animals would need constant attention:

Very probably the traveler may not be conversant with the management of horses, or, if he be, and come from Great

Britain, it is impossible he can be acquainted with such roads as he will have to travel in this country. He must not only have the fatigue of driving his horses over such horrible sloughs, rocks, swamps, and precipices, as no English waggoner would allow to be passable, but when he puts up at night, he must be his own hostler; he must unharness, feed, and clean his own cattle, or they will stand in their dirt, and starve.[33]

In 1811, with the surveys and various preliminaries completed, actual construction of the National Road began. One of the evils that this new national highway was supposed to correct was a rough road that became progressively rougher. First the right-of-way was cleared, or "cleared and grubbed" (stumps and roots pulled out) to a specified width of sixty-six feet. Once the debris was removed, the road surface itself, a strip of stone twenty to twenty-two feet wide, was laid down the middle. This strip was composed of two layers: the lower, made of stone able to pass through a seven-inch ring, was laid to a depth of about twelve inches. Next the upper layer, comprising stones small enough to pass through a three-inch ring, went down to a depth of six inches. Then sand and gravel were scattered over the surface and packed into place by rolling heavy logs over it.[34]

Using two different sizes of stone would eventually lead to trouble, as Pennsylvania turnpike officials had already learned. In October 1807, one of them, in describing their road-building procedure, also gave a warning:

> First, [we lay down] a stratum of [stone] six inches deep, broken small enough to pass through a ring of five inches diameter, on which the remaining six inches of stone, broken to a smaller size to pass through a ring of two and a half inches, are laid with the greatest evenness. [However,] experience convinces us that, if the whole body of stone was to be broken down to the smallest size, the road would be more durable, and of an even surface; the larger stones will, in time, work up to the surface by the action of heavy carriages, and prove highly detrimental.

In addition, "good and sufficient drains [must] be kept always open on each side, so that no water remains on the surface."[35]

But although Gallatin quoted this letter in his report, the construction went ahead according to the original proposals.

As finally laid out, the road started at Cumberland, Maryland, and from there went west through hilly, wooded country for about twenty miles, following the existing route toward Morgantown. But once past Tomlinson's Inn (near present-day Grantsville), the road turned gradually northwest, into the thickly timbered hills of southern Pennsylvania, and maintained its northwesterly heading across the Youghiogheny River and the Allegheny ridges to Uniontown, some forty miles distant. Most of its course between Tomlinson's and Uniontown followed a seldom-used, much older route, first known as Nemacolin's Path and, in the late 1750s, as Braddock's Road because of the English general who broadened it during the French and Indian War. There were several hard pulls on this stretch, especially over Laurel Hill, just west of the Youghiogheny, and over Chestnut Ridge, a few miles east of Uniontown. (Early travelers often confused these points, referring to Chestnut Ridge as Laurel Hill, or vice versa.)

Once the road reached Uniontown it would follow an existing, well-traveled route that ran northwest to Brownsville, crossing the Monongahela River there and then continuing to Washington, about twenty-five miles southwest of Pittsburgh. At Washington the road would turn west again, bound for the upper Ohio River at Wheeling. In keeping with the standards set for earlier turnpikes, the angle of the roadway was never to exceed five degrees from the horizontal, which itself was steep enough–a grade of nearly nine percent, or a rise of nine feet in every hundred. Besides the road work, numerous bridges would be needed, including two big ones over the Youghiogheny and the Monongahela.[36]

Early in 1812, after the work started, Superintendent David Shriver saw the need for

> some provision for keeping the road in repair, after it shall be
> received from the contractors; for [the] present road, passing
> over ground so broken, subject to the wash of large quantities
> of water discharged from steep valleys adjoining, as well as

the operations of the seasons upon it in its green and unsettled state, and the great use which, from its local situation, will immediately be made of it . . . will very soon [require major repair. Therefore,] I would respectfully suggest the propriety of demanding such a toll as will be sufficient to keep it in good and perfect order.[37]

THE TOPIC OF CHARGING TOLLS ON A national roadway would cause hot debates for the next twenty years, but there were other points of contention as well, as U.S. Rep. Charles Mercer of Virginia declared in an 1818 speech to the House:

The commencement of the only public work of considerable magnitude which owes its existence to the resources of the union, was long delayed for the assent of one of the states through which it passes. Local jealousies have [posed] other obstacles to its final success, which have [seriously] impaired its utility, and are likely to endanger its preservation. Maryland has refused to authorize a toll for the repairs of the Cumberland road, (which Pennsylvania would have cheerfully conceded) in order that Baltimore may more advantageously contend with Philadelphia, for the western trade across the Alleghany; and two little towns in Pennsylvania have had the pernicious influence to bend from its direct course, so as to suit their own narrow interests, this important channel of intercourse between the eastern and western states.[38]

Sectional squabbles and toll debates would continue, but as events were about to show, there could be little debate about the accuracy of Shriver's predictions regarding the road's heavy use and subsequent need of repair.

Between 1811 and 1813, at least five contractors worked on the road, but progress was slow. In December 1812, Shriver could report, "The contracts for the first ten miles of the western road are completed, with but few exceptions. . . . The road is open, and used daily by travellers. On the second letting, comprising nearly eleven

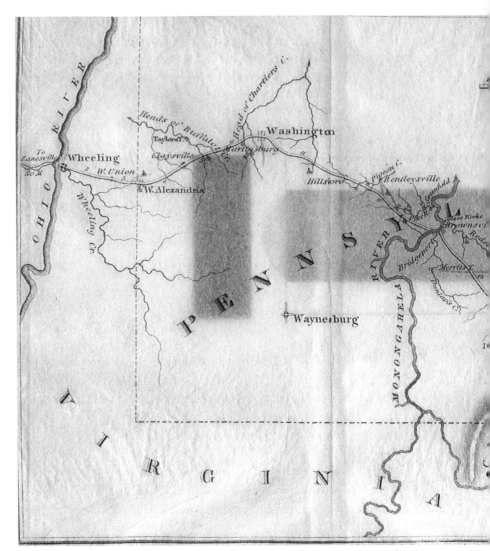

Map of the National Road Between Cumberland and Wheeling was engraved for the 1822 edition of John Melish's *Description of the United States & Travellers Directory.* The Casselman River bridge was located near "Tomlinson's," an inn marked on the map above the "L" in "Maryland" (see frontispiece). Note the location of British General Edward Braddock's grave alongside the north side of the road on the eastern slope of the Chestnut Ridge. Much of the National Road from Cumberland to just west of Chestnut Ridge followed the route carved out of the wilderness by the ill-fated 1755 Braddock Expedition. Pittsburgh, not shown on this map, is located about 40 miles north of Brownsville, along the Monongahela River. (*Courtesy of the David Rumsey Map Collection, www.davidrumsey.com*)

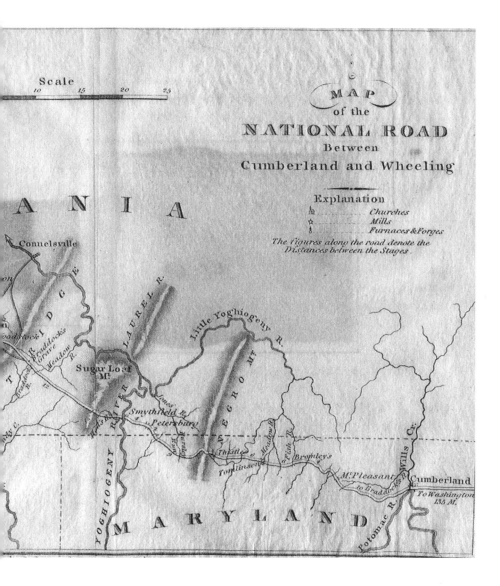

Scale
10   15   20   25

MAP
of the
NATIONAL ROAD
Between
Cumberland and Wheeling

Explanation
           Churches
           Mills
           Furnaces & Forges
The figures along the road denote the
Distances between the Stages.

miles in addition, the contractors (for the time) have made considerable progress." But a year later, in December 1813, he had to admit:

> The second letting, eleven miles, has [still] not been finished, as was expected and provided for by contract the 1st of November last; four miles thereof are now used by travelers, and require but little dressing to the sideways to be complete, four more are nearly so, and it is confidently expected the whole will be finished next summer. On the third letting, about eighteen miles, there is but little done. . . .
>
> [However,] the contractors are making great exertions to procure laborers, and a number of persons, from the evident utility of the work, have become anxious for its speedy progress. . . . Provisions for keeping the road in repair, and for the prevention of abuses to the work, similar to that of other turnpikes, are every day becoming more necessary.

One year later, and still east of Uniontown, Shriver could report that the eleven-mile stretch of the second letting "is now generally used by the traveler." Elsewhere, "about eight miles is in great forwardness and nearly completed, [while] on ten but little progress is made, except the mason work, which is nearly finished."

This report pointed out the fact that different contractors performed their work in different ways—some were efficient, others not. As Shriver would later comment, "If this great national undertaking does not progress with a rapidity equal to the wishes of Government or the anxiety of individuals, the cause may be easily traced to [two] sources . . . the inefficiency of the existing mode of letting out contracts, and the very inadequate supply of hands."

There was another irritant as well—the fact that, "Frequent abuses take place upon the road, such as throwing down the walls, digging down the banks, felling trees, . . . locking of wagon wheels, placing fences within the sixty-six feet, and many other improper acts."[39]

Locking the wheels on downgrades was a long-standing practice. Fortescue Cuming took note of it while traveling by stagecoach near Pittsburgh in 1807:

> [W]e changed an excellent set of grey horses, for as good a
> one of bays ... three miles more brought us to the top of the
> Coal hill, the descent of which to the Monongahela, almost a
> mile, is so steep that two of the wheels of the stage wagon
> had to be locked, and I frequently wished myself out of it, but
> it was impossible to stop to get out, so I comforted myself
> with the reflection that no unfortunate accident had yet hap-
> pened to the stages on this hill, which giving me courage, I
> was enabled to enjoy the views so inexpressibly fine, which
> are perpetually varying, as the road winds down the hill.[40]

Cutting more ruts in the usual dirt roads did them little additional harm, but it did considerable harm to road surfaces made of
finely broken, newly laid stone by exposing the bare earth beneath
and so hastening the erosion process.

No doubt the War of 1812 had an effect on construction, but
whatever the reasons, workers continued to be scarce. So even
before hostilities ended, some of the contractors tried to lure
British soldiers into the labor force. In December 1814, this advertisement appeared in Brownsville's *American Telegraph*:

> The Contractors on the Western Turnpike want to employ
> about ONE THOUSAND GOOD HANDS, to whom prompt
> payment and One Dollar a day will be given. ... If it is politic
> to encourage desertion from the ranks of our enemy, by offer-
> ing them a bounty in land on condition that they immediate-
> ly settle on it, it is equally or more immediately important to
> obtain the aid of these men in completing this National
> Highway—and especially when the wages offer so strong an
> inducement.[41]

In 1814, a dollar a day for labor was respectable pay, but the
work nonetheless continued to drag. As Shriver commented at
year's end, "I had nearly [established] a location from the end of the
work contracted for, to Uniontown, about twenty-one miles, and
should have reported the work; but as the contractors did not proceed with that speed I expected, I thought it prudent to defer this
report, and take time to re-examine the ground [because] much

time, pains, and care [are] necessary in fixing on the best ground, and shortest distance through this mountainous country."[42]

In March 1816, a Senate committee, taking note of the tardiness, reported that:

> If Congress persevere with becoming spirit in this great public work, we shall soon see one of the best roads in the world over the chain of mountains which separate the western from the Atlantic waters, and which, but few years since, were supposed to present insurmountable obstacles to a safe and easy intercourse. . . . [But] it is alike a source of surprise and regret to the committee that the work has been [allowed] to linger for a period of more than nine years. A vigorous prosecution of it now can alone, in any degree, repair the past neglect; and, in the estimation of the committee, no subject is more deserving the favour of Congress.

One reason for the delays, the committee surmised, was the reluctance of local officials to open a smooth road to the west and thus lose some of their constituents to a country that "already holds out sufficient lures to the inhabitants of the Atlantic states to migrate thither." The committee, however, regarded this view as faulty and short-sighted:

> The error of this [policy] is proved by the infallible test of experience, applied to the past and present population of the States and Territories west of the mountains. The emigrant [moves] with intention to reside for life in his new habitation; and when he determines upon such removal, he bestows but little attention upon . . . whether the road on which he has to travel is a very good one, or in the condition of the principal State roads now used. This policy, therefore, although it cannot prevent him from going to the west . . . will materially affect his future connexions with the eastern country, in all the ramifications of a mutually profitable trade and intercourse.

Expanding this theme, the committee's report declared:

> Good roads have an influence over physical impossibilities. By diminishing the natural impediments, they bring places

and their inhabitants [closer] to each other. They increase the value of lands and the fruits of the earth in remote situations. . . . They promote a free intercourse among the citizens of remote places, by which unfounded prejudices and animosities are dissipated, local and sectional feelings are destroyed, and a nationality of character, so desirable to be encouraged, is universally inculcated.[43]

With these resounding words came a recommendation that $300,000 be allocated to push construction forward. The money helped. By December 1817, Treasury Secretary William Crawford could report:

The road is completed from Cumberland forty-five miles west of that place . . . and, from the activity with which the work is carried on by the contractors, there is reason to believe that it will be completed [to Uniontown] early in the ensuing year. Contracts have also been made for completing upwards of thirty miles of the road west of the Monongahela. . . . [T]hese contracts embrace such parts of the roads between the Monongahela and the Ohio as presented the most serious difficulties to travelling and the transportation of heavy articles between those rivers. . . . There is also just reason to believe that the whole of the distance yet to be undertaken, both on the eastern and on the western side of the Monongahela, may be advantageously let in the course of the ensuing year; and that the road from Cumberland to the Ohio may be completed in the best manner in two years from the present time.[44]

For once, the estimate was reasonably accurate. By the summer of 1818, the road had progressed to the point that wagons and coaches could get to Uniontown with little or no trouble. Then, by taking the old road coming into Uniontown from the northeast, they could follow it northwest, through Brownsville and Washington, all the way to the Ohio River without undue hardship. The existing pathway between Washington and Wheeling was a roundabout one, but the new road would correct that.[45]

The westernmost stretches of the road had been costly. As the *Baltimore Patriot* and other papers commented caustically in

December 1818, "A report has been made on the subject of the Cumberland Road. The last 36 miles have cost $616,000—more than 17,000 dollars a mile."

In rebuttal, the *Albany (NY) Argus* offered this comment:

> By an article in a late paper it appears that the last thirty-six miles of this road have cost more than seventeen thousand dollars a mile. [But the fact that] the Cumberland road, besides affording an easy passage over an extensive tract of mountainous country, will be of very great commercial importance is obvious; as it will open as direct a communication as the face of that country admits of, between the Potomac, which falls into the Chesapeake bay, and the Monongahela which unites with the Allegany at Pittsburgh.[46]

Besides, more and more travelers were using it—and complimenting it. After James Flint, rowing a skiff down the Ohio, made his way to Wheeling in November 1818, he noted in his journal that

> Wheeling is a considerable town on the left bank of the river, ninety-six miles [by water] from Pittsburgh. It is expected that the new road from Baltimore to this place will be completed in the course of a year. This being a national highway, on which no tolls are to be levied, and the shortest connection between a sea-port and the Ohio, a great increase of trade is consequently anticipated. Hereafter, Baltimore will be the most proper landing place for Europeans who would settle in western America. At present the carriage of goods from Baltimore to Wheeling is cheaper than from Philadelphia to Pittsburgh. From this it is evident, that the new route is already the shortest and the cheapest.[47]

INDIVIDUAL TRAVELERS ON THE ROAD at that time were numerous, but one of the more interesting was an escaped slave named Frisby, who apparently had a real talent for eluding would-be captors:

> One Hundred Dollars Reward. Ran Away from Union Town, Pennsylvania, on the march from Bowling Green, Virginia, to

Wheeling, on the Ohio. . . . Frisby is about 5 feet 8 or 9 inches high, stout and well made, remarkably broad across the shoulders, about 35 years of age; has some grey hairs in his head and beard, and lisps a little when he speaks. He reads and writes a little–is a professor of the Christian religion, of the order called Methodists–and is, in fact, by occupation a carpenter. He was raised by Gov. Bowie, of Md., in whose neighborhood is his wife, belonging to Judge Key, where it is probable he will go, if he should not remain amongst that class of persons in Pennsylvania, denominated Quakers. . . . The above named negro was apprehended at Bedford, in Pennsylvania, in July last; in October was conveyed to Pittsburg, where he was put on board the Barge Gov. Clarke, destined for New-Orleans; which was commanded by a Captain Oliver C. Johnston, from whom he made his escape, not far from Shawnee Town, on the Ohio. . . . [W]herever he may be, he will endeavor to pass himself as a free man, and no doubt will produce documents made by himself for that purpose. The same Reward as offered and paid for his apprehension in July last, will again be paid for putting him in jail, and keeping him there so that I can get him, or Two Hundred Dollars for delivering him to Messrs. Brandt & Co. Merchants, in New-Orleans.[48]

When James Flint and the elusive Frisby traveled it, the road was still not finished, and in June 1819, Superintendent Shriver inserted notices in western Pennsylvania papers requesting proposals "for constructing the whole or any part of the United States Road, Between Uniontown and Washington. . . . Contractors are to furnish the materials, and finish the work they respectively undertake, before the first day of October 1820."

At the same time, the *Baltimore Patriot* printed this item:

THE GREAT WESTERN ROAD . . . At the late session of Congress, upwards of half a million dollars was appropriated to finish this road to the Ohio river; the Bank road [between Baltimore and Frederick] is also rapidly progressing, and will be nearly completed in 1820. A very short distance will only then remain to be turnpiked, and Baltimore will have a turn-

pike road to the Ohio river. The sum of one hundred thousand dollars will effect this grand object. . . . It will be a matter of astonishment if the great object is longer neglected; it
has already been neglected too long; it wants but little exer-
tion—yet let not one man, nor one section of the country,
leave it to another. Let all assist—let all unite their exertions
and the work will SOON BE DONE.[49]

John Woods, who traveled the "Great Western Road" in the
summer of 1819, wrote:

From the north branch of the Potomac river, we passed a very
hilly country, to a new road, called the National Turnpike.
This road is to extend from Cumberland on the Potomac, to
Wheeling on the Ohio, a distance of more than 120 miles; the
first 62 miles, from Cumberland to Union town, on the west
side of the Allegany Mountains, was just finished, and is a
good road, though hilly. The road west from Union town to
Wheeling, was begun in many places, and many men were
employed on it when we passed along it. This grand national
road is intended to connect all the western country with the
seat of government, as there is water communication from
Cumberland to the city of Washington, on the east by the
Potomac, and from Wheeling on the Ohio, with . . . all the
western country, by the means of the Ohio, Mississippi,
Missouri, Cumberland, Tennessee, and other rivers. This
national road is free, as there are no gates on it; for as it was
made by the nation, so it is to be kept in repair by it. We
entered this road, five miles west of Cumberland, and soon
after stopped at Mr. Carter's tavern, called "the Travellers'
Rest," at the foot of the Allegany Mountains.

After clambering over the ridges, Woods and his party came to
the village of Smithfield, where the National Road crossed the
Youghiogheny River. There Woods found

three taverns, viz. a stone house, the Globe; a frame one, the
Rising Sun; and a good log one, the Yougany; and about
twenty other houses, mostly of logs. A noble stone bridge [is]

over the river, the centre arch ninety feet span, said to be the largest in the United States. The Yougany is one of the head streams of the Monongahela. Leaving the river, we followed the course of a small stream, to the Elephant tavern, kept by Major Paul, (late in the American service), where we slept. This town is noted as a waggon house; there were eight stopped there at the time we were there, mostly drawn by six horses each, and none less than five.

After leaving the Elephant tavern,

We now again ascended, and at length reached the top of Laurel Hill [actually Chestnut Ridge], the last ridge of the mountains. . . . Here we had the first, and a most extensive view of the west side of the mountains. As the air was clear, we could see objects distinctly; much cleared land in sight, and many fine springs; indeed, they were numerous all over the mountains, but there were but few houses. This day we descended gently down the hill; the road was steep and winding. As we advanced, the timber increased in size, mostly oak, and towards the bottom it was immensely large. . . . We had now entered the western country, but we were still in the old settled part of it, Union town having been built more than thirty years. It is a large place, mostly of brick buildings; it has a bank, twelve or fourteen taverns, a flour, a saw, and a carding mill, on a small stream near the town. . . . From Union town, the turnpike was only begun at different places, but many men were employed on it. . . . Land better as we approached Brownsville, on the Monongahela. Brownsville is a thriving place, with some iron-works; at high water many people embark here for Pittsburgh. As the national road crosses the Monongahela at this place, there is a bridge to be built over the river; it was about 300 yards when we forded it, but it is much wider when the water is high. From the river we went six miles, mostly through woods, to the Golden Lion Tavern. A woman milking her cow, on the side of the road, gave us some milk, and offered us some apples.[50]

Krepps Inn built in 1822 along the National Road was located just west of Brownsville, Pennsylvania, and served travelers for more than 100 years. It was unoccupied in 1963 when this photograph was taken. Note the large twin chimneys on the gable ends. (*Historic American Building Survey/Library of Congress*)

During the same summer, Thomas Hulme was just to the west of Woods and his party, in Wheeling, reaching it from Pittsburgh after a journey by coach over the Pennsylvania state road. In July 1819, he noted in his journal:

> Cross[ed] Wheeling Creek several times to-day; it is a rapid stream, and I hope it will not be long before it turns many water-wheels. . . . Went with a Mr. Graham, a quaker of this place, who treated us in the most friendly and hospitable manner, to see the new national road from Washington city to this town. It is covered with a very thick layer of nicely broken stones, or stone rather, laid on with great exactness both as to depth and width, and then rolled down with an iron roller, which reduces all to one solid mass. This is a road made for ever; not like the flint roads in England, rough, nor soft or dirty, like the gravel roads; but smooth and hard. When a road is made in America, it is well made.[51]

Even more enthusiastic was a "Traveller to the West," who had earlier voyaged down the Ohio and was now returning east through Wheeling by stagecoach:

> [A]ll the bridges are of solid hewn stone, with from one to three arches. From Wheeling the road crosses a considerable stream no less than 7 or 8 times, within ten miles. From Uniontown, at the foot of Laurel-hill [Chestnut Ridge], the highest and most westerly of the several ranges of mountains, to Cumberland, a distance of 60 miles, it is completed; and the ascent or descent does not exceed from 5 to 7 degrees. No one who for business or pleasure has occasion to visit the western country, will grudge his proportion of the public expense in erecting this stupendous high way. It is of infinite value in a national point of view, as connecting and cementing the western with the Atlantic states. What was formerly a hazardous journey of weeks, is now performed in 4 days. . . . Imagine a narrow way over these mountains, necessarily on a side hill, with deep ruts worn by the heavy six horse teams constantly passing and repassing–an awful precipice at the right or the left, constant danger of oversetting from the lower rut always being the deepest and the impossibility of carriages passing each other in many places from one fourth of a mile to a mile in extent.–Contrast this with the road I have attempted to describe, on which you can now come down these mountains in safety, the horses going almost at full speed, and you will have some idea of its utility in facilitating the intercourse between the Atlantic and the western states. Nothing in our country can exceed the grandeur and beauty of the scenery, from the top of Laurel hill, West, and Sideling hill, East and North.[52]

Many other voices echoed these praises of the road, but a few did not. As one paper remarked tersely, "This road is not liked in Pennsylvania." The reason was clear: traffic once carried through Pennsylvania was now shifting south to the smooth, toll-free National Road. Philadelphia's *Franklin Gazette* spelled it out:

The commerce of the western country is of such vital importance to Philadelphia, that nothing is more astonishing than
the tranquility with which its approaching loss is viewed by
her citizens. The completion of the Great National Road from
Wheeling to Cumberland, and the connecting of the latter
place with Baltimore, are measures that should excite serious
alarm among the men of property in Philadelphia, and awak-
en their exertions. Wheeling, a town on the Ohio River, 100
miles below Pittsburgh [by water], is about being connected
to Baltimore by a route, shorter and cheaper, and better than
any that at present exists between the Eastern and Western
waters of the United States. The distance will be but 252
miles, the greater part of which is now turnpiked; the whole
[including the Bank Road between Baltimore and
Cumberland] will probably be completed in less than two
years—and 121 miles of the road, (the best in the United
States) will be free from toll. . . . [So] the only practical means
of retaining this valuable commerce [will be] by the construction of a good free turnpike road [in place of the existing
road], and the establishment of safe and rapid communication
upon it with Pittsburg. . . . [But] let it be free of toll and kept
in excellent order.[53]

Well aware of the threat, other Pennsylvanians were working
hard on improvements. And the state road needed improvement,
as Thomas Hulme's journal of 1818 suggested:

Pittsburgh, June 3.—Arrived here with a friend as travelling
companion, by the mail stage from Philadelphia, after a journey of six days. . . . The ridges of mountains called the
Allegany . . . extend[ed] across our route nearly 100 miles, or
rather, three days, for it was no less than half the journey to
travel over them; they rise one above the other as we proceed
Westward, till we reach the Allegany, the last and most lofty
of all, from which we have a view to the West farther than the
eye can carry. I can say nothing in commendation of the road
over these mountains, but I must admire the drivers and their
excellent horses.[54]

One observer, reporting on Pennsylvania's road-building effort at that time, suggested that it was a battle all the way:

> The third section from Chambersburgh to Bedford is 53 miles in extent; of these 53 miles 24 are finished, 10 more are contracted for, and 19 remain to be contracted for. . . . Besides being the most extensive section, of any of those forming, this third section passes over a country almost wholly mountainous. . . The fourth section is 27 miles in extent, from Bedford to Stoystown; of these 16 are completed [and] 3 are contracted for.

Even worse was the fifth section:

> The fifth section between Stoystown and Greensburgh is 36 1/2 miles in extent; of these 17 are completed, 15 1/2 are contracted for, and but 4 remain to be contracted for. . . . This section presented a greater number of obstacles than any other on the route; the large streams upon it are more numerous than upon any other, and the chestnut and laurel mountains need only to be mentioned to those who have ever passed them to prove the extent of the difficulty. . . . [Nevertheless,] we are happy to be able to state, that the company formed in this city, for transporting merchandize and passengers by lines of waggons travelling day and night, between Philadelphia and Pittsburgh, contemplate commencing their operations early in the spring.[55]

As Samuel Breck explained it in an 1818 pamphlet:

> The Transporting Company, authorised by a law of last session, have a capital of one hundred thousand dollars. They have despatched four wagons daily (Sundays excepted) since the month of May last; two from Philadelphia and two from Pittsburg, and are now making preparations to double that number. These wagons take fresh horses every ten miles, and travel day and night. . . . After next summer, when the road will be finished the whole way, they will send, if necessary, ten carriages daily, at as low a freight as four dollars, and perform the journey of 300 miles in 8 days.[56]

The company was short-lived, but its operational plan reflected the fact that the better the road, the faster the travel on it.

The turnpike was not finished quite as soon as Breck expected, and was rough in spots, but it did have its compensations. Adlard Welby, traveling the "third section" from Chambersburg to Bedford in August 1819, mentioned that the road

> has been lately formed, is judiciously laid, and would be excel-
> lent were the stones covered with gravel, or rather were they
> broken small; as it is, one is shaken to pieces without the pos-
> sibility of avoiding it. [But t]hroughout the mountains and
> their neighbourhood, you almost universally meet with most
> excellent water, affording a delicious beverage during the hot
> weather; the trunk of a tree hollowed out is set up like a
> pump, with a spout near the top, from which the water, con-
> stantly rising towards its level, runs in a clear and cool stream.

A little farther west, Welby found the traveling easier: "We approached [Bloody Run] for the last nine miles by a new and excellent road just finishing, which is laid a considerable way along the Juniatta, the banks of which are beautifully edged with wood-land. Some alterations and repairs [were] done to the dearborn and waggon here."

Taking note of his surroundings, Welby commented further, "Many parties from various nations and of different modes of trav-elling are on the road for the West, and we hear of great numbers having passed during the spring and summer, all making towards the great point of attraction, the western country."[57]

By the fall of 1819, most of Pennsylvania's state road had been properly "turnpiked." But it was still a toll road, and at that time, the country's attention tended to center on its newly completed National Road.

After this road reached Wheeling in 1819, construction did not resume again for several years. Nor was there a pressing need for it, because at Wheeling, emigrants simply descended the Ohio River, or continued west on Zane's Trace–all the way to the Mississippi, if they chose, first by way of Zane's route to Maysville, then by way of the Maysville road to Lexington; from Lexington the road led through Frankfort to Louisville, from Louisville to

Vincennes, and from Vincennes to the Mississippi. Soon this pathway—west of Frankfort, at least—would be known as the Great Western Mail Route because it was one of the most heavily used avenues to the Mississippi, even after the National Road made its way through Ohio into Indiana.

When John Woods reached Wheeling in 1819, he noted that it was "a thriving place, with some iron-works; [and] the great road for all the western country, crossing the Ohio at this place, will always add much to its importance."[58]

But Thomas Hulme did not think much of Woods's "great road for all the western country."

OWNERS of CATTLE

I intend driving the cattle I have on hand, to the Eastward in August. Those who know themselves indebted to me, are, *generally* informed, that I will take cows of all ages that are fit for beef, and steers from two to five years old, tho' they should not be fat—I will attend at New-Market on the 3d and 4th of August, and at the Sinking Spring, on the 5th and 6th, for the purpose of receiving any cattle that may be brought in; those of my acquaintance who have good young cattle, and are disposed to wait for the money until my return, will get a generous price for all they bring in, to either of the above named places, or to this place, before the 10th of August.

JOSEPH KERR.

Chillicothe, June 10th, 1808.

A notice for a cattle drive in the *Scioto Gazette*, Chillicothe, Ohio, June 1808.

Traveling it some thirty miles west of Wheeling (where it was still known as Zane's Trace), he complained that it was "by no means well laid out; it goes strait over the tops of the numerous little hills, up and down, up and down. It would have been a great deal nearer in point of time, if not in distance (though I think it would that, too), if a view had been had to the labour of travelling over these everlasting unevennesses."

Despite the unevenness, Hulme met, in one eight-mile stretch, "10 wagons, loaded with emigrants." Other traffic was there as well. Not far west of Zanesville, David Thomas ran into a cattle drive with "upwards of 300 head of cattle destined for the Philadelphia or Baltimore market. The road was filled to a great distance, and their long line seemed to recall the pastoral days of Theocritus."[59]

Emigrants were coming into Ohio in a steady stream, and into northern Kentucky as well. But west of Louisville, the road leading toward the Mississippi through Indiana Territory and Vincennes could seem long and lonely, as could the road from Vincennes across southern Illinois to St. Louis. William Blane left a graphic description of the Illinois prairie:

> I do not know any thing that struck me more forcibly than the sensation of solitude I experienced in crossing this, and some of the other large Prairies. I was perfectly alone, and could see nothing in any direction but sky and grass. Leaving the wood appeared like embarking alone upon the ocean; and upon again approaching the wood, I felt as if returning to land. Sometimes again, when I perceived a small stunted solitary tree that had been planted by some fortuitous circumstance, I could hardly help supposing it to be the mast of a vessel. No doubt the great stillness added very much to this strange illusion. Not a living thing could I see or hear, except the occasional rising of some prairie fowls, or perhaps a large hawk or eagle wheeling about over my head. In the woods I have often observed this silence and solitude, but it struck me more forcibly in these boundless meadows.[60]

On roads crossing such terrain, it was wise to be cautious. In April 1819, a letter arrived at Baltimore from Vincennes:

> I witnessed a terrible scene some moments since. A gentleman by the name of McCall, an associate judge of our court, has just been murdered by some 3 or 4 Miami Indians. The cart which bears him is yet within sight of my door—his wife sits beside him, in the attitude, and with all the appearance of despair, accompanied by her two children. Father of mercies, how horrible a sight! The very paper before me appears to be sprinkled with blood![61]

Later the same year, a Vincennes paper printed this account:

> HORRID MURDER. A short time since, we adverted to the frequency of crime in the western country, and copied from an Illinois paper an account of a murder committed at the United States Saline [near Shawneetown]. We have now the disgusting task of recording another, as brutal and barbarous as any which has stained the annals of the west. Unless more exertion

is made for the conviction of the perpetrators of such deeds, the great roads in Illinois will soon rival the most dangerous parts of Italy and Germany; and travellers, as in those countries, will be obliged to go in bands, particularly armed against the murderous assaults of monsters in human shape, whose trade is robbery, and whose pastime is spilling human blood.

Three men were travelling on foot from St. Louis to Vincennes. Their names were Squires, Morris, and Wagner. At the persuasion of Wagner, they passed Lewis's tavern, about four miles, and encamped in a thicket on Friday night last. In the dead of the night, Wagner rose and with a large knife cut the throat of Squires, who was an old man, and expired without a struggle. The wretch then attempted the same act on Morris, but fortunately the first stab awakened him, and in the struggle the murderer seized the old man's cane, and beat Morris until he supposed him to be dead. He then robbed them, and left them. Morris revived, and was discovered by some travellers on Saturday, as he was strolling about the prairie in a deranged situation; [they] humanely conveyed him to Lewis's. . . . Such is the plain narrative of this bloody business. Morris states that he had 70 dollars in notes on the Bank of Chillicothe, and 10 dollars in silver, which are all missing.[62]

A voyager on the Ohio River in western Indiana described the local method of handling such matters. While he was at a riverside tavern,

two men called in armed with rifles, and made enquiries for some horses they suspected to be stolen. They told us they had been almost all the way from [New] Albany, to Shawnee town after them, a distance of about 150 miles. I asked them how they would be able to secure the thieves, if they overtook them, in these wild woods; "O," said they, "shoot them off the horses." This is a summary mode of executing justice, thought I, though probably the most effectual, and, indeed, the only one in this state of society.[63]

Traveling the roads through unsettled country also meant crossing any number of creeks and rivers. The emigrant arriving at such a stream could reach the far bank in one of three ways: he could find a ford and wade or swim across; he could ride across on a ferry; or he could simply walk across on a bridge. When construction began on the National Road in 1811, bridge-building was already one of the country's accomplished arts, those bridges across the Delaware in Pennsylvania standing as notable examples.

Soon enough, however, the stone bridges on the National Road became famous on their own. The first of note was a single-arch bridge across the Little Youghiogheny in western Maryland, built in 1813 at a spot called the "Little Crossings." (It is now known as the Casselman River Bridge). The span of its arch–eighty feet–was broad enough so that roadside critics claimed it would collapse when any substantial weight rolled over it, but the bridge held (and still does). A more impressive feat was the three-arch "Big Crossings" bridge across the Great Youghiogheny, built at a then-startling cost of $40,000.[64]

West of the Alleghenies, however, few stone bridges were in place. A bridge in the wilderness, of course, could be nothing more than a couple of logs thrown across a stream. But a wider stream, or a river, required something more, and the enterprising frontier dweller could then build a ferry by lashing a number of logs together. It was usually simpler and less time-consuming than building a bridge.

Early in 1796, a petition made its way to the U.S. Senate from Ebenezer Zane:

> [T]he petitioner sets forth that he hath, at considerable trouble and expense, explored, and in part opened, a road northwest of the river Ohio, between Wheeling and Limestone, which, when completed, will greatly contribute to the accommodation of the public as well as of individuals; but that several rivers intervening, the road proposed cannot be used with safety until ferries shall be established thereon. . . . [T]he petitioner will engage to have such ferries erected, provided he can obtain a right to the [adjacent] land, which is now the property of the United States.

The spectacular three-arch "Big Crossings" bridge across the Youghiogheny River was built in 1818 as part of the original National Road. The river was dammed in 1942, which submerged the town of Somerfield (formerly Smithfield) and the bridge. During periods of drought, the bridge is visible, here photographed by Vincent G. Ferrari in 2001. The stone span remains well preserved and is an underappreciated historical and architectural treasure. (*Vincent G. Ferrari*)

Generously–perhaps a little too much so–the Senate awarded him "three tracts of land, not exceeding one mile square each, at [the] Muskingum, Hockhocking, and Scioto, where the proposed road shall cross those rivers, for the purpose of establishing ferries thereon."[65]

Some of the ferries in the western country had a special feature or two that provoked comment. The 1808 edition of Zadok Cramer's *Navigator* described one of them, on the Muskingum below Zane's Trace: "At the mouth of this river a ferry boat is carried rapidly across by means of a rope extending from bank to bank, and a windlass ingeniously worked at each end."[66]

To cross the Ohio River, a "Traveller to the West" found, in 1819, "a horse ferry boat at Cincinnati, which plies once in every half hour to Newport and Covington, the two opposite villages on the Kentucky side. The distance from Cincinnati to Lexington is 90 miles. I was surprised to find no stages between these two places; but the intercourse is trifling, as Lexington receives her Western supplies by way of Louisville, and her Eastern, by Limestone." [67]

A traveler near the Ohio River in the 1820s penned an engrossing account of a ferryman and his patrons:

> Some few miles below Augusta, on the Kentucky shore, there stands at this time on the bank of the river, a small double log cabin, the former proprietor of which united for a long time the character of farmer, tavern-keeper, magistrate and ferryman . . . he was a jolly fellow, full of fun. . . . Among the evenings that I have spent with this jocose landlord, there is one I shall long remember—It was in the latter part of October, near the close of the day, when in company with two or three fellow travelers I arrived at [his] door; the clouds which had been lowering all the afternoon now assumed a more dark and threatening aspect; the vivid lightning which played along the verge of the horizon was followed by loud peals of thunder; the wind with irresistible force ascended the valley of [the] Ohio and in a few moments the rain descended in torrents. We were offering congratulations to each other upon our comfortable situation as we drew near the fire, when the trampling of horses was heard, and a voice from without crying "halloo the ferryman." The door was opened and exhibited to view a young couple covered with mud and drenched by the rain who desired to be ferried over the river without delay, as they were in great haste. The landlord cast his eyes toward the clouds, from which rain was still descending with great violence, shook his head and desired them to dismount, declaring that his boat should not cross the river again that night. "Johnny, tell him he must set us over and be hanged to him," whispered the young lady with great earnestness, "for that plaguy dad of mine will surely be here before midnight, and then the jig is all up. . . ." Johnny bade his dear Sukey, as he was pleased to call her, hold her tongue lest she should be overheard, and again bawling to the landlord proffered him five dollars if he would ferry him over—but in vain; the landlord was inexorable, and after some little consultation they dismounted, and approached the fire, from which we gladly retreated in order to avoid the water that dripped from their garments in great profusion. As we walked to the other

end of the room one of my fellow travellers, who readily con-
jectured the business of the hopeful couple at the fire, tapping
me on the shoulder, whispered "there's a runaway match for
you, and as our landlord is ex officio a justice of the peace, he
shall marry them this very night, and rare sport we'll have of
it too." . . . Matters were very soon arranged to the satisfaction
of the parties, and the fair Sukey immediately withdrew to the
landlady's apartment in order to exchange her muddy gar-
ments for the bridal one which she had brought in a handker-
chief suspended at the horn of her saddle.

While the landlord and travelers waited for her, Johnny told
them of their escape from her family's home:

[W]ith as much haste as possible, placing her on one horse
and mounting the other myself, we left the house just as the
old man opened the door. We have travelled night and day
since we started, but so closely has the old fellow pursued,
that he was in sight of us when we landed on this side of
Licking river; but for the sake of a dollar which I gave the ferryman, he agreed not to set him over for an hour, and thus
enable us to escape, and here you see us, half starved, and as
wet as a drowned rat." At this moment the bride came bouncing into the room quite metamorphosed, and chucking
Johnny under the chin, informed him that she was now ready
and that there was no time to be lost. . . . Our landlord now
arose, and taking down an antiquated volume from the shelf
over the fire place which contained the church of England
ceremony, desired the bride and groom to rise, and with all
imaginable gravity commenced reading the service; but ere he
had proceeded two pages a loud knocking was heard from
without. "Good luck," exclaimed Sukey with the utmost consternation, "I'll warrant that is my old dad; do sir, I pray, make
haste and finish." The landlord beckoned to my officiating fellow traveller to step to the door and prevent its being opened
until the proper time, and passing a bowl of punch, which had
been prepared for the occasion, to the bride and groom,
desired them to be of good cheer, as he would soon be done.
The ceremony was resumed, as well as the cries from without

for admittance; and at the moment when the landlord was pronouncing them man and wife, the door flew open, and to our great astonishment in [strode] an elderly little gentleman, exclaiming with a loud shrill voice "man and vixen–what does this all mean?" . . . He advanced with a quick step and indignant look towards his daughter, exclaiming "you good for nothing jade, you, I have got you at last, have I?" "Yes dad," replied Sukey, "but Johnny has got me too."[68]

Among other things, this story shows that travelers in need of a ferry were often at the ferryman's mercy. In 1807, Christian Schultz spent a hair-raising night in the woods south of the Ohio, surrounded by wolves, after two long delays in crossing the river because of absent ferrymen. There was also a risk in using a dilapidated or poorly built ferry; Adlard Welby, crossing the Ohio from Kentucky to Indiana in 1819, was not overjoyed at the prospect: "Three miles beyond Louisville the western road again brings you to the Ohio; and by a very ill conducted and apparently rather dangerous ferry we were wafted over (after waiting for our turn with many waggons & c. above three hours), and entered the State of Indiana at the town of New Albany."[69]

A well-known ferry across the Ohio was the one between the foot of Zane's Trace and Maysville, as John Woods noted in 1819: "Maysville is a considerable place, and enjoys a good trade with the back country. . . . Much good building going forward. A large ferryboat, worked by horses, plies between Maysville and a small town opposite; it takes over passengers, horses, carriages, and stock; as a road on the opposite side [the Trace] takes most of the land-travellers through the state of Ohio."[70]

More succinctly, William Faux, who used it at about the same time, said, "We passed through pleasant Maisville, in Kentucky, on the banks of the Ohio, which we had first to cross on a large teamboat, worked by eight horses, on to which we drove, stage and all, without quitting the stage."[71]

STAGECOACH LINES

THE RAPID RISE OF STAGECOACHING between the Alleghenies and the Mississippi River resulted in part from a decision reached by the U.S. Post Office in 1803. In November that year, James Jackson, the head of a congressional committee looking into the subject of mail transport by coach, presented a list of questions to Postmaster General Gideon Granger. One of them asked whether carrying the mail "in stage or covered wagons" on an existing route between Virginia and Georgia had answered expectations. Other questions were, "Is it expedient to extend . . . the carriage of the mail in stage or covered wagons? And what mode will be most advantageous? By private contract, or otherwise?"

Granger left no doubt as to his preferences; he favored expanding stagecoach mail and employing private contractors to handle it:

> The increase of our population, agriculture, and commerce . .
> . and of travel to and from different States, and distant parts of
> the same State; the superior security and regularity with which
> the mails are carried when under cover, and guarded by the
> traveller; the constantly increasing and enormous size of many
> of the mails on the great post roads, owing principally to an
> extended and extending circulation of newspapers; the vast
> convenience furnished to the traveller, and to the country
> through which the [stages] pass . . . all [require] giving every
> reasonable encouragement to those who will adventure in
> establishing and supporting regular lines of public carriages.

Especially important, in Granger's opinion, was:

The establishment of lines of stages from . . . Chambersburg, in Pennsylvania, to Pittsburgh, and from thence, by Chillicothe in Ohio to Lexington, in Kentucky, and from that place to Knoxville, in Tennessee, and from thence by Staunton, to Richmond, in Virginia. Many embarrassments and difficulties will present themselves in passing the mountains, and completing the establishments in the Western States. But it is believed that, with a reasonable encouragement, the necessary arrangements might be effected in a short time.

There was another subject to deal with as well. As the committee stated:

[T]he late cession of Louisiana by France to the United States renders it an object of primary importance to have the nearest and most expeditious mode of communication established between the city of Washington and the city of New Orleans, the capital of that province; not only for the convenience of Government, but to accommodate the citizens of the several commercial towns in the Union. . . . [A]t present, the mail is conveyed on a circuitous route from this place to Knoxville and Nashville, in Tennessee, and from thence, through the wilderness, by Natchez, to New Orleans–a distance of more than fifteen hundred miles.[1]

However, exploring the terrain between Knoxville and New Orleans to find the most direct route between the two would not be an overnight job, and in the meantime Granger turned to other matters. In July 1804, mail coaches owned by John Tomlinson & Company began running once a week from Philadelphia to Pittsburgh–an important step. Three months later the *Washington (DC) National Intelligencer* printed a letter describing this trip:

Pittsburgh. . . . I have the pleasure of announcing to you my safe arrival here, after a very pleasant journey of less than 7 days from Philadelphia. Ladies perform this trip with much ease and safety; there were two in the stage with us. The hors-

PHILADELPHIA AND PITTSBURGH
MAIL STAGES.

THE proprietors, with pleasure now inform the
public that they run their line of STAGES twice in
the week, to and from the above places.
They leave John Tomlinson's, Spread Eagle,
Market street Philadelphia, every Tuesday and Friday morning at 4 o'clock; and Thomas Ferree's,
Fountain inn, Water street, Pittsburgh, every Wednesday and Saturday, perform their trip in seven
days—for each passenger 20 dollars, 14 lb. baggage,
for extra baggage to pay 12½ cents per lb this line
runs through Lancaster, Elizabeth town, Middle
town, Harrisburgh, Carlisle, Shippensburgh, Cham-
bersburgh, M'Connells town, Bedford, Somerset,
Greensburgh, &c.
As usual they continue to run these line of stages in conjunction with Mr. Scott, from Philadelphia to the city of Washington via Lancaster,
Columbia, York, Hanover, Petersburgh, Frederick
town, &c. three times a week, summer establishment, and twice a week in winter. Also their
daily stages from Philadelphia and Lancaster, continue as heretofore.
All baggage transported by any of the above
lines of stages is to be, and remain at the risque of
the owner. The proprietors of the above lines
respectfully thank the public for their past favours,
would be glad they would increase them, and they
will pledge themselves neither expence nor attention shall be wanting on their part to make
theire several lines respectable.
            JOHN TOMLINSON & Co.
  Nov. 12   mw&f3m

A notice in the *Aurora General Advertiser* (Philadelphia) in November 1804, advertising passenger room on mail stages from Philadelphia and Pittsburgh. The stages left each city twice a week for the seven-day journey across the state. The price was $20, nearly $300 in today's economy, and included 14 pounds of baggage. Extra baggage was charged at 12 1/2 cents a pound.

es in this line, I believe to be superior to any other on the continent, and the drivers very careful and accommodating. The Inns where the stages put up are excellent, [and their] charges are truly moderate; my expenses the whole distance (320 miles) . . . amounted to only the small sum of 8 dolls. 2 cents. The proprietors really merit every encouragement, and the thanks of the public.

In response to this letter, a New York paper said:

[I]t must be a charming thing to travel between Philadelphia and Pittsburgh. A pleasant journey of less than seven days– ladies perform the trip with much ease and safety. . . . A very inviting detail truly. This silken sort of travelling is indeed delightful. Who does not long to go to Pittsburgh? *Eight dollars and two cents* in three hundred and twenty miles! And then the stage runs as smooth as a ball on a billiard table.

Hush–it would be a dreadful sin to suspect that the writer, instead of being a traveller who had reached Pittsburgh on his way to New-Orleans, is one of the proprietors of the stage, and penned the [letter] in his office in Philadelphia.[2]

On occasion, Tomlinson and his Pittsburgh-bound coaches had more serious problems than a skeptical editor. In December 1806:

A daring outrage was committed on the Western Mail Stage . . . about half a mile from the Bridge on the Lancaster Turnpike Road, on its rout to the westward, by two or more footpads [highwaymen], who attempted to seize the horses, at the same time calling out to the driver to stop and deliver, which was not obeyed.–Instantly a piece was discharged at him, but happily the contents struck the fore part of the stage by his side and he escaped unhurt. The assassin who fired was so near that the wadding of his piece fell on fire in the stage amongst the passengers, nine in number. The horses ran off from the fright, and it being dark no attempt was made at detection at the time. For apprehending of the villains, Mr. Tomlinson offers a reward of 100 dollars.[3]

WEST OF PITTSBURGH, IN OHIO, stagecoach service was barely getting started; Granger's statement in 1803 about effecting the necessary arrangements there "in a short time" had proved optimistic. In April 1806, well before construction of the National Road began, he wrote to Nathaniel Willis, a prominent citizen of Chillicothe, on the subject of carrying the mail along Zane's Trace between Chillicothe and Wheeling:

I wish you to make enquiry and inform me if you find any person willing to undertake to carry the mail in stages. . . . [I]n the meantime I wish you to have the mail carried on horseback on that route until it is so improved that stages can pass upon it with proper expedition. . . . [So] call upon the several supervisors of the roads and endeavour to persuade them to improve it. A line of stages would be of great advantage in

carrying the mail and afford considerable accommodation to
the inhabitants & I hope to see one erected as soon as the
road is in proper order. I do not wish you to set your stages
in motion between Chillicothe and Frankfort until they are in
operation between Wheeling and Chillicothe, but as soon as
that is the case yours must be in motion.[4]

After a number of difficulties, Willis apparently got his lines
moving. In October 1806, mail-coach schedules for points both
east and west appeared in Chillicothe's, *Scioto Gazette,* followed by
a note: "Cash Given For Oats At the Stage Office, Chillicothe."[5]

In August 1807, while hiking Zane's Trace from Maysville to
Chillicothe, Fortescue Cuming "arrived at Heistant's tavern, four
miles from Marshon's, where we met the Lexington stage." Not far
from there, Cuming came to

Talbot's, which is a good two story house of squared logs,
with a large barn and excellent stabling, surrounded by a well
opened and luxuriant farm, with a fine run of meadow. . . .
[Talbot] has lately rented this house and farm from Mr. Willis
of Chilicothe, the contractor for carrying the mail from
Wheeling to Lexington. Observing a new stage wagon in the
yard, my host informed me that it was one which Mr. Willis
intended in a few days to commence running between
Chilicothe and Ellis's ferry [opposite Maysville], so that it,
and the one already established, will each run once a week on
different days.

Then Cuming, still eastbound on Zane's Trace and passing
through what was then New Lancaster, had an introduction to
local customs:

After supping at the inn where the stage stopped, I was shewn
to bed up stairs in a barrack room the whole extent of the
house, with several beds in it, one of which was already occupied by a man and his wife, from the neighbouring country,
who both conversed with me until I feigned sleep, in hopes
that would silence them, but though they then ceased to
direct their discourse to me, they continued to talk to each

other on their most private and domestick affairs, as though there had been no other person in the room.

Cuming had another unusual encounter some thirty miles to the east:

> I crossed the ferry to Zanesville, and dismounted at an inn where the stage generally stops. On entering I walked into a room, the door of which was open, where the first object that met my eye was the corpse of a female, laid out in her shroud on a bier. There was no person in the room but another female who was seated near the corpse, and to whom I apologized for my abrupt entrance, explaining my reasons for being in advance of the stage. She answered by wishing she had some mode of preventing the stage from driving up to the house, as her sister had died that morning, and it would be inconvenient to accommodate travelers that night, on which I remounted, rode to the post office, where I found the stage delivering the mail, from whence in consequence of my information, the driver took us to Harvey's very good inn, where we found an excellent supper, clean beds, a consequential host and hostess, and the highest charges I had hitherto paid in Ohio.[6]

At that time, apparently, the coach to Zanesville from Wheeling ran once a week. In the 1808 edition of *The Navigator*, Zadok Cramer noted that Wheeling had "a post office that receives and dispatches the mail to the eastward by stage twice a week, and once a week to the westward." He noted further: "The United States road from Cumberland, striking the Ohio at Wheeling, will tend very much to accelerate the growth of the town. That favourable circumstance, added to its being an excellent place for embarkation, will doubtless render Wheeling a place of considerable importance in a few years. It is now a place of business, and has a great thoroughfare of people from all parts of the United States travelling through it."[7]

After 1815, the "great thoroughfare of people" passing through Wheeling into Ohio found stagecoaches more readily available. By November 1816, for example, Philip Zinn was advertising twice-

WASHINGTON CITY & GEORGETOWN STAGES.

A detail from an advertisement in a September 1815 issue of the *National Intelligencer* (Washington, DC) showing a coach-and-four.

weekly coach service between Chillicothe and Columbus, the new state capital. At Chillicothe, Zinn's passengers could take other coaches traveling east or west along Zane's Trace. By mid-1819, his ads specified that, "One trip will be performed with a large and elegant new stage and four horses. A second trip will be performed with a smaller stage and two horses."[8]

Zinn's operation may well have profited from the increasing settlement in central Ohio. One observer, writing from Wheeling in July 1819, commented:

> After a ten days' visit at Lexington, I took the mail stage, as the most expeditious mode of travelling through Chillicothe and Zanesville, to this place, about 50 miles S.W. of Pittsburgh, travelling about 50 miles per day. . . . The country on the great road from Limestone to Wheeling is well settled. . . . Chillicothe, Lancaster, and Zanesville are handsome towns, and the country generally has the appearance of having been settled 50 years. From Zanesville to Wheeling, more particularly, the land is broken and very hilly, making it necessary to chain our stage wheels 20 times a day.[9]

John Woods, heading for Wheeling from Pittsburgh by coach in August 1819, had a different problem:

Having purchased a new rifle for 18 dollars, and taken a place in the Wheeling stage for Washington [Pennsylvania], for which I paid 2 dollars 50 cents, I supped and slept at the Pittsburgh Hotel; charge for supper and bed 50 cents. [The next day] I left Pittsburgh, in the stage, before daylight, and crossed the Monongahela, by the new bridge. . . . The stage-coach was very different from an English one; it was much more like a light waggon; it was covered at the top, but open on the sides, with leather curtains to let down in case of rain or cold. The road being rough, we could not keep these curtains down, as there was no sort of fastenings to them; and as it rained very hard several times, we got wet.[10]

William Faux had left Washington for the west almost a year earlier: "By mutual agreement, a band of philosophers, last evening, met to smoke me off to the western wilderness; and smoke we did till one o'clock this morning, when they escorted me to, and saw me safely packed in Uncle Sam's western mail, and bade me a hearty farewell for three months. Thus, with some regret, left I city, summer, and civilization behind me."

Faux's regrets increased after he crossed the Ohio. Leaving a "stage-house" on Zane's Trace thirty miles west of Wheeling at 3 a.m., his coach soon had a mishap:

At four this morning, on the driver getting down to lock the wheel, the horses started, and instantly struck a stump of a tree, and upset the mail with a crashing fall, which bruised my side, cut my face, and blackened my eye; the two leaders escaped into the forest, and we saw them no more. The driver went in pursuit of them, and left me to guard and sleep one hour and a half in the damaged vehicle, now nearly bottom upwards. . . . At five, the driver returned, and with two horses only, we got under way, and moved on through Cambridge and Washington to breakfast, and at sun-set reached our inn at Zainsville.[11]

Newspaper accounts of such incidents could sometimes cause trouble for the paper, because stagecoach lines losing passengers from bad press had a way to retaliate. As the *Baltimore Patriot* explained indignantly: "The Zanesville Messenger informs us, that the contractor for carrying the mail from that place, has refused to let his drivers carry the Messenger, as heretofore, because it contained, the preceding week, an article headed 'accident,' relating to the upsetting of the stage. This is *one* way of muzzling [the] press."[12]

Theoretically, road conditions should have been better farther east, but the reality was quite the opposite. In October 1815, the *Albany (NY) Advertiser* said simply, "A third accident with the stage.–The stage overset last week, below the Little Falls, and materially injured Mr. James Delvin, a respectable inhabitant of [Utica]."[13]

Mail stages had been trundling west from Albany for some twenty years prior to this incident. By July 1804, Jason Parker's line was running from Albany to Utica three times a week, and twice weekly from Utica to Geneva. And by the spring of 1811, Parker had taken in partners and was sending coaches all the way to Buffalo and Niagara Falls.[14]

MAIL STAGE
FROM
ALBANY TO NIAGARA FALLS.

LEAVES Albany every morning at 4 o'clock A. M. and arrives at Utica the same day at 7 P. M.—Leaves Utica every Monday, Wednesday and Friday at 4 A. M. and arrives at Geneva and Canandaigua the following days— Leaves Canandaigua every Monday and Friday morning, and arrives at Buffaloe the following day, and returns in like manner.

A Stage runs every day from Buffaloe to the Fells. Extra carriages may at all times be obtained on the route.

FARE.

From Albany to Utica $5 50
From Utica to Geneva   5 00
From Utica to Canandaigua 5 75
From Canandaigua to Buffaloe, 6 cts per mile.

The subscribers having formed themselves into a company for the purpose of running a Stage on the above-mentioned route, solicit the patronage of the public. The proprietors of this line are so well known, that the traveller may rest confident that the best of horses and carriages will be employed, with careful and trusty drivers, and that nothing shall be wanting to add to the comfort and convenience of the passenger.

Seats may be taken at Dunn's Tavern, Albany ; at Powell's Coffee-House Schenectady, and at Bagg's tavern, Utica.

POWELL, PARKER, BAKER & Co.
PARKER & POWELL,
HOSMERS & Co,
LANDEN & Co.

An advertisement from July 1811 in the *National Intelligencer*, announcing a new mail stage and passenger service between Albany, New York, and Niagara Falls. "The best of horses and carriages will be employed."

THE FIERCE FIGHTING AROUND LAKE ERIE and along the Niagara River during the War of 1812 interrupted this operation–the British burned Buffalo to the ground late in 1813–but it resumed shortly thereafter. However, from 1804 to 1819, the roads improved little, if at all. John Duncan left a graphic account of a stagecoach trip west along the same route–the route of the Erie Canal–in 1818–1819. Writing in October 1818, he said:

> The stage waggon which is still used in this part of the country, corresponds exactly with the picture and description which [Isaac] Weld [gave in 1795]. The body is rather long in proportion to its breadth, and contains four seats, each containing three passengers who all sit with their faces toward the horses.
>
> From the height of the seats it is open all round, and the roof is supported by slender shafts rising up at the corners and sides; in wet weather a leathern apron is let down at the sides and back, to protect the inmates. The wagon has no door, but the passengers get in by the front, stepping over the seats as they go backward; the driver sits on the front seat with a passenger on either hand. The heavier kinds of boxes and trunks are fastened behind, upon the frame of the carriage, but the smaller articles and the mail bag are huddled under the seats in the inside, to the great annoyance of the passengers, who are frequently forced to sit with their knees up to their mouths, or with their feet insinuated between two trunks, where they are most lovingly compressed whenever the vehicle makes a lurch into a rut. The body of the waggon is suspended upon two stout leathern straps, passing lengthwise under it, and secured upon strongly propped horizontal bars before and behind.

He wrote a more detailed account in February 1819:

> The American stages are of three kinds. The old-fashioned stage-waggons, which have been described in the letter from Buffalo [above]; an improved construction of these, with doors, and three seats instead of four, which are chiefly found in Massachusetts; and post coaches, as they are called, which have been recently introduced on the roads between New York and Baltimore, and are beginning to make their appearance in some other places. The post coaches are something like one of our [English] six-seated stages, but with an additional seat in the centre, which enables them with close pack-

ing to contain nine inside; the roof in place of being flat is quite round, [so] of course nothing can rest upon it; the luggage is contained in a kind of bag behind, and the driver sits on a low seat in front; one passenger may sit beside him but there are no other outside.

Much more graphic was Duncan's description of a coach ride west across New York, on what New Yorkers called the Great Western Turnpike:

The roads through which we drove (it was literally through,) had so shaken our waggon, that after nine hours' jolting one of the straps gave way, and we were brought to a stand by the carriage sinking down upon the pole. [However,] Americans are not easily disconcerted. There was a rail fence by the road side, from which the driver selected a stout rafter, long enough to reach from the footboard in front to the after axle, the body of the waggon was hove up by our united energies, and the wooden substitute for a spring was thrust under it. We then resumed our seats and jolted on, quite unconscious of any additional inconvenience from riding on a rail. At the next inn we obtained another waggon.

Scarcely had we begun to move forward when we descried the stage from the westward coming slowly up, with the passengers straggling here and there around it. We learned on meeting that they had just recovered their feet after an upset, and the mud on their clothes sufficiently corroborated the statement; happily no one was hurt, the stage having opportunely turned over against a steep bank by the side of the road. They told us that our turn was coming, but we thought that the roads before us could hardly be worse than those behind, and that with patience and caution we might manage to get through. . . . Off we again started, and while struggling up a very steep hill, our carriage descended into a gap with so violent a shock, that the bolt or pivot on which the front axle turned snapped in two, and the horses had nearly dragged the front wheels from under the body of the waggon. Our driver however was happily provided with a spare bolt, the passen-

gers got out, a stout rail from the nearest fence was thrust
under the carriage, and up to the ankles in mud, part on each
side, we managed by dint of strength to sustain the waggon
till the axle was replaced in its proper position, and the new
bolt inserted.

The passengers got a brief respite shortly after passing through
Auburn:

About five in the afternoon we reached the Cayuga lake,
which is here very nearly a mile in width, and is crossed by a
wooden bridge supported upon piles. The wheels of our char-
iot rolled along the level platform, with a smoothness to
which we had long been strangers; and so luxuriant seemed
the contrast, that on getting to the farther end, some of the
passengers proposed that we should turn the horses and
enjoy it a second time!

The respite would be needed. Not far west of Cayuga Lake:

A new variety of American roads now commended itself to
our attention. A wearisome swamp intervenes between
Waterloo and the Seneca Lake, and a yet more wearisome log
causeway affords the means of crossing it. This substitute for
a road is composed entirely of the trunks of trees, laid down
layer above layer, till a solid but rugged platform is elevated
above the level of the marsh. The logs are piled upon each
other without any kind of squaring or adjustment, and the
jolting of the wheels from one to another is perfectly horrible.
Bad however in the superlative degree as such riding is, it was
connected in the present instance with additional circumstances of annoyance, not usually attendant. By the heavy and
long continued rains the swamp had been converted into a
lake, which gradually rising in height had at last completely
covered the wooden road.
    Night had sunk down upon us, and though there was a
glimmering of moonlight, it had to struggle through a dense
atmosphere of clouds; our charioteer, however, feeling secure
in his knowledge of the channel, drove dauntlessly forward,

An "American Stage Waggon," from an edition of Isaac Weld, Jr.'s, *Travels through the States of North America, and the Provinces of Upper and Lower Canada.* Weld's engraving shows a carriage he took in 1798, a type that would remain in common use well into the nineteenth century. Weld noted that modes of travel in the United States were similar to Europe, but the great distances and "very indifferent" taverns often made a journey tiresome. (*Yale University*)

the horses dashed into the water, and very soon our bones bore testimony to the correctness of his pilotage. Well was it for us that the driver's skill was not inferior to his daring, for had he gone to either side of the proper line, horses and waggon, with all that it contained, would probably have found in the marsh their last earthly resting place. Two or three times it seemed as if such a consummation was approaching:—several logs had floated out of their places and left yawning gaps in the causeway, across which our horses might be said to swim rather than walk, and the wheels followed them with a plunge, so sudden and so deep, that it felt as if the bottom of the road had literally fallen out, and our whole establishment were going after it.

About ten o'clock we reached the Seneca lake, and were in hopes that Geneva, the village on its bank, was to terminate our day's toils. In this however we were disappointed. The innkeeper averred that it was absolutely necessary that the mail should go forward to Canandaigua, sixteen miles farther; he assured us that the road was much better than those we had travelled, promised us a comfortable carriage, good horses, and an excellent driver, and said that we should certainly accomplish it in less than four hours. Persuaded against our own judgment to rely on these promises, we consented to go forward; and a young man with a bugle horn was put into the carriage beside us, to cheer us forward with its courage-stirring notes. I did not at first suspect the object of this accompaniment, but it soon became obvious that it was intended to prevent our falling asleep. I already mentioned that the stage waggon was open all around, and you would of course attribute the necessity of this to the heat of the climate. It was subservient, however, to another important purpose as well as that of keeping us cool. When the wheels on one side descended into a rut, the passengers immediately threw themselves by a simultaneous motion towards the opposite, and those who were close by the side thrust their heads and shoulders through the opening; this sudden shifting of the centre of gravity counterpoised the waggon's tendency to upset, and we had become by practice so expert in the manoeuvre, that often, when the vehicle seemed to tremble on the very turn, the weight of our heads turned the scale in our favour. The prudent landlord at Geneva however knew well, that if we fell asleep, as our long continued fatigues would strongly dispose us to do, our heavy heads in place of being thrust out of the carriage would necessarily make a great addition to the leeward weight within, and to a certainty capsize the machine. He therefore very thoughtfully provided us with a trumpeter, who by singing songs, relating his marvelous adventures, and ever and anon wakening the warlike energies of his instrument, managed to keep us sufficiently awake to continue our exertions on behalf of the balance of power.[15]

AT THE TIME DUNCAN WROTE his account, stagecoach service was beginning much farther west. As Lexington's *Western Monitor* reported in June 1817: "A line of stages commenced running on Monday last from Louisville to Maysville, by the way of Frankfort, Georgetown, and Lexington, which will be continued in a few weeks to Wheeling, Va. A line also, we understand, is soon to be established from Frankfort to Nashville. This is an enterprise of vast importance to this part of the country."[16]

Mail coaches had been rolling into Nashville from Knoxville for at least ten years prior to this notice, and another line, estab-

> ### WESTERN STAGES TO TENNESSEE.
>
> FROM Thorny Point, the landing place of the Steam Boat Washington, by the way of Fredericksburg, Orange Court House, Gordonsville, Milton, Charlottesville, Staunton, Lexington, Virg. Fincastle, &c. &c. &c. to Tennessee.
>
> Leave the Columbian Inn, in Fredericksburg, every Sunday morning at 8 o'clock, and return to the same place every Friday.
>
> The public are respectfully informed that the above route is now very pleasant to and from the Westward and Washington City, having the aid of a Turnpike Road for 20 miles above Fredericksburg, and the advantage of an agreeable passage in the Steam Boat Washington.
>
> *April* 15—3twtf   THE PROPRIETORS ·

Tennesee was admitted to the Union in June 1796, and as this advertisement in an April 1816 issue of the *National Intelligencer* shows, a regular weekly stage and "steam boat" line ran from Washington, DC, to the Volunteer State.

lished in the spring of 1816 and advertised as "Western Stages To Tennessee," came into that state from Virginia after first passing through Charlottesville, Staunton, and Fincastle. For westerners, Nashville was especially important; one observer called it "the last great point of departure, where all the letters from the various parts of the union are collected, to be forwarded through the wilderness to the Mississippi Territory and New-Orleans, and of course the place where all letters from New-Orleans and Natchez are also collected, to be forwarded to the different states." Stagecoach service from Nashville along the Natchez Trace would have been a desirable end, but the trace—because of swamps, floods, felled trees, and other reasons—continually proved itself hostile to wheeled vehicles.[17]

Such vehicles were far better suited for the National Road, which by 1818 was commanding most of the country's attention. In that year, Samuel Breck of Pennsylvania wrote:

> This national road . . . is constructed (and constructing) of the
> most solid materials; and is supposed to be very superior to

any turnpike or other road in America. A line of stages now runs three times a week, by the way of this road, from Baltimore and Washington. The distance from Baltimore to Wheeling is about 270 miles; the stage runs it in five days. There is now established in Baltimore, a complete uninterrupted stage connection to Louisville, in Kentucky.[18]

The new line of stages resulted in part from a notice inserted in eastern newspapers by the U.S. Post Office in May 1818, even before the National Road reached Uniontown: it specifically called for contractors to carry the mail, in stagecoaches, from Hagerstown via Hancock, Cumberland, Uniontown, Brownsville, and Washington, to Wheeling. By September of that year, with large advertisements headed "Washington, Baltimore & Wheeling Mail Stages," such a line was in place, promising trips of only four days to Pittsburgh and four and a half days to Wheeling. Beyond that, "The stages for Louisville, Kentucky, leave Wheeling on Tuesdays, Thursdays, and Saturdays . . . forming a complete line, without any loss of time, from Washington and Baltimore to Louisville, Kentucky, via Wheeling or Pittsburg."[19]

And with these words, the first great era of western stagecoaching began.

PART TWO

1819–1832

IN OCTOBER 1825, THE *Vincennes (IN) Western Sun* reported, "Within two days past, upwards of one hundred waggons, heavily loaded, containing movers and their effects, with droves of cattle, sheep, negroes, & c. have passed through this town, on their way to the state of Missouri."[1]

Timothy Flint, already in Missouri at the time, wrote that:

> the immigration from the western and southern states to this country poured in a flood, the power and strength of which could only be adequately conceived by persons on the spot. We have numbered a hundred persons passing through the village of St. Charles in one day. The number was said to have equalled that for many days together. From the Mamelles I have looked over the subjacent plain quite to the ferry, where the immigrants crossed the upper Mississippi. I have seen in this extent nine wagons harnessed with from four to six horses. We may allow a hundred cattle, besides hogs, horses, and sheep, to each wagon; and from three or four to twenty slaves. . . . [T]he whole group occupies three quarters of a mile. . . .
>
> Just about nightfall, they come to a spring or a branch, where there is water and wood. The pack of dogs sets up a cheerful barking. The cattle lie down and ruminate. The team is unharnessed. The huge wagons are covered, so that the roof completely excludes the rain. The cooking utensils are brought out. The blacks prepare a supper, which the toils of the day render delicious; and they talk over the adventures of the past day, and the prospects of the next. Meantime, they are going where there is nothing but buffaloes and deer to limit their range, even to the western sea. . . . Nothing can or will limit the immigration westward, but the Western Ocean. Alas! for the moving generation of the day, when the tide of advancing backwoodsmen shall have met the surge of the Pacific. They may then set them[selves] down and weep for other worlds.[2]

(Overleaf) *United States of America* by H[enry] S. Tanner (1829). Henry Tanner's map was one of the most popular of the eastern United States and went through a number of editions over the next two decades. Mileage numbers are given between towns. Ohio became the 17th state in 1803; as this map shows, by 1829, Louisiana, Indiana, Mississippi, Illinois, Alabama, Maine, and Missouri had been admitted to the Union. Note that Mexico borders Louisiana, Oregon Territory has been established, while vast areas under American Indian control are indicated. (*Courtesy of the David Rumsey Map Collection, www.davidrumsey.com*)

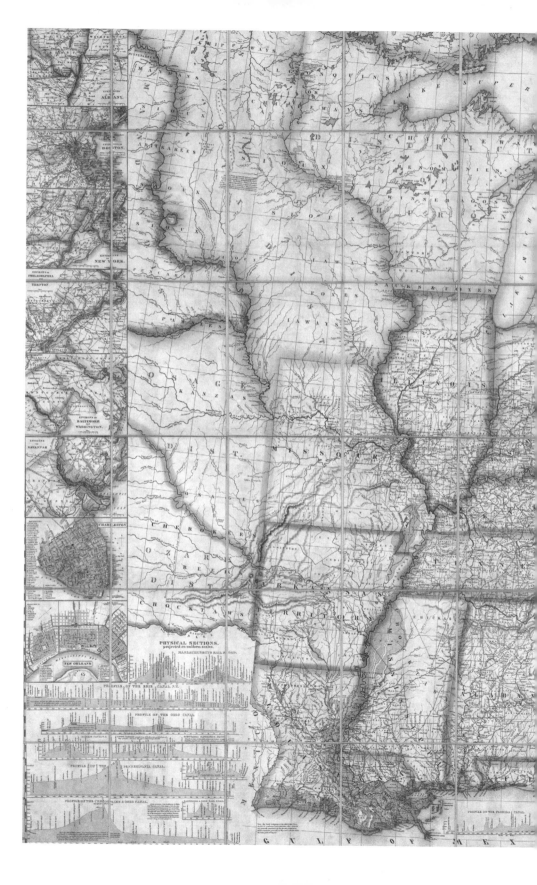

UNITED STATES
OF
AMERICA.
by H. S. Tanner. 1829.

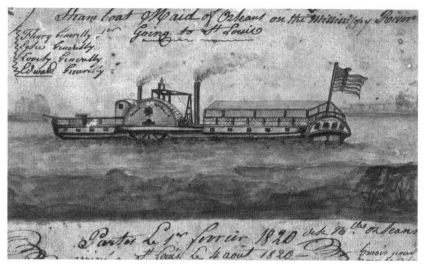

The earliest known picture of a steamboat on the Mississippi River, the *Maid of Orleans*, drawn in 1820 by a French passenger. The *Maid of Orleans* was built in Philadelphia in 1818. (*Tulane University*)

4

WATERWAYS

In December 1811, a Virginia paper inserted this notice: "Rosevelt's Steam Boat, built at Pittsburg, reached Louisville (Falls of Ohio) in 64 hours sailing–a distance of more than 600 miles. She sails *against the current* at the rate of 13 miles in two hours and a half." The upstream rate of travel was a mere five miles an hour, and yet this boat, the *New Orleans*, sent a tremor through the west. Another paper declared:

> The recent establishment of a steam boat on the western waters, carries in itself consequences much more important and exclusive, than the canal of Languedoc to France, or perhaps the celebrated dykes of Holland. The friends to American improvements, must take pleasure in knowing that this steam boat in all its parts, engine, boiler, and machinery, has been constructed at Pittsburg. The western country is indebted to the enterprise of two of our citizens, Messrs. Livingston and Fulton, for [such an] important improvement in the navigation of the Mississippi.[1]

It was indeed an important improvement, the culmination of more than a century of development, beginning with the primitive steam engines of Denis Papin and Thomas Savery in the 1690s, progressing through the big Newcomen engines used in the 1720s to pump water out of English coal mines, and coming to rest–temporarily, at least–with the refinements designed by James Watt in the late 1760s. Then, between 1790 and 1804, American inventors, among them Oliver Evans, John Stevens, and Nicholas Roosevelt, patented no fewer than fifteen varieties of the steam engine, some of which were boat-related. Other patents followed, most notably those issued between 1809 and 1811 to Daniel French, John Stevens, and Robert Fulton.[2]

But for another ten years after the 1811 voyage of Roosevelt's *New Orleans,* the vessels powered by men, or wind, or both, continued to hold sway on western waters. In 1818, Morris Birkbeck estimated that "Nine-tenths of the trade is yet carried on in the usual craft; flatboats, barges, piragues, & c." Then, in 1819, the *Western Engineer,* as part of Stephen Long's expedition to the Rocky Mountains, managed to churn its way more than three hundred miles up the Missouri River. Commercial steamboats were quick to follow. In late May of that year, the steamboat *Independence* puffed up the Missouri from St. Louis to Boon's Lick, a distance of some two hundred miles, in seven sailing days. But arriving there at the same time was "the large and elegant keel boat *Governor Clark,* from St. Louis, with merchandize, & c. . . . Also, two large keel boats, from Madison County, Kentucky, with freight, and a number of families, intending settlement in this quarter." And for twenty years after the *Independence* steamed up the Missouri, steamboats, keelboats, flatboats, and various other craft coexisted on western rivers.[3]

In 1819, William Amphlett, referring to the Mississippi, wrote: "Its course is very crooked, and the current so strong, that wind alone will not impel a vessel upwards. Keelboats, with the assistance of poles and oars, may ascend it; but all-powerful steam is the best auxiliary here." Any number of boatmen would have agreed with him. Elsewhere he commented: "For those who choose to emigrate to the Western States via New Orleans, there is always the accommodation of keel and steam boats to ascend the Mississippi and its principal branches. From New Orleans [upstream] to Natchez, the voyage by keel-boats will take from 12 to 18 days, according to the state of the current. By steam-boats the same distance can be run in half the time."[4]

With the rapid multiplication of steamboats, the route to the west that Amphlett alluded to became far more popular. It was a variation—a reversal—of a long-used pathway to the western country. Now, instead of the usual overland journey from the east and a downstream voyage to New Orleans, a traveler could first sail to New Orleans, then take a steamboat up the Mississippi to St. Louis, or continue steaming up the Ohio to Louisville or Cincinnati, and begin his explorations from those points.

The steamboat's biggest advantage, of course, was its ability to move upstream against a strong current with little more effort on the crew's part than supplying fuel to the furnace that heated the boiler. Forcing a keelboat upstream still required the endless, back-breaking labor of rowing, poling, or cordelling (in which the crewmen, trudging along the riverbank with a long line in hand, dragged the boat behind them). As a result, steamboats played a major role in populating the upper Mississippi, especially after the federal government began leasing the lead mines there to private companies late in 1822. Within five years, places like Galena, Illinois, and Dubuque, Iowa, were boom towns, with most of their needs supplied via waterways. (Young Lt. Philip St. George Cooke, who arrived at a Galena tavern one night in 1828, counted in the gaming room "eight or ten different tables, each surrounded by players . . . all swearing or talking loudly; many intoxicated, disputing, and quarreling." The next morning, a man was found at the river's edge, quite dead "from a wound of his carotid artery.")[5]

Samuel Cumings's *Western Pilot* of 1829, a successor to Cramer's *Navigator,* included this note:

> I embarked a few years since, at Pittsburgh, for Cincinnati, on board of a steam boat—more with a view of realising the possibility of a speedy return against the current, than in obedience to the call of either business or pleasure. [At that time] the steam boat had made but few voyages back to Pittsburgh. We were generally skeptics as to its practicability. The mind was not prepared for the change that was about to take place in the West. It is now consummated; and we yet look back with astonishment at the result. [Now the rudest woodsman] is struck with the sublime power and self-moving majesty of a steam boat;—lingers on the shore where it passes—and follows its rapid, and almost magic course with silent admira-

tion. The steam engine in five years has enabled us to antici-
pate a state of things, which, in the ordinary course of events,
it would have required a century to have produced.[6]

Still, keelboats and flatboats remained very much in evidence.
They could serve very well as downstream craft, and were far
cheaper to build and maintain than steamboats. Furthermore, keelboats could negotiate shallow waters more easily than their steam-
powered cousins, a virtue especially valuable in the fall, when rivers
were low. As James Hall said in the mid-1820s: "The steam-boats,
which are numerous, are strong, beautiful, and swift, and are provided with excellent accommodations; but these can only run
when the water is high, and this mode of conveyance is in some
cases too expensive for the circumstances of the emigrant. In either
of these events . . . other boats are resorted to. The keel is a long,
sharp vessel, drawing but little water."

Hall himself rode a keelboat down the Ohio, and in a letter took
special note of the crew's activities:

> I present the following beautiful specimen, verbatim, as it
> flowed from the lips of an Ohio boatman . . .
>
> *Here's to you, and all the rest,*
> *And likewise her that I love best;*
> *As she's not here to take a part,*
> *I'll drink her health with all my heart.*
>
> [This] will convince you that I have not decided in favour
> of the "River Melodies" on slight grounds. By some future
> opportunity I will send you some more of them; in the mean-
> while I bid you good night, in the words which the rowers are
> even now sounding in my ears, as they tug at the oar, timing
> their strokes to the cadence:
>
> *Some rows up, but we rows down,*
> *All the way to Shawnee town,*
> *Pull away–pull away!*[7]

For the cautious voyager, keelboats had yet another advantage
over steamboats: there were no boiler explosions to drive scalding

An advertisement, top left, for the services of the steamboat *Maid of Orleans* in the *Missouri Gazette*, March 1820. Two notices of steamboat services, bottom left, along the Ohio River in the *Cincinnati Gazette*, September 1821. A boat-builders advertisement, right, in the *Western Herald* (Steubenville, Ohio), January 1829.

steam or slabs of iron across the deck. Cuming's *Western Pilot* of 1829, speaking of St. Louis, said, "A great number of keel boats, and river craft of all descriptions, bound to all points of the boatable waters of the Mississippi, are seen at all seasons of the year lying in the harbor."[8]

The redoubtable journalist Anne Royall saw much the same thing near New Orleans: "The steam-boats which ply the Mississippi river, and its tributary streams, stop up the river some distance, in the suburbs. . . . Next to these, the barges, then keelboats, and next the flat-bottoms, and last of all the rafts . . . extend from three to five miles in length and in the busy season six miles from end to end. The flat bottoms alone at this time were two miles in length!"[9]

Keelboats and flatboats were lying side by side when, in the spring of 1830, a sudden storm blew up on the lower Ohio near Shawneetown:

> An unpleasant scene of activity and bustle was presented at our shores yesterday. A strong south wind, which continued with violence all day, agitated the river to a degree seldom, if ever, before equaled. A number of flat and keel boats were moored at our landings [and] one of them, a keel from the Wabash, belonging to Mr. John Wise, of Vincennes, was stove by the waves, and sunk with a greater part of her cargo on board;—some were sunk without being stove—while others were preserved by the untiring [efforts] of their crews, and the friendly assiduities of some of our citizens. [However, we] understand that the damage sustained can be repaired, without further loss to the proprietors than the expense attending the refitting of their boats.[10]

A practice that became fairly common on the rivers was to employ steamboats and keelboats in tandem, and on at least one occasion this turned out to be very fortunate for the passengers. In the fall of 1830,

> the steamboat Neptune, from St. Louis, bound to New Orleans, with a cargo of lead and two keel boats in tow, struck upon a snag and sunk in thirty feet [of] water at the mouth of the Ohio in so short a time, that the crew and passengers had not an opportunity of saving their clothes or baggage. The keel boats were cut adrift just in time to prevent their sinking with her, and on them were saved the lives of the crew and passengers, who must otherwise have perished.[11]

Snags on the rivers—usually submerged or floating tree trunks, called "planters" or "sawyers" depending on their position—sank numerous vessels every season. Planters were nearly vertical, anchored on the river bottom, while sawyers were nearly horizontal, lurking at or just below the surface.[12]

The rivers, of course, held dangers other than snags. Shortly before he went to the gallows for his crimes, John Washburn wrote a lengthy confession describing the robberies and murders he and his companions had committed along the Mississippi and its tributaries. After one robbery aboard a Natchez steamboat in the late 1820s:

> We went down to Lovett's house [at Natchez under the hill] and found that he and Jones were doing a first rate business. They informed us that they had committed several robberies during our absence, which principally consisted of burglaries. They said they had been watching a man belonging to a flat boat, and put us on the track he had gone. Carter and myself went in search of him, and overtook him about thirty five miles below Natchez. We went on board the boat and called for some liquor; Carter pulled a pistol from his pocket and shot the owner of the boat in the left breast, as he was drawing the liquor for us. A boy of about 12 years of age came running to assist his master; I caught hold of him by the nape of the neck and the back of his pantaloons, and threw him overboard. He endeavored to catch hold of the gunwale of the boat, but I struck him on the head with a billet of wood—he sunk to rise no more. We landed the boat and plundered it of two thousand dollars in money. We then returned to Natchez.
> . . .
> For those crimes Lovett, Jones, Carter, and myself were [soon] arrested, and after three weeks confinement we all four broke jail and escaped. We went to Memphis; there we divided the whole treasure and separated. . . . Lovett and myself went to Smithland, at the mouth of Cumberland river. There we were again arrested for the same charge we had been confined for in Natchez jail. We remained in Smithland jail three months, and once more broke jail and escaped to Nashville

by the stage. At Nashville we rented a room in a house of ill fame, kept by a woman named Patsy Foster. At this woman's house we remained concealed three months. We used to keep within doors the whole of the day and go out at night.[13]

By the late 1820s, Nashville, on the Cumberland, was only one of many ports for steamboat traffic, which increased steadily thereafter. And with the steady increase in steamboats, a new and distinctive character made his appearance: the riverboat gambler. Early in 1830, on an Ohio River steamer, the well-known author Mrs. Frances Trollope sniffed, "the men became sufficiently acquainted to game together, and we were told that the opportunity was considered as so favourable, that no boat left New Orleans without having as cabin passengers one or two gentlemen from that city whose profession it was to drill the fifty-two elements of a pack of cards to profitable duty."[14]

Besides gamblers, passengers of all other professions crowded onto the New Orleans steamers. Anne Royall said that, of all the scenes along the levee, "the number of people taking their passage up the river is the most astonishing sight of the whole. It would seem they were rained from the clouds!!" A few miles upriver, however, now aboard the *Beaver*, she witnessed something considerably more dramatic:

[A]t length we came up with the *Paul Jones*, Capt. Carruthers. . . . When we came up with [her], we were just steering from the left to the right hand coast. The *Paul Jones* turned at the same time, and we had a fair race. Our object was to keep our advantage, and the *Paul Jones* seemed determined we should not, and put on all stream. The *Beaver*, however, reached the point first, and here a hard contest took place. The *Paul Jones* came up alongside and endeavored to force the *Beaver* back by aiming her bow across the bow of the latter, and though she kept her place, she was unable to gain a hair's breadth on the *Beaver*. Thus we continued for an hour, side by side, often coming in contact, to the great alarm of some ladies on the stern of the *Paul Jones*, who squealed out every time the boats struck. For miles we could have stepped off one boat on the other. I watched the countenances of the captains, who were

both good natured men, and discovered by their smiling there
was no danger. . . . Such was the warmth of the conflict, however, that not a man on either boat spoke a word, and though
the captains wore a smile, the pilots seemed to hold their
breath. At length the *Paul Jones* gave way, though we kept
sight of her several hours.[15]

THE RADICAL CHANGE STEAMBOATS made in river travel was well
illustrated by a piece appearing in the *Cincinnati Register* in 1833,
which summarized the previous thirty years on the river:

I have seen the time when the only boat that floated on the
surface of the Ohio, was a canoe, propelled by poles used by
two persons, one in the bow, and the other in the stern. I have
seen the day when the introduction of the keel-boat, with a
shingle roof, was hailed as a mighty improvement in the business of the West. I remember the day when the arrival of a
Canadian barge (as the St. Louis boats were called at the head
of the Ohio) was an important event in the transactions of a
year. I remember the day when a passage of four months from
Natchez to Pittsburg was called a speedy trip for the best craft
on the river; and when the boatmen, a race now extinct,
leaped on shore after the voyage, and exhibited an air of as
much triumph as did the sailors of Columbus on their return
from the New World. I remember the time when the canoe of
a white man dared not to be launched on the bosom of the
Alleghany. I remember the time when a trader to New
Orleans was viewed as the most enterprising amongst even
the most hardy sons of the West: on his return from his 6
months' trip, he was hailed as a traveller who had seen the
world. I remember the day when the borders of the Ohio
were a wilderness, and N. Orleans was 'toto orbe divisa,' literally cut off from the whole world. . . . I have lived to see two
splendid cities, one devoted to manufactures, the other to
commerce, spring up where, in my boyhood, nothing
appeared like civilization but the hut of the soldier or of the

settler. I have lived to see a revolution produced by a mechanical philosophy, equal to that effected by the art of printing. It has changed the character of Western commerce, and almost proved that the poetical wish of 'annihilating time and space,' was not altogether hyperbolical. By it Pittsburg and New Orleans have become near neighbors. I have lived to see the day when a visit to New Orleans from Cincinnati requires no more preparation than a visit to a neighboring country town. I remember when it required as much previous arrangement, as a voyage to Calcutta. I have lived to see vessels of 300 tons, arriving in twelve or fifteen days from New Orleans at Cincinnati; and I calculate to see them arrive in ten days. . . . All these things I have seen, and yet I feel myself to [number] amongst the young sons of the West.[16]

5

ROADWAYS

By 1820, both the National Road and the new Pennsylvania state road were complete, and catering to band after band of happy travelers. Those using the National Road, however, were no doubt happier than those on the Pennsylvania pike, because the National Road was toll-free. The cost for improving the Pennsylvania road had come to more than a million dollars, and while the state bore the greater part of this amount, more than a third of it came from privately funded turnpike companies, which expected to make a profit on the venture. So the road was a toll road, and the tolls were substantial. As the *Lancaster* (PA) *Journal*, at the western terminus of the once-famous Lancaster Pike of the 1790s, reported in 1822:

> It may be proper to state, that the amount of toll which must be paid at this time, on the trip from Pittsburg to Philadelphia and back on a six horse team and broad wheel wagon, by the cheapest route, is nineteen dollars and twenty cents [equivalent to more than $300 today], and that the toll on a narrow wheeled wagon and six horses, for the same trip, is twenty-nine dollars and thirty cents: which is an average of about twenty-four dollars on each load; and at the present price of carriage, is upwards of twenty-one percent of the wagoner's whole receipts, on his outward and inward load. The effect of this upon the interests of Pennsylvania, must be too clear to every mind. . . . The national road runs from Baltimore to

Wheeling on a line nearly parallel with our principal road and but about thirty miles south of it. . . . This road was finished in the year 1820, at an expense to the nation of one million eight hundred thousand dollars, and declared free . . . and being a good road and toll free, [it] must gradually draw away our trade, and in fact has already drawn away a considerable part of it . . . and when the trade is once diverted to its new channel, we can never hope for its return. If we will not know the ways of wisdom in the days of our prosperity, she will leave us to our own in the days of our adversity.

To solve the problem, "wagons having [a] wheel tire of at least four inches in width, engaged in the transportation of merchandize, and of our agricultural and manufactured products, may pass to a market toll free; and in order to effect this, it is proposed that an additional subscription to the stock of the several [turnpike] companies, shall be made by the state."[1]

Toll issues aside, the Pennsylvania and National roads were good ones, but together they made up only a small percentage of the country's roadways. Even a part of the Maryland Bank Road, extending west from Frederick to meet the National Road at Cumberland, was in miserable shape. Late in 1821, the *Baltimore Patriot* printed a letter headed "A Disgrace To Maryland":

A turnpike road from Baltimore to Wheeling is completed, except about ten miles from Hagerstown to Boonsborough. . . . Now we are authorized to state a fact which occurred this week. The Hagerstown stage which left Baltimore on Friday morning did not arrive until after 12 o'clock at night–it took from five to six hours to go from Boonsborough to Hagerstown, a distance of ten miles; it took five or six hours on yesterday morning, to return the same distance–and the passengers walked several [miles] of the road; this will be the case, more or less, until next April. It is a disgrace and a shame to the state that this short space between Boonsborough and the Bank Road is not turnpiked. Let an effort be made now, and the road can be completed, and at a low rate, before another year expires.[2]

William Blane confirmed this account in 1822: "From [Frederick] to Hagerstown, the road was the worst I ever travelled over, in a wheeled carriage. It was so full of holes and large pieces of rocks, that I am convinced nothing but the lowness of the stage prevented our being upset. But a regular turnpike road is begun, and will be completed in a year or two."[3]

Although one of the worst in the country in 1822, this road was one of the best within two years. As the *North American Review* noted early in 1825, "The great national road from Wheeling to Cumberland has been continued [east] by the [financial support of the] banks in Baltimore, and three other banks in the western districts of Maryland [so that] now the line of communication between Baltimore and Wheeling is complete, over one of the best roads in the world." And so it was. Journalist Anne Royall, after passing over part of it by stagecoach, said:

> I sat on the front seat [of the coach], and every now and then [my German-born] driver would ask me "how I was pleased?" "Very well." "Ah! I warrant you shall say as you vas never better trifed in all your life;" which was true enough, for better horses or a better road is not to be found in the world, than the road from Boonsboro' to Hagerstown. The road is a great curiosity, being turnpiked with white stone, broken into small regular pieces, and laid as firm as the original rock; no floor could be more level; it was one entire smooth pavement; it appeared more like sailing or flying, rather than riding over land; not a jar or jolt the whole way; and I was proud to confirm the driver's prediction, that I never had so pleasant a drive before nor since, excepting my return on the same pavement.[4]

Royall's delight was due to the fact that the road had been built by a new process, one worked out by John Loudon MacAdam, a Scottish engineer. So highly regarded did MacAdam's notions of a proper roadway become that his book, *Remarks on the Present System of Road Making*, passed through eight editions from 1816 to 1824. Basically, MacAdam's system called for a road surface made of clean broken stones, an inch in size throughout, without clay or other binders to hold them together. Stones broken to a small and

uniform size, with their jagged, squared-off surfaces, would inter-
lock with each other and thus hold their position, instead of shifting and slipping (like marbles in a bowl) when hooves or wheels
passed over them. As MacAdam phrased it:

> Every road is to be made of broken stone without mixture of
> earth, clay, chalk, or any other matter which will imbibe
> water, and be affected with frost; nothing is to be laid on the
> clean stone on pretence of binding; broken stone will com- .
> bine by its own angles into a smooth solid surface that cannot
> be affected by vicissitudes of weather, or displaced by the
> action of wheels, which will pass over it without a jolt, and
> consequently without injury.

In MacAdam's view, proper drainage was essential; water was a
roadway's chief enemy, and he warned that using different sizes of
stone for the roadbed did nothing more than facilitate water damage:

> It is well known to every skilful and observant road-maker,
> that if strata of stone of various sizes be placed as a road, the
> largest stones will constantly work up by the shaking and
> pressure of the traffic, and that the only mode of keeping the
> stones of a road from motion, is to use materials of a uniform
> size from the bottom. In roads made upon large stones as a
> foundation, the perpetual motion, or change of the position of
> the materials, keeps open many apertures through which the
> water passes.[5]

(Curiously, much of this information had been within public
grasp well before MacAdam published his first edition. The attach-
ment to Gallatin's report of 1808 describing the turnpike built near
Philadelphia in 1801–04 had stated that if the whole body of stone
was to be broken down to a smaller size–two-and-a-half inches, in
that instance–the road would be more durable than when using
two sizes of stone.)[6]

Maryland road builders were not the only ones to adopt
MacAdam's method: army officers were about to do so as well.
This fact carried a good deal of weight, because in the 1820s and

1830s, the U.S. Military Academy at West Point housed one of the best engineering schools in the country, and Army officers were to superintend both the building and repair of the National Road once it crossed into Ohio.

Late in 1821, the commissioners for the road (one of whom was David Shriver, the original superintendent) scouted the country along Zane's Trace from the Ohio to the Muskingum River, then reported grimly:

> The ground throughout the entire distance is very hilly and broken; the principal streams run nearly at right angles with the course of the location; and the hills bordering those streams have to be passed in a lateral direction . . . otherwise a descent and ascent sufficiently gentle could not be had. . . . Another difficulty to be overcome in locating a road through this tract of country arises from the nature of the ground itself, [because] in the spring seasons particularly, the surface of the hill sides are found sliding into the valleys below, or stopping in their course where the ground becomes more level.[7]

But the road builders had encountered problems just as serious— or more so—east of the Ohio, and solved them, as proved by the endless hooves, boots, and wheels now crunching over the road there. In working on the route west of Wheeling, the builders now had ten years of experience to rely upon, and the MacAdam process as well.

Meanwhile, the original stretch of road east of Wheeling continued to carry heavy traffic. One traveler, reaching Cumberland in 1822, was awestruck by its appearance: "[T]he Alleghany Mountains, which here consist of five or six distinct ridges, extending over a space of fifty or sixty miles, [are] covered, to their very summits, with a strong growth of timber, mostly precluding the sight of every other object but the majestic road, which seems to stretch across an interminable wilderness, with the stride of a giant."[8]

Equally enthusiastic was James Hall:

> In some places the road is hewn into the precipitous side of the mountain, and the traveller, beholding a vast abyss

beneath his feet, while the tall cliffs rising to the clouds over-
hang his path, is struck with admiration at the bold genius
which devised, and the persevering hardihood which executed, so great a work. Those frightful precipices, which once
almost defied the approach of the nimble footed hunter, are
now traversed by heavy laden wagons; and pleasure carriages
roll rapidly along where beasts of prey but lately found a
secure retreat.[9]

The "pleasure carriages" rolling along the road could include
gigs (horse-drawn, two-wheeled carts holding one or two people),
buggies, coachees (smaller, four-passenger versions of a stagecoach), dearborns, and perhaps one or two examples of a vehicle
introduced to Baltimore early in 1819, the "Tracena. A new mode
of travelling, combining the advantages of carriage, horse, and foot.
It has a saddle as a horse, it has wheels as a carriage, yet the rider
derives his progress from his own feet. It exhibits the principle of
skating on land. . . . These horses are cheap, they are safe, and do
not fall without the rider's consent." In other words, it was an early
version of a velocipede, predecessor of the bicycle.[10]

Traveling the National Road in a more conventional vehicle, a
stagecoach, in 1822, William Blane noted some interesting details
about what he saw:

Leaving Cumberland, I proceeded on the great National
Road which crosses the Alleghany Mountains, and which
reaches from Cumberland to Wheeling, a distance of 125
miles. The road begins to ascend almost immediately, and
passes through a rough and mountainous country, thickly
covered with forest, which is chiefly of oak, here and there
interspersed with pine and cedar. . . . Deer, bears, wolves, wild
turkies, and indeed all kinds of wild animals, are uncommonly plentiful in these mountains, owing to the rocky nature of
the ground, which will in all probability prevent its being cultivated for centuries. It is only at considerable intervals, that
even by the road side, a small spot of settled or cleared land
can be seen, while at a distance from the road, the country is
perfectly 'wild.' Another circumstance that in a great measure
preserves the large game, is that during the summer and

autumn these mountains are so terribly infested with rattlesnakes, that the hunters are not much disposed to enter the woods.

While the stage was stopping a short time in order to water the horses, and to allow the passengers to take some refreshment at a small inn on this mountain, I observed that two hunters, who had just come in with some turkies they had killed, were each of them carrying one of the long heavy rifles peculiar to the Americans. As one of them, an old man, was boasting of his skill as a marksman, I offered to put up a half-dollar at a distance of fifty yards, to be his if he could hit it. Accordingly I stepped the distance, and put the half-dollar in the cleft of a small stick, which I thrust into the ground. The hunter, slowly raising his rifle, fired, and to my great astonishment struck the half-dollar. This was the first specimen I had seen, of the unrivalled accuracy with which the American hunter uses his rifle.[11]

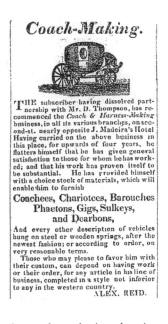

Coach-Making.

THE subscriber having dissolved partnership with Mr. D. Thompson, has recommenced the *Coach & Harness-Making* business, in all its various branches, on second-st. nearly opposite J. Madeira's Hotel Having carried on the above business in this place, for upwards of four years, he flatters himself that he has given general satisfaction to those for whom he has worked; and that his work has proven itself to be substantial.   He has provided himself with a choice stock of materials, which will enable him to furnish

Coachees, Chariotees, Barouches
Phaetons, Gigs, Sulkeys,
and Dearbons,

And every other description of vehicles hung on steel or wooden springs, after the newest fashion; or according to order, on very reasonable terms.
Those who may please to favor him with their custom, can depend on having work or their order, for any article in his line of business, completed in a style not inferior to any in the western country.
ALEX. REID.

A coach maker's advertisement in a March 1831 issue of the *Scioto Gazette* (Chillicothe), Ohio.

Construction of the National Road west of Wheeling, in Ohio, started in 1825, and by December of that year the secretary of war could report:

Contracts have been already made for about twenty-eight miles of the road, and which are in course of execution. In directing the manner of its being made the McAdam plan was adopted, recommended by its cheapness and superior quality. The superiority of this mode over that formerly pursued in the construction of turnpike roads is ascertained most satisfactorily, by twenty years' experience in Great Britain . . . and also from a small experiment made in this country. The result, as far as we have proceeded in the execution of this measure, has exceeded our most sanguine expectations. By dividing the road into very small sections, so as to enlarge the sphere of competition and to exclude speculations, the cost is reduced to $4,300 per mile, presenting a most favorable comparison with the expense incurred, being $12,900 a mile, in the construction of the road on this side of the Ohio. . . .

Nearly the whole extent of road embraced by the contracts has been cleared, cut, graded, and shaped, so as to be ready for receiving the first course of metal, as it is called, meaning the stone broken to a small size, agreeably to the McAdam plan. It is not intended to lay on the first course, to consist of a thickness of three inches, until May next; the second course, also of three inches, will be laid after the first course shall have become consolidated and compacted by the pressure of a heavy roller, and it is believed will be found, after having been compacted by the same process, to afford the requisite solidity to the road. If it should prove to be otherwise, a third course of three inches will be laid.

The continuation of the Cumberland road west of Zanesville has been laid out as far as Columbus.[12]

So MacAdam's teachings became part of the federal road-building process. But his book had appeared too late to affect the construction of the original stretch of the road, east of Wheeling. As one result, this stretch soon needed repair—and needed it badly. The two sizes of stone used for its surface, the heavy travel, and the winter weather in the Alleghenies had all taken their toll. In March 1823, for example, a little note had appeared in the *Washington (DC) National Intelligencer*: "A friend, who is journeying Westward, writes to us from Wheeling that he found the National Road in a very bad condition, and he fears that the Twenty-five Thousand Dollars, appropriated by Congress to mend it, will not put even one-half of the Road in proper repair."[13]

NOT THAT THINGS WERE ANY BETTER farther west, well beyond the National Road's reach. William Blane, who had already seen his share of rough roads, was to see even more:

The roads [in Kentucky] being very bad, I determined to buy a horse, and indeed riding is the only practicable and safe manner of travelling through most of the Western States. . . . [The road between Maysville and Lexington] was beyond all comparison the worst I had ever seen. It was full of holes, and in many places nearly up to the horse's knees, in mud intermixed with large stones and pieces of rock, which seemed as if put there on purpose to annoy equestrians. To convey any idea of such a road by mere description is impossible.[14]

Conditions were much the same in Missouri. In 1825, the *Missouri Intelligencer* in Franklin commented:

It is not often that we extend our perambulations beyond the purlieus of the press; but when we do so, we are forced to lament the neglected condition of our highways, which every where admonish us that barbarism still lingers in a country pretty well peopled with Christians. It is true [that] nature has here and there laid open a pathway (through a prairie) which serves to contrast the smooth with the rough, but it can never, even in the imagination, 'make the rough smooth.' In journeying from St. Charles to this place [Franklin], by a route traveled more than any in Missouri . . . we had hoped to find safety in the mail stage. But in spite of the care and skill of the driver, we were more than once thrown neck and heels into the very jaws of Peril.[15]

That year, Abraham Bradley issued a new map showing roads reaching into the west that had not appeared on earlier editions. One such road followed the north bank of the Missouri River from St. Charles across the state, through Franklin, to "Liberty C.H." (court house), near the border of "Konzas." A parallel route, starting in St. Louis and following the river's south bank, ended at Fort Osage, again just shy of the "Konzas" border.

Well south of this road was another such route, starting west from the banks of the Mississippi opposite Memphis and leading to Little Rock, Arkansas. Meeting the Arkansas River there, it continued west, roughly following the waterway's course, all the way to the outpost of Fort Smith and even beyond, to Fort Gibson, Oklahoma.

South of that lay another route, which ran west from Natchitoches, Louisiana, to Nacogdoches, Texas, then continued across the Trinity and Brazos rivers, beyond which point Bradley labeled it the "Road from Mexico." Actually, after crossing the Brazos, the road dipped southwest and continued to San Antonio. During the 1820s, Texas was beginning to attract more attention from newspapers in the East, and also from those individuals considering a westward move. Roads leading there, in fact, had been mentioned as early as 1812, in Amos Stoddard's *Sketches of Louisiana,* and in William Darby's *Emigrant's Guide* of 1818. By 1825, the enterprising Stephen F. Austin, following the initiative of his late father, Moses, had persuaded three hundred American families to relocate to Texas, the first group of many to go there.[16]

Not shown on the Bradley map of 1825 was yet another road– the fabled Santa Fe Trail, blazed by William Becknell and his companions in 1822. But the trail did appear on another U.S. map of 1825, this one drawn by David H. Vance and published by Anthony Finley. Vance called it the *Route of the Traders from Missouri to New Mexico.* Starting first from Franklin and later from Fort Osage in western Missouri, it struck the Arkansas River in Kansas and followed it west nearly to the Front Range of the Rocky Mountains before turning south and crossing Raton Pass into New Mexico. Santa Fe was nearly eight hundred miles from Fort Osage, but the profits to be earned made the trip worthwhile. Army Lt. George Brewerton, who spent a good deal of time in the West, described the men involved in the business as "Santa Fe traders, who counted their gains in thousands, and whose signatures were good in St. Louis to almost any amount."[17]

Like the Bradley map, Daniel Hewett's *American Traveller, or National Directory* of 1825 did not mention the Santa Fe Trail, but it presented the preferred pathways to numerous other points in the West. Hewett's Western Route No. 2, for example, provided directions, "From Washington to St. Louis, and thence to St. Charles, Franklin, and Council Bluffs." Council Bluffs, he noted, was "about 650 [miles] above the junction of the Missouri with the Mississippi. . . . It is an important station, the highest up the Missouri, that is occupied by the United States as a military position." Distant as it was, Council Bluffs was much closer to St. Louis than the destination offered by Hewett's Western Route No. 1, "From Washington to St. Louis, and thence to the Pacific Ocean."[18]

Most emigrants, however, wanted information about the roads closer to home. In that regard, the National Road was always a topic of interest, despite its deteriorating condition. The German Duke Bernhard of Saxe-Weimar-Eisenach, traveling east through Ohio in 1826 and following the old trace from Zanesville toward Wheeling, first encountered the new stretch: "We met [at Fairview] with part of the great national road . . . [which] is covered six inches thick with small stones, having a ditch on each side; they were working slowly at it; Fairview is now at the end of the road." Farther east, "We frequently [rode] along the new national turnpike road, on which they were working rapidly. This road carefully avoids the numerous hills, cuts through several of them, and has, where it is requisite, solid stone bridges."

One of the peculiarities of bridge building in Ohio (and western Pennsylvania) was the "S" bridge (at least four of which still survive). When the National Road crossed a stream diagonally, the typical arched bridge, for reasons of efficient construction, had to span the stream at right angles; and since the bridge was now at an angle to the road axis, it was given curved approaches at either end to meet the road squarely.

Regardless of bridges, however, there was a notable difference when the new road met the old:

> In Wheeling we took the stage on the great national road to Washington in Pennsylvania. We soon ascended a high mountain, from the top of which we could discover on one side the beautiful valley of the Ohio, [with] the woody mountains bordering the valley; and the town of Wheeling, with its orchards and gardens on the other. . . . The national road, which is finished seven years ago, requires considerable repairs, or at least to be kept in better order. Since it has been finished nothing has been done to it. The tracks are deep, and the road is very rough.[19]

Frances Trollope followed the same route from Wheeling east early in 1828, tucking herself into a "cold corner in a rumbling stage-coach":

The coach had three rows of seats, each calculated to hold three persons, and as we were only six, we had, in the phrase of Milton, to "inhabit lax" this exalted abode, and, accordingly, we were tossed about like a few potatoes in a wheel-barrow. Our knees, elbows, and heads required too much care for their protection to allow us leisure to look out of the windows; but at length the road became smoother, and we became more skillful in the art of balancing ourselves, so as to meet the concussion with less danger of dislocation.

We then found that we were travelling through a very beautiful country . . . and the very circumstance of a wide and costly road (though not a very smooth one) which in theory might be supposed to injure picturesque effect, was beautiful to us [as well]. . . . This road was made at the expense of the government as far as Cumberland, a town situated among the Alleghany Mountains, and, from the nature of the ground, must have been a work of great cost. I regretted not having counted the number of bridges between Wheeling and Little Washington, a distance of thirty-four miles; over one stream only there are twenty-five, all passed by the road. They frequently occurred within a hundred yards of each other, so serpentine is its course.

Once east of Washington, the mountain scenery commanded Mrs. Trollope's attention—but not for long:

As our noble terrace-road, the Semplon of America, rose higher and higher, all that is noblest in nature was joined to all that is sweetest. The blue tops of the higher ridges formed the outline; huge masses of rock rose above us on the left, half hid at intervals by the bright green shrubs, while to the right we looked down upon the tops of the pines and cedars which clothed the bottom. . . .

The first night we passed among the mountains recalled us painfully from the enjoyment of nature to all the petty miseries of personal discomfort. Arrived at our inn, a forlorn parlour, filled with the blended fumes of tobacco and whiskey, received us; and chilled as we began to feel ourselves with the mountain air, we preferred going to our cold bed-rooms

The Nixon Tavern, Fairchance, Pennsylvania, built in 1810, represents the rough-hewn aspect of rural inns along the National Road and other routes during the early nineteenth century. The inn described by Frances Trollope in 1828 may have been similar in appearance. When this photograph was taken in 1934, the tavern was still occupied. (*Historic American Building Survey/Library of Congress*)

rather than sup in such an atmosphere. We found linen on the beds which they assured us had only been used *a few nights*; every kind of refreshment we asked for we were answered, "We do not happen to have that article."

The next morning cheered our spirits again; we now enjoyed a new kind of alpine witchery; the clouds were floating around, and below us, and the distant peaks were indistinctly visible as through a white gauze veil, which was gradually lifted up, till the sun arose, and again let in upon us the full glory of these interminable heights. . . . From one point, preeminently above any neighbouring ridge, we looked back on the enormous valley of the West. It is a stupendous view; but having gazed upon it for some moments, we turned to pursue our course, and the certainty that we should see it no more, raised no sigh of regret. [The Alleghany region] is a world of mountains rising around you in every direction, and in every form; savage, vast, and wild; yet almost at every step, some lovely spot meets your eye, green, bright, and blooming.[20]

Following the same route east that year, Anne Royall noted that, when leaving Wheeling, "we take the celebrated Cumberland road, which leads us directly up on a considerable eminence back of the town. . . . It certainly was a stupendous undertaking to make a road of such magnitude, over such uneven ground." But, she added sadly, the road "is going to decay."[21]

West of Wheeling, new stretches of the road continued to take shape, and by mid-1829, requests for contractors to work on it were appearing in newspapers as far afield as the Indiana-Illinois border. However, the problems in the East were more pressing, and the report of the chief engineer in November of that year included this comment: "Repairs of the Cumberland road, between Cumberland and Wheeling.–The superintendent appointed to direct this work was instructed to adopt the MacAdam system of road making, and to apply the funds to repairing the worst parts of the road, the sum appropriated being entirely inadequate to effect a complete repair of it." In July 1832, Lt. J.K.F. Mansfield, then assigned to superintend the repair work, found the road in "a shocking condition, and every rod of it will require great repairs; some of it is now impassible." His instructions were to resurface it with broken stone "not exceeding four ounces in weight," roughly one-and-one-quarter- to one-and-one-half-inches square, slightly larger than MacAdam's original prescription.[22]

The refurbishing would be costly–so costly, in fact, that in the official view there was only one feasible way to pay for it: the National Road was about to become a toll road.

OTHER ROADS–FARTHER WEST but major routes nonetheless–also needed attention. As more mail was carried by stagecoach in the 1820s and '30s, so more complaints were heard about the delays in delivery. In part, these delays were a result of the usual problem of bad roads and lack of funds to repair them. As for repair of these roads, any number of federal officials wanted the states to deal with it, while any number of state officials thought it was the federal government's responsibility. As one of the arguments for federal intervention stated: "The distance between . . . Vincennes and St.

Louis, is made up of about one-fourth of timber land, and three-fourths of prairies, from five to twenty miles across. The settlements are therefore scattered, and far between, and confined to the vicinity of the timbered land. . . . To make the necessary causeways and bridges, and to keep the road in a proper state of repair, is beyond the capacity of the people who reside upon it."

Whatever the problems, the road, a continuation of the great western route from Zane's Trace through Lexington to Louisville, remained an important one, and early in January 1830, the Indiana General Assembly took special note of it:

> [T]he Western Mail Stage route, from Louisville in Kentucky, via New Albany [to] Vincennes, through the state of Illinois, to St. Louis in Missouri, is of great importance to the citizens of this state and the Union, and should receive the attention of the general [federal] government. . . . [But] owing to the great emigration westward, the road is almost rendered impassible, and whereas the general government has lately [ordered] the Mail to be conveyed in Stages, from Louisville to Vincennes, a distance of nearly 100 Miles, in a day and a half, it is considered almost impossible [to do so] unless the general government should aid in the improvement of said road.

To accomplish this, the lawmakers proposed a law "appropriating one section of land for each mile the said road may run between the above mentioned points, to enable the state to raise funds, for the purpose of constructing a clay turnpike road, with suitable bridges," along the route.

Postal officials agreed that the Louisville-St. Louis road

> is one of the most important mail roads in all the western states, being the principal line of connexion between the fertile and flourishing states of Illinois and Missouri, and all the other northwestern states, and, indeed, all the old Atlantic States. It must, for many years, be the channel of communication through which the Government shall transmit and receive all its intelligence relative to the mines in the region of Galena and Prairie du Chien, the military posts of the Upper

Mississippi, Missouri, and their tributary streams, and the whole northwestern Indian frontier. . . .

In relation to the quality of the road . . . general reports represent it as a road greatly inferior to what most of the roads on our leading stage routes are. The complaints during the present season have been almost constant of the very bad state of the roads generally, but especially between Louisville and Vincennes. It may be expected that the complaints will be still louder now that the time for performing the whole trip is thirty-six hours less each way than was allowed prior to the first of the present month. The repair of the roads would, unquestionably, be highly beneficial to the public interest, and very gratifying to this Department; but in what way it should be done, whether by the authorities of the States, or of the General Government, is a question which the Postmaster General does not consider himself competent to decide.[23]

One man who did feel himself competent to decide the fate of a given route–the Maysville Road, the extension of Zane's Trace into Kentucky–was President Andrew Jackson. Running southwest from the Ohio River at Maysville into Lexington, it was only about sixty-five miles long, but was nonetheless an important part of the long-used pathway to Louisville and the Mississippi. According to one account, a company hired a man for one month "to record the number of persons, wagons, horses, cattle, & c. which passed over the road; and the average for a day, derived from this record, amounts to three hundred and fifty-one persons, thirty three carriages, and fifty-one wagons."

By the late 1820s the road was in dire need of improvement; so bad was it, in fact, that one observer called it

one of the worst in all our country. In winter it is almost impassable, owing to the depth of the soil, which readily forms deep mud holes. Such is the difficulty of getting along, that the wagoners have sometimes to join themselves in gangs to lend each other assistance. Double teams are often hitched to the same wagon; and not unfrequently they become so deeply mired that the neighbors have to turn out to aid the teamsters; and in winter it often happened, after sticking in the mire, that they are frozen up entirely. The same state of things exists in relation to the mail.

A Kentucky company formed to handle the repair job found that the needed funds were lacking. Company officials then asked the federal government to subscribe to $150,000 worth of their stock, claiming that their route was, in effect, part of the National Road. In April 1830, after a debate of nearly three days, the House of Representatives finally agreed, approving the Maysville bill by a vote of 102 to 86. Remarks made during the debate, however, show how skeptically some congressmen viewed the plan. One of them said:

A sandstone mile marker along Zane's Trace on Route 22, near Kinderhook, Ohio. The carved letters and numerals have been made legible by blacking in. (*Library of Congress*)

> In the Pennsylvania Senate, on a bill making further appropriations for roads and canals, a member, Mr. Seltzer, said, "That the gentleman from the city had given us an eloquent speech, but had sung the old song—a song which he had sung many times before. . . . It has been sung from year to year—'give us more money to extend a little further, and the canal will be profitable.' When the money has been received, and the extension made, they come here, and the song is sung over again, 'give us a little more, and it will be profitable.' The State has already expended more than twelve millions of dollars, and not one mile of canal has been completed.[24]

(Actually, parts of the canal had been completed by that time, but the point made about the "same old song" was nonetheless a good one, and one that applied to many infrastructure projects, the Maysville Road included.)

Jackson was no more in favor of the plan for the road than the good congressman, and he decided to veto the bill. In Jackson's view, it was far more important to pay off the national debt than to spend money on new projects. Once that debt was paid, he thought, a surplus would build up that could be distributed to the states for internal improvements.

There were other objections as well. In his veto message (probably written in collaboration with Vice President Martin Van Buren), Jackson noted that the Maysville Road bill was "a measure of purely local character"–entirely within the borders of a single state–and that nothing in the Constitution authorized the federal government to become a shareholder in a state corporation. To do so, Jackson said, would be "corrupting" and lead to "the destruction of states' rights" because the federal government would "wield its power in your elections and all the interior concerns of the state."[25]

Nevertheless, a good many Kentucky residents did not see things that way. Traveler Simon Ferrall, who was passing through Maysville at the time, noted, "A great deal of excitement was just then produced among the inhabitants of Maysville by the president's having put his veto on the bill, passed by congress, granting loans to the 'Maysville and Lexington road' and the 'Louisville canal' companies. The Kentuckians were in high dudgeon, and denounced Jackson as an enemy to internal improvement, and to the western states."[26]

Jackson's veto ended one debate and started others. But, left to its own devices, the State of Kentucky, with the help of its most prominent citizen, Henry Clay, managed to raise enough money to refurbish the road by 1835. In a sense, this action was a signal of the gradual improvement that was to come for other roads leading west.

Stagecoach Lines

Because stagecoach drivers often enjoyed the admiration and regard of others, many a young man wanted a job handling the reins. One youngster in western Virginia, however, told this tale about asking an older man's advice—an older man with a marriageable daughter named Edith:

> So, the other day, says I to him, "Mr. Pembroke, I have a notion to get into some regular business. . . . I have a notion of becoming a stage driver."
>
> "A stage driver!" repeated the old man, and shook his head, "that will never do, child," said he; "you are young and giddy—a stage driver is thrown into much company; he has many invitations by the passengers to drink when he does not need it, and is led into bad habits unless he keeps a more than mortal watch over his conduct. Besides, my lad, there are many young women, allured by the gay whistle of the stage driver, who contrive to get into his stage under one pretence or another, and he is apt to be led astray. . . ."
>
> "If that won't answer," said I, "what would you think of my becoming a carter, and driving a waggon to Pitt? I am an excellent hand among horses."
>
> "Worse and worse," cried he. "Ay, the boy is mad. A teamster to Pitt, to be sure! You would be ruined, you, so young; why man, you ought by all means to be married before you undertake any business attended with so many temptations.

Don't you know," continued he, "that the prettiest girls in all the country are to be found at those houses where the waggons stop; don't you know you would fall in love, head over ears, with half a dozen, and ten chances to one, that, in despair of which to take, you would go and hang yourself, you young dog. Don't go to that business until you get married."

. . . I was not a little piqued at his answer, and so, for mischief, I put another question to him. "And what, sir," said I, soberly, "would you think of my taking to town a drove of grass-hoppers? I am told they fetch a capital price to feed mocking birds."

"A drove of grass-hoppers! You impudent rascal," said he, raising his cane, which as it fell towards my head, was arrested by the arm of Edith, poor girl, who had sprung to my rescue.[1]

Early in September 1818, the first coach owned by the new Baltimore-to-Wheeling stagecoach line clattered over the National Road into Brownsville. It was a momentous event. Among the principals of the line were James Reeside of Cumberland, Basil Brashear of Brownsville, and James Pemberton of Wheeling. But conspicuously absent from this list were other names that would soon come to symbolize fast travel on the National Road: Stockton and Stokes.[2]

Richard Stockton was in the coaching business by mid-1815, operating in Baltimore as Stockton & Clarke, and directing most of his attention to points in the East. However, one of his lines ran north to Lancaster, Pennsylvania, and so could meet coaches bound for Pittsburgh and the Ohio River. By mid-1817, Stockton coaches were gradually shifting westward, now running to Frederick and Hagerstown, Maryland, and by mid-1818 to Chambersburg, Pennsylvania.[3]

By the spring of 1821, the firm, now operating as Stockton & Stokes, was running coaches all the way from Philadelphia to Wheeling. But the partners also stayed attentive to other markets. In April 1823, they advertised their "New Line Of Mail Coaches, Between Alexandria and Winchester . . . Connecting with the Tennessee Line, at the latter place, via Staunton, & c." [4]

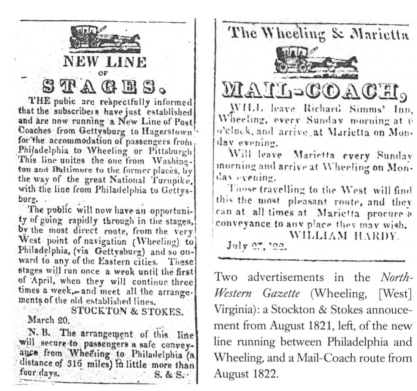

NEW LINE
OF
STAGES.

THE pubic are respectfully informed that the subscribers have just established and are now running a New Line of Post Coaches from Gettysburg to Hagerstown for the accommodation of passengers from Philadelphia to Wheeling or Pittsburgh This line unites the one from Washington and Baltimore to the former places, by the way of the great National Turnpike, with the line from Philadelphia to Gettysburg.

The public will now have an opportunity of going rapidly through in the stages, by the most direct route, from the very West point of navigation (Wheeling) to Philadelphia, (via Gettysburg) and so onward to any of the Eastern cities. These stages will run once a week until the first of April, when they will continue three times a week, and meet all the arrangements of the old established lines.
STOCKTON & STOKES.
March 20.

N. B. The arrangement of this line will secure to passengers a safe conveyance from Wheeling to Philadelphia (a distance of 316 miles) in little more than four days.   S. & S.

The Wheeling & Marietta

MAIL-COACH,

WILL leave Richard Simms' Inn, Wheeling, every Sunday morning at 6 o'clock, and arrive at Marietta on Monday evening.

Will leave Marietta every Sunday morning and arrive at Wheeling on Monday evening.

Those travelling to the West will find this the most pleasant route, and they can at all times at Marietta procure a conveyance to any place they may wish.
WILLIAM HARDY.
July 27, '22.

Two advertisements in the *North-Western Gazette* (Wheeling, [West] Virginia): a Stockton & Stokes annoucement from August 1821, left, of the new line running between Philadelphia and Wheeling, and a Mail-Coach route from August 1822.

During the 1820s, the road from Richmond through Charlottesville to Staunton, in Virginia's Shenandoah Valley, was a well-used one, and a number of westbound travelers took note of it: "At Charlottesville you are almost sure to get into a crowded coach, but fortunately the road to Staunton is very good, and affords some magnificent mountain and valley views. Our Virginia friends are sound economists, and follow Adam Smith's principle of keeping the market rather understocked in the commodity of stage coaches."

And sure enough,

We left Charlottesville [for Staunton] in a coach with nine passengers; and when we were just about starting, the coach-agent, bringing to the coach door a decent looking country girl, made the following apostrophe–'will no gentleman have the politeness to ride outside, to make room for this young lady?' three voices instantly answered, I will; the sounds having proceeded from an Irishman, just arrived in the country, a Philadelphian and a Virginian. The Philadelphian suited the action to the word, and without more ado vacated his seat. I mention this to show, that in this country civilization has invaded even the stage coaches.

Less civilized was the road between Charlottesville and Staunton, which "has an awfully dangerous appearance, running up the side of a steep mountain, and having no parapet wall. The safety, however, lies in the horses, who cannot by any means be persuaded to run off the road. The coaches, horses, and drivers are good, and the latter take the precaution of locking one of the hind wheels, in going down steep or long hills. With the wheel locked, they drive down very fast."[5]

Evidently not all coach horses were so reliable. In the summer of 1822, several newspapers told of a mishap on the National Road:

On Sunday night, 31st ult. between 9 and 10 o'clock, the last set of horses on the National Road from Wheeling, took fright, within about 4 miles of Washington, and ran off with the stage and four passengers in it. . . . They turned off as usual, when they came to the watering place at Mr. Smith's, and the driver endeavored to dash them against his house, but they turned off short to the turnpike, and went off a perpendicular bank, of five or six feet high, but did not upset the stage. At this moment, the driver exclaimed "we must all be killed," yet he kept his seat, though both the large mail bags were thrown out. The front horses had reached the precipice on the opposite side [when] the driver turned them down the turnpike. Mr. Benjamin Butler, of Williamsport, [jumped from] the stage a few rods from Mr. Smith's and Mr. Christie of Kentucky soon after. Mr. M'Grew of this place [Pittsburgh], and Mr. Potter, of Philadelphia, remained in the stage unhurt, and the horses were taken up in less than a half a mile from Mr. Smith's.–Mr. Christie escaped with a sprained an[k]le, but Mr. Butler appeared to have fallen on his head, and was found

senseless, weltering in his blood. . . . Under such appalling circumstances, when death appeared inevitable to all, it is not
surprising that Mr. B. should leave the stage; but it adds
another, to the many proofs, that it is generally most safe to
remain in the carriage.[6]

Anne Royall had her own concerns when meeting a tipsy stage
driver while she was changing coaches on her way to Hagerstown:

[A] chubby German, rather more than half drunk, came up to
the door of the stage, in which I was still sitting, to know
which was my baggage? I asked him if he was the
Hagerstown driver? He replied, he was: good!

"Do you think you are sober enough to drive a coach?"

"Vy, yes, I always trifes pest ven I iss half trunk."

"But, friend, I rather think you are more than half; you have
a Royal cargo, you must mind what you are about; if you do
not act as straight as a line, I will have you up when I get to
Hagerstown; do you carry the mail?"

"Pe sure I toes."

"You are a pretty fellow, to be trusted with the mail; I shall
see into this; we must have sober men, if they can be found
to carry the mail. Do you think you can drive me to
Hagerstown by dark?"

"I vill try."

By this time his hat was off, and thinking, no doubt, from
the firmness of tone, and the authoritative manner I assumed,
I could be no less than some great personage, he stood trem-
bling to help me in the Hagerstown stage.

The door of the tavern, before which we stopped, was
crowded with people of tolerable appearance, some of whom
belonged to the Hagerstown stage; it was amusing to see their
silent amazement at the manner in which I addressed the
driver. I dare say they would have traveled through the
United States, without it ever coming into their heads to call
these drunken fellows to account. It is needless to say that the
driver was my humble servant, and friend, during our drive.
The stages, in these parts, are very large and strong, and have

four seats, sufficiently large for four persons each. There were
nine passengers, ten with myself, in the stage. Every eye was
upon me; all was wonder! Who can she be? Who can she be?
was whispered. They were not left long to conjecture; a clerk,
who lived in Baltimore, one of the agents of the line, let out
the secret. I had seen him, it appeared, in Stokes and
Stockton's office; and, after renewing our acquaintance, he
took a seat with the driver–[so,] as matters stood, it was quite
necessary for the driver to do his duty. . . . [And] it was only
dark when we arrived in Hagerstown, which lies on the great
road to Wheeling.[7]

Farther west, most travelers were apparently willing to take
their chances with drunken stage drivers or road hazards, provided they could find a coach available. To them, a welcome
announcement appeared in the St. Louis *Enquirer* in September
1820:

We are gratified in seeing it announced that a line of Stages is
established to run from Louisville through Vincennes to St.
Louis.–This will be an invaluable accommodation to travelers
to the West, who have hitherto been obliged to resort to
tedious and vexatious means of conveyance. We are glad also
to see the progress of public improvement. Comfortable
farms and good houses are creating on the St. Louis road, and
a stage coach with passengers will soon be humming across
those vast and cheerless prairies, where, but a short time
since, the wolf and deer were the principal inhabitants, or
men in savage attire, as ferocious and wild as they.[8]

Presumably, the *Enquirer* was equally gratified to learn of a
stagecoach humming across vast and cheerless prairies even farther west: in late March 1821, Benjamin Owen began running
coaches once a week from St. Charles, Missouri, west along the
river to Franklin, halfway across the state. According to Owen, the
coaches would leave Benjamin Emmons's hotel in St. Charles at 6
a.m. on Monday and arrive at Mr. Means's hotel in Franklin by
Wednesday evening, covering the 140 miles in about two and a
half days.

GENERAL MAIL AND PILOT

COACH-OFFICE,

CORNER OF BUFFALO AND CARROLL-ST. DIRECTLY OPPO-
SITE THE EAGLE TAVERN.

Top, an engraving of an "American stage-coach" based on a sketch made by
Captain Basil Hall of the Royal Navy during his travels through the United States
in the 1820s. Below, an advertisement from the Rochester 1827 directory, showing a carriage similar to that which carried Captain Hall.

How long Owen stayed in business is uncertain, but by January
1824, a new line was in place, carrying the U.S. mail and running
directly to Franklin from St. Louis in three days. The price of a
ticket: $10.50, "Ferriage included," with, "All baggage at the risqué
of the owner." In 1824, Franklin was still the eastern terminus of the
Santa Fe Trail, so an occasional passenger coming in on the coach
may well have continued his journey all the way into New
Mexico.[9]

At about the same time, in Ohio, two prosperous innkeepers named William Neil and Jarvis Pike had decided to enter the coaching business, and purchased the assets of Philip Zinn, who had been running coaches between Chillicothe and Columbus since 1816. Within the next year or two, they took over other operations, such as Marsh & Barney's Columbus and Portland (later Sandusky) line; and by May 1826, Neil's name appeared on a lengthy advertisement for the "Cincinnati, Dayton, Columbus and Portland Line Of Mail Stages," which "Runs Through In Four Days."[10]

Late in 1827, an ad by Neil and Pike appeared in the *Ohio State Journal*: "We wish to purchase from Eighty to One Hundred Head Of Horses, suitable for the Harness. . . . We also wish to employ a number of Stage Drivers and Hostlers; none but those of steady habits need apply." Within a month, another Neil ad promised to run post coaches between Columbus and Chillicothe no less than six times per week.[11]

By the late 1820s, the term "post coach" was generally understood to mean the best coach available, one better adapted for the comfort and safety of the passengers than the old stage wagon. The style had come into vogue some ten years earlier, and John Duncan had described one during his travels through New York in 1818–19: a round-top coach with a capacity of nine inside, a separate seat outside for the driver, and a boot at the rear for the luggage. In all probability the coach body rested on C-springs, or "patent elliptic springs" to make life easier for the occupants.[12]

The Ohio Stage Company again emphasized the "post coach" aspect in an 1829 ad in the *Cincinnati Annual Advertiser*, which, incidentally, showed how far the operation had progressed since its beginning. Signed by Robert Neil as "Agent," it proclaimed that passengers patronizing the "Wheeling, Lake Erie & Cincinnati Lines of Post Coaches . . . can be conveyed in any direction they wish. . . . Passengers go through in from three to four days, from the Lake to Cincinnati, and in three days from Wheeling to Cincinnati. These Lines are connected with the great Mail Lines, or National Road to Baltimore, Philadelphia, and New-York, and also with the Lines to Lexington, Louisville, Nashville, and St. Louis."[13]

One of the lines mentioned in the ad, running along the great "Western Mail Stage route" from Louisville to St. Louis, passed through Vincennes. And in mid-1826, an open letter appeared in the columns of the *Vincennes (IN) Western Sun*, commenting on the repeated failure of coaches coming from Louisville to meet their schedules, and reminding the paper's readers that

> the mail should in all cases be carried according to contract– if two horses would not do for the stage, four must be put in– if four would not answer the purpose, six must be attached to it. . . .
>
> How comes it, then, that gen. D. Green [Duff Green, friend of Andrew Jackson], the Editor of the [United States] Telegraph, living at Washington, with a salary of three thousand dollars per annum for his editorial labors–with a contract for carrying the mail from Louisville to this place in a stage, from the first day of May last–and who has been regularly reported, from that time to this, as having failed–has had no notice taken of his failures?
>
> Has not [the Postmaster General] dealt differently with other contractors on this route? And has he not–although he has been notified of the failure to bring on the mail in a stage according to contract, written a modest little note, informing "That gen. Green would be on soon, and the evil, he hoped, would be remedied?"
>
> Is it not a fact, that Mr. A.L. Mills, the other contractor, (and a better one there is not on the line from Washington to St. Louis,) has come on regularly with a stage, expecting to receive passengers, and in consequence of the failure on the other part of the line, been subjected to a very considerable loss?[14]

Apparently complaints such as this finally had an effect, because by 1830, despite bad roads, postal officials had decreased the travel time:

> The mail is now transported on this route, from Louisville to Vincennes, in Indiana, 124 miles, in 34 hours. It is detained two hours at Vincennes for distribution, whence it is trans-

ported to St. Louis, an estimated distance of 170 miles, in 46 hours; making the whole period, from the time of its departure from Louisville, to the time of its arrival in St. Louis, three days and ten hours. This increased celerity, which commenced on the 1st of the present month [January 1830], is given to that mail in consideration of its great importance.[15]

One factor in maintaining the "increased celerity"was changing horses as often as practical–every 10 miles or so–because only fresh teams could keep up the pace.

An element that tended to improve stagecoach service generally, and especially in terms of lowering fares, was an increase in competition. One example was the privately owned People's Line, which in July 1831 titled its advertisement "No Monopoly–No Extortion, No Imposition," a stab at Stockton & Stokes: "[T]he public must be generally aware of the late desperate struggle of Messrs. Stockton & Stokes to perpetuate their monopoly by defeating the arrangements of the People's Line, for the conveyance of its passengers West."[16]

But the near-monopoly continued. By the fall of 1831, Stockton & Stokes was advertising a daily mail coach which covered the distance from Baltimore to Wheeling in only three days. This meant ninety miles a day–fast traveling indeed. At that time, in fact, Stockton & Stokes stood as one of two giants in Mississippi Valley stagecoaching. The other was Neil, Moore & Company of Ohio. Moreover, the two firms were cooperating with one another.

7

CANALS

In the fall of 1819, an editor in Utica, New York, wrote proudly:

> On Saturday the 23rd of October 1819, his Excellency the Governor, the Canal Commissioners, and a large number of gentlemen from this place had the exhilarating satisfaction of making the first trip from Utica to Rome, on the Great Canal. A boat built for the navigation of the Canal arrived here from Rome on Saturday morning. . . her arrival was greeted by the ringing of bells and the hearty cheers of a large concourse of admiring spectators. At a quarter past 9 the Governor, attended by the Canal Commissioners and fifty or sixty others, went on board the boat; it was drawn by one horse and made its way thro' the water in the handsomest style. We have seldom seen more heartfelt joy than was manifested on this occasion [by] those who viewed the departure from Utica of this, the first boat which the waters of the Canal had ever borne.

The editor closed his piece with a sentiment shared by many others: "[This] is a work which has never been exceeded in grandeur of design, and, in its practical effect, will undoubtedly conduce vastly more than any measure which could have been devised, to the wealth, prosperity, and political importance of our own State, and to the general good of our common country."[1]

For many years prior to 1800, men of vision had talked about a canal across New York State, linking the Atlantic with the Great

Lakes. A glance at any good map showed one reason why such a plan seemed possible: the Mohawk River, rising not far from Lake Ontario and flowing more than a hundred miles east to the Hudson. To those considering a canal, the Mohawk's east-west course was not the only element that made it attractive: in its passage to the Hudson, the river cut through a notch in the Appalachian wall and thus eliminated one of the great hindrances to a westbound waterway.

Even with these advantages, however, major problems presented themselves. One of the greatest was the sharp rise in terrain for the first hundred miles west of the Hudson River. Between Troy and Utica, a distance of about 110 miles, the elevation increased some 400 feet. The sharpest upheaval actually occurred in the eastern end of this stretch, in the 20 miles between Troy and Schenectady, which saw a rise of more than 200 feet. (The Cohoes Falls, looming above the Hudson, accounted for a third of this distance.) A rise so sharp meant that the locks would have to be built one just above the other, like a giant flight of stairs. Factors such as this caused no less a figure than Thomas Jefferson to regard any attempt to build such a canal system as "little short of madness."[2]

So, although a full-length New York canal was often discussed, tangible efforts in that direction were rare. Jedediah Morse's *American Gazetteer* of 1797 summarized the situation at that time:

> Mohawk River, in New-York, rises to the northward of Fort Stanwix [Rome], about 8 miles from Black, or Sable River, a water of Lake Ontario, and runs southwardly 20 miles to the fort, then eastward 110 miles, and after receiving many tributary streams, falls into the Hudson river. . . . The produce that is conveyed down this river, is landed at Schenectady, on its S. bank, and is thence conveyed by land 16 miles, over a barren, sandy, shrub plain to Albany. It is in contemplation either to cut a canal from Schenectady to the navigable waters of Hudson river, or to establish a turnpike road between Schenectady and Albany. This fine river is now navigable for boats, from Schenectady, nearly or quite to its source, the locks and canals round the Little Falls, 56 miles above Albany, having been completed in the Autumn of 1795; so that boats

full loaded now pass them. The canal round them is nearly 1/4 of a mile, cut almost the whole distance through an uncommonly hard rock. The opening of this navigation is of great advantage to the commerce of the State.[3]

To further improve navigation, the firm that had built the Little Falls canal, the Western Inland Lock Navigation Company, soon built two more, one at nearby German Flats and another at the summit level above Rome. Short and disjointed as they were, these canals nevertheless reduced transportation costs along the route by a half or more.

After passing through Little Falls and German Flats in 1807 on his way upriver, Christian Schultz left a colorful description:

On the approach to the Falls the scenery of the country experiences a sudden and picturesque change; the river becomes contracted to about one-third its usual breadth; on each side the mountains rise to a towering height, the sides of which, though inaccessible, are covered with lofty trees, which fasten their roots in the fissures and crevices of the rocks, and firmly maintain their station in spite of storms and tempests; while, as you advance, the river seems lost in a wilderness of rocks and precipices. In ascending these Falls you pass through eight locks into the canal, where each ton of merchandize pays a toll of two dollars and twenty five cents. . . . certainly too high, and generally complained of. . . . [But the] canal, which is four or five miles long, is a beautiful piece of water, passing through the flats of the town of Herkimer.[4]

In mentioning these canals, Albert Gallatin's report of 1808 noted that two of them originally had wooden or brick locks, which had failed the test of time. Between 1802 and 1804, stone locks "of solid masonry" had replaced them, "a circumstance which increased considerably the expense of the undertaking."

The "expense of the undertaking" was the pertinent point. A long-distance canal, spanning the length of the Mohawk (which Gallatin gave as 125 miles), and extending west from its headwaters through Oneida Lake to Lake Ontario, would cost an estimated $2,200,000. (This figure included the $420,000 needed to cover fifty-five well-built stone locks, each with an eight-foot lift.) Moreover, a westbound vessel passing through such a canal would still find itself in Lake Ontario, with no water link to Lake Erie. To connect one lake with the other, a second canal would be needed around Niagara Falls. And this, Gallatin estimated, would cost an additional million dollars.[5]

Although Gallatin's report did not suggest it, there was another canal route to consider, one that ran south of Lake Ontario, bypassing it completely, and reached all the way to Lake Erie's eastern shore. While the Lake Erie route would require more time, more digging, and more money, there were at least two objections to the Lake Ontario plan: the difficulty of cutting a canal around Niagara Falls, and, perhaps more important, the fact that canal traffic, once in Lake Ontario, would find it all too easy to swing north to Canada. So in March 1808, the New York Legislature authorized "an accurate survey of the most eligible and direct route for a canal to open a communication between the tide waters of the Hudson and Lake Erie." Early in 1809, surveyor James Geddes completed a lengthy review of the terrain east and south of Lake Ontario; then, echoing earlier voices on the subject, reported that an "interior route" all the way to Lake Erie was feasible. Major obstacles lay astride this route, of course. Aside from the multiplicity of locks needed at the eastern end, digging all the way to Lake Erie meant overcoming a problem equally challenging near the western end: the Niagara Escarpment, miles of solid rock that the builders would either have to breach or surmount to get to the lake.[6]

Nevertheless, the thought of a canal's advantages continued to exert a strong pull on those involved with transportation. As American inventor Robert Fulton wrote late in 1807, "on a road of the best kind, four horses, and sometimes five, are necessary to transport only three tons. On a canal, one horse will draw twenty-five tons, and thus perform the work of forty horses." [7]

In an impassioned speech to the House of Representatives early in 1810, New York Congressman Peter Buell Porter declared:

> If you can constitutionally create banks for the accommoda-
> tion of the merchant, but cannot construct canals for the ben-
> efit of the farmer—if this be the crooked, partial, side-ways
> policy that is to be pursued, there is great reason to fear that

our western brethren may soon accost us in a tone higher than that of the constitution itself. . . . Let the U.S. and the state of New-York undertake a canal from the Hudson to the lakes; and, so far from draining your treasury by the operation, it will give you in five years–I pledge my reputation on it–an overflowing treasury. There can be no mistake about this business, sir, it is a matter of plain calculation. The government of the state of New-York have long seen the advantages of such a navigation. . . . They wait only in the expectation that the general government will aid them in this great work; and this is certainly a just and reasonable expectation, inasmuch as the work would benefit the property of the U.S. to a much greater extent than that of the state of New-York.[8]

Accordingly, late in 1811, DeWitt Clinton, governor of New York and a staunch advocate of the canal, tried to get federal support for it, but to no avail. Various legalistic reasons were presented for the lack of cooperation, but it was whispered that sectional rivalries and jealousies were the real reasons for refusal.

However, states in the West continued to push for it. As early as November 1811, the Tennessee General Assembly sanctioned not only a New York canal, but one through Ohio as well: "[A] canal navigation between the Great Lakes and Hudson river in the state of New-York, provided it should be extended by [a] canal between the waters of Lake Erie, and Muskingum river, a branch of Ohio river, would prove to be highly beneficial to the Western States in general." Tennessee then called for a grant of federal money for the New York project.[9]

With such support–vocal, if not financial–backers of the enterprise would not be deterred, and in mid-1812, newspapers all over New York announced that "the Grand Canal Bill has become a law of this state. Its strong and principal feature is an authorization to the commissioners to borrow five millions of dollars on the faith of the state for the term of 15 years, at an interest not exceeding six per cent, to aid in prosecuting this great and noble undertaking." It was more than great and noble–it was a major gamble, taken by men of exceptionable faith, exceptionable ability, and exceptional determination.[10]

Meanwhile, interest in the enterprise was extending well beyond New York. In March 1816, an Ohio paper wrote enthusiastically:

> A memorial has been presented to the Legislature of New-York, bearing the signature of many of the most respectable citizens in that patriotic state, on the subject of the contemplated Grand Canal, (the largest in the world, except that of China,) an object well worth the consideration of an enlightened Legislature! There is sublimity and boldness in the very idea of such an undertaking–and should it be accomplished, the greatest advantages would result not only to the state of New-York, but the UNION at large.

Ohio had reason to be enthusiastic about the idea, because, in company with Michigan, it bordered Lake Erie and so would be a direct beneficiary of the canal's westbound traffic. So, with the federal government withholding its support, Clinton and company approached Ohio and Michigan for loans. Ohio Governor Thomas Worthington urged cooperation from his legislature:

> I communicate to you copies of a letter from DeWitt Clinton, esq., president of the board of canal commissioners, in the state of New York. That state contemplates making a canal, which will connect the navigable waters of the Hudson river with lake Erie. The advantages of such a water communication to the state of Ohio generally, and in a particular manner to the northern part of it, are so manifest, that I am persuaded you will not hesitate to give to the subject that careful examination its great importance requires.[11]

But again, tight-fisted legislators balked, and no support was forthcoming.

However, urged on and actively supported by Governor Clinton, the builders pushed ahead. Largely because of the obstacles both east and west, actual construction of the canal began in the middle–at Rome, near the headwaters of the Mohawk River–on the Fourth of July, 1817. This middle section, called the "Long Level" because it would require few if any locks, fell roughly between Utica and Syracuse. It would require less time and money to complete, thus allowing use of the canal sooner (and earlier collection of tolls), if only for a limited distance. Moreover, it would give the workers a measure of experience before they attempted the more difficult tasks ahead. As a pro-canal pamphlet of 1818 explained it:

> The Commissioners, very properly, have first undertaken the completion of the Middle Section; because the completion of this line, which communicates with the Mohawk, will afford immediate advantages on its being finished. . . . Nearly four thousand men, with fifteen hundred horses and cattle, are now vigorously employed on this part of the route. . . . The Great Western Canal will be finished. [And if] four thousand men cannot advance the work with sufficient rapidity, eight thousand can.[12]

Based partly on studies of the major canals in England and the Middlesex in Massachusetts, the canal bed, running generally parallel to the Mohawk River, was to be forty feet wide at the top, twenty-eight at the bottom, and four feet deep. To prevent seepage, the bed was lined with clay. Because dimensions of the bed, the locks, and the boats all had to complement each other, the early boats were sixty to seventy feet long and seven to twelve feet wide; the locks to receive them were ninety feet long and fifteen wide. Along one side of the canal bed was the towpath for the horses or mules that pulled the boat.[13]

Interest in the canal continued to spread. During a difficult stagecoach journey across New York in 1818, John Duncan noted in a letter home, "Had time and opportunity admitted of it I should willingly have spent a few hours at Utica, in acquiring information about the progress of the western canal, which is to pass close by the town."[14]

From Rome the builders dug southeast, toward Utica. The crow-flight distance between the two was less than twenty miles, but not until October 1819, more than two years after the groundbreaking, did the first boat nose through the canal from one village to the other. One construction problem had followed another, but the learning experience proved to be invaluable.

In 1820, near Rochester, an Englishman named John Howison commented on the progress:

> Next morning I proceeded to the village of Pittsford, and, while they were preparing breakfast for me, walked to the Grand Canal, which passes within a quarter mile of the place. Here I found about a dozen labourers actively employed in digging and embanking. The country being level, and the soil easily worked, they made rapid progress in the excavation; the parts of it that were completed measured forty feet wide, and four feet in depth. The workmen told me that they were boarded by the contractor, and received only half a dollar a day; a wage which shews how much the price of labour has declined in the populous parts of the United States. The commissioners for the Grand Canal divided the line into sections of one mile each; these were publicly contracted for, and the person who made the lowest tender had, of course, the preference. Many of the first contractors realized a great deal of money by the business; but there is now so much competition in the purchase of the sections, that the persons desirous of obtaining them are obliged to offer at the lowest rates possible.

Once he reached Auburn, Howison had a chance to ride the canal east all the way to Utica, but on a vessel smaller than usual. During the ride, he learned something about American politics:

> On going aboard the boat, I found its accommodations of a much meaner description than I expected. It was about thirty feet long, had a small cabin fore and aft, and was drawn by two horses, at a rate of nearly four miles an hour. The water in the canal was four feet deep, and tolerably transparent, but I could not perceive that it had any current. I soon entered into conversation with the captain, and the following dialogue passed between us.
> "Have you any canals like this in Britain?"
> "No, none so extensive."
> "Well, now, sir, this is a great thing for our country, a'nt it?"
> "Yes; you owe all this to DeWitt Clinton."

Watercolor of the Erie Canal by John William Hill, 1829. The canal exceeded its original five-million-dollar cost estimate by two-million dollars, but was operating in the black within ten years. (*University of Rochester*)

"Well, I don't know—some say yes, and some say no, but he had plenty to help him; however, you, being a foreigner, must judge impartially."

"DeWitt Clinton had some assistance, of course, but to him must be ascribed the merit of completing the canal."

"I know that's the general idear in Britain. You all think DeWitt Clinton a great man there."

"Yes; we think him the first statesman in America."

"Well, he's considerable of a statesman, though all don't think so now; but in a country like ours, the governors are continually changing, and the people alter their opinions, and are led about like a pig by the nose. . . . Ah, sir, the people of the United States will believe any thing; and if one takes the proper way, it is as easy to lead them as it is to lead [a] ringed ox."

. . . [Our] canal boat stopped at a small village called Syracuse, a little after sunset. All the passengers slept on board; and in the morning, at dawn, the horses were again yoked. We traveled the whole day without interruption, and reached Utica about nine at night. . . . The canal passes ·

through the middle of it (though the water had only been admitted within one mile of the town at the time I was there).[15]

But the workers soon completed the cut, and in November 1821, the *Utica Gazette* was

> happy to state, that the Canal from this place [eastward] to the Little Falls has been completed within the time contemplated, and opened for the purpose of navigation. . . . In passing Frankfort, Herkimer, and Germantown, many gentlemen came on board, and before the voyage was completed, every boat was thronged with passengers, and the bridges and towing path were lined with admiring spectators. At the Little Falls, the arrival of the boats was announced by a national salute and the cheers of a great number of people who had assembled to witness the scene.[16]

Newspapers in the far west took notice as well. In January 1822, a piece on the "Western Canal" in the St. Louis *Missouri Gazette* mentioned, among other benefits, the increased revenue to the state of New York and the "vast saving of expense in transportation."[17]

The canal boats that effected this transportation eventually fell into three classes: packet, line, and freight. Packet boats were the most luxurious and carried only passengers, while line boats might carry passengers, or freight, or both. Emigrants traveling on a budget could, if they chose, book passage on a freight boat, paying bottom price but sometimes having accommodations to match. One observer noted, "Passengers are carried in freight boats for 1-1/2 cent[s], or about three farthings a mile, exclusive of board, and travel about 60 miles in 24 hours. In the canal packets the fare, including all expenses, is generally four cents, or about twopence per mile. The boats run day and night, and accomplish about 80 miles in 24 hours."[18]

Some boats made better time than others because three horses towed them instead of two; furthermore, some teams were changed more frequently. To facilitate this, in fact, boats sometimes carried a fresh team on deck, to be harnessed to the towline when needed. Because the towpath lay to one side of the canal bed, the towline was attached to the boat not at the bow (which would have caused it to rub continuously against the bank), but at a point about halfway between bow and stern.

By October 1823, canal planners and workers had accomplished two major goals: they had finished the east section, with its multiplicity of locks, all the way to Albany, and had built the longest of all the canal's aqueducts—an impressive, eleven-arch span—over the Genesee River at Rochester. So a vessel leaving New York City now had complete waterborne passage all the way up the Hudson through Albany to the Rochester wharf.

Another phase of construction ended at about the same time. This was actually a separate entity, begun in 1818, called the Champlain Canal. It ran north instead of west, joining the Hudson River to Lake Champlain, and was sixty miles long when completed.

Settlers beyond the Mississippi, however, found the canal's westbound channel more interesting. In December 1823, the *Missouri Intelligencer*, published in Franklin, 160 miles west of St. Louis, stated that the passage of a boat through the "Grand Western Canal" into the Hudson was "a proud day, not only for New York, but for all the western country." Moreover, it quoted laudatory comments from a paper no less prestigious than the *Times* of London.[19]

When William Blane arrived in Albany that year, he noted especially that "as it is here that the great Canal, reaching from Lake Erie, enters the Hudson, it will soon become a place of great importance. This stupendous Canal, which, like the great wall of China, forms a visible line on the terrestrial globe, has raised the State of New York to the highest rank in the Union."

Once Blane started west, he opted for dry land all the way to Utica. For those who followed him, it soon became standard practice to travel by land at least as far as Schenectady, sixteen miles from Albany, to avoid the long delays involved in raising a canal boat through twenty-seven locks.

Now at Utica, Blane

> embarked in one of the passage-boats which navigate the canal, and proceed at the rate of four miles an hour by night

and by day. They are as comfortable as their size will admit. The cabin, which occupies nearly the whole of the boat, is well furnished; and the fare is very good. . . . On the second morning after leaving Utica I disembarked at Rochester, having travelled on the canal 160 miles. Rochester is a very flourishing little town, situated on the Gennessee River, which the canal crosses on a superb stone aqueduct 780 feet long.

From Rochester, Blane took a coach for Lewiston, passing through "a very large cedar swamp, the road through which was a 'corderoi' one. . . . Our rickety old stage jolted so terribly, that we had to get out and walk the whole distance, assailed on every side by myriads of musquitoes."[20]

Gliding smoothly through a canal was far preferable to jolting over a corduroy road—one with logs laid side by side across the road surface. So, to avoid the repeated bumping, more and more travelers flocked to canal-side. In May 1824, with passage open a fair distance west of Rochester, the *Poughkeepsie Journal* ran this item: "Cheap Travelling.—The Rochester paper announces that packet boats now daily depart east and west on the Canal, and the fare is so good and cheap that no one who consults economy *can now afford to travel on foot*. . . . The canal continues to be thronged with boats, filled with the products of the north and west, and with merchandize, emigrants, & c. & c."[21]

At the same time, Irish workers between Lockport and Lake Erie were chipping away at the Niagara Escarpment, using hand tools when possible and also copious amounts of blasting powder to break the stone loose. At Lockport, five pairs of locks finally took shape: Boats ascending used the five on one side, those descending the five on the other. In company with the Genesee aqueduct, these locks, and the adjacent cut through the rock, aroused more excitement than any other feature on the canal. When the much-loved General Lafayette, French hero of the Revolutionary War, made his tour of the United States in 1824, his aide took special note of the place:

> On a height near Lockport we met a troop of from seventy to eighty citizens on horseback, and under this escort entered the village, where the general was saluted by an extraordinary

kind of artillery. Hundreds of small blasts, charged with powder by the workmen engaged in quarrying the bed of the rock
to form the canal, exploded almost at the same moment, and
hurled fragments of rock into the air, which fell among the
acclimations of the crowd.

Surviving this barrage, Lafayette and his entourage made their
way to the canal basin, "where the boat was waiting to convey us
to Rochester. Before we embarked, we had great pleasure in view-
ing the handsome locks, cut out of the solid rock."

Even more dramatic was the experience Lafayette and his party
had when their canal boat stopped halfway across the great aqueduct above the Genesee:

> [W]e followed [the general on deck], and what was our
> astonishment and admiration at the scene that presented
> itself? We were apparently suspended in the air, in the centre
> of an immense crowd which lined both sides of the canal; sev-
> eral cataracts fell rumbling around us, [and] the river
> Genessee rolled below [us] at a distance of fifty feet; we were
> some moments without comprehending our situation, which
> appeared the effect of magic; at last we found that the part of
> the canal on which we were, was carried with an inconceiv-
> able boldness across the Genessee river by means of an aque-
> duct of upwards of four hundred yards in length, supported
> by arches of hewn stone.[22]

In October 1824, a year after completion of the Genesee
Aqueduct, the last fragment of the Niagara Escarpment finally fell
away. The channel chiseled through this escarpment–a rock-
walled canyon some thirty feet deep–soon had its own name: the
Deep Cut. Most of the follow-up work was finished by August
1825, when the German Duke Bernhard of Saxe-Weimar made an
appearance:

> We left Schenectady early in the morning on board the pack-
> et-boat Samuel Young, which had engaged to take us to
> Utica, eighty miles distant, by an early hour the next day. It
> was a large boat, and, as the passengers are obliged to spend

the night on board, is provided with separate apartments for
the ladies. The canal again ran along the well-cultivated valley of the Mohawk, and the country, on account of the foliage
of the trees upon the heights, was beautiful. [But] our company was very numerous, [so during] the night, as there was a
want of berths, the beds were placed upon benches, and, as I
was the tallest person, mine was put in the centre upon the
longest bench, with a chair as a supplement. . . . I spent an
uncomfortable night, on account of my constrained posture,
the insects which annoyed me, and the steersman, who
always played an agreeable tune upon his bugle whenever he
approached a lock.[23]

Two months later, in October, Governor Clinton dipped up a
vase of water from Lake Erie, carried it by canal boat to Albany,
and triumphantly poured it into the Hudson. It was a fitting conclusion to what had become an eight-year project. After the event,
a New Yorker waxed poetic:

"Tis done! 'tis done!–The mighty chain
Which joins bright Erie to the Main,
For ages, shall perpetuate
The glory of our native State.[24]

And so it did. William Blane called it "a work that the oldest
established European empire would be proud of, and which of its
kind is perfectly unrivalled in any part of the world."[25]

The canal had no lack of traffic thereafter. One of the most
interesting accounts of travel on it was penned by Anne Royall in
1827:

The number of locks between Albany and Schenectady, viz:
twenty-seven, renders it more pleasant to go by land to that
city, through which the Erie Canal passes; here the canal
packets meet you, in which you proceed at a pretty good rate
to Utica. . . . These packets are very pleasant, fitted up in the
inside like steamboats, with dining-rooms, and separate
rooms for gentlemen and ladies, which are accommodated
with births similar to the steamboats. The fare, including
board, is four cents per mile, without board, three cents. . . .

A woodcut of the aqueduct carrying the Erie Canal over the Genesee River at Rochester. This image was drawn and printed by Everard Peck around 1823, before the aqueduct was completed. The actual structure has eleven spans, not seven. (*Rochester Public Library*)

The distance from Schenectady to Utica is seventy-nine miles and a half; the packet runs this distance in twenty-four hours, passing through twenty-six locks. The packets are drawn by three stout horses who proceed at a brisk trot, and are relieved every ten miles by fresh horses and a fresh driver. The packets carry the mail. This manner of travelling is extremely pleasant, much preferable either to the stage or the steamboat, being alike safe from the accidents of both; nor are you liable to be covered with dust as you are in the stages, or crowded to suffocation.

The evening was pleasant and the country fertile through which we sailed; rich meadows, fields of every species of grain, flocks of sheep, cows, geese, and children in abundance are seen from the canal; you often see those white-headed little urchins on the brink of the canal with a fishing rod in their hands, but what success they meet I had not the opportunity to enquire.

The horses snorted, pricked up their ears and trotted merrily on; pleased with them, pleased with the country, and pleased with myself, I was sorry that night shut out the beauty of the scene and I had to go down into the cabin. These boats are drawn, as was said, by three horses; the freight boats are drawn by two and often one. The rope (for they are drawn by ropes) is very long, an hundred yards perhaps, and the horses by this means are a considerable distance ahead of the boat, which is kept straight by a rudder; there is but one tow-path which is sometimes on one side and sometimes on the other of the canal. The first boat we met, I expected to see a combat of ropes as I could see no possible means of avoiding it, both running in the teeth of each other, but they slipt by as it were by magic, without butting, or hitting, or tangling of ropes. I had so much to engage my attention that I could not spare time to ask how one rope could directly cross another without tripping up the horses' heels. Next morning, I watched this legerdemain, when I observed the teemsman belonging to our boat check (not stop) his horses, and the boats passed. By checking the horse the rope drops into the water and on the path; the other boat and teem therefore slipped over it in a twinkling. Boats going west must lower to those going east, this being perfectly understood by the teems-men; they pass by each other with that ease and facility that would elude the eye of the keenest observer.

These packets have accommodations for thirty passengers, and very civil captains; the ease with which you slip along and the ever varying scenery, is very pleasing to the traveller. The only annoyance is the scraping of the boat against the locks when it is let in; the sudden rising of the boat causes it to drive from side to side, which often awakes those who are asleep; after the first night, however, one gets used to it. These boats have no decks except a small place at each end, and though a person could sit or stand with ease on the top of the boat, it would be dangerous, on account of the numerous bridges over the canal, there being a bridge at every man's farm. These bridges occur nearly every half mile and add much to the beauty and the variety of scenery, being in the form of a crescent, neatly painted, with handsome railings. Over those bridges the teem-driver trots in a trice when he is obliged to change sides on the canal, but in other cases he goes under the bridge.[26]

Anne Royall may have found the bridges charming, but most other canal travelers did not. Captain Basil Hall, who in 1828 booked passage in a packet boat with his wife and small daughter, had this experience, which started off well enough:

> [T]he windings of the canal brought us in sight of fresh vistas, new cultivation, new villages, new bridges, new aqueducts, [now] mingled up with scattered dwellings, mills, [and] churches, all span new. The scene really looked one of enchantment. . . . Nothing on earth, however, it should seem, is without some drawback, and our day dreams accordingly were much disturbed by the necessity of stepping hastily down off the deck, as often as we had to pass under one of the innumerable little bridges built across the canal. Their height was barely sufficient for the boat to shoot through, and at first, when called by the steersman, "Bridge!–Passengers!–mind the low bridge!" it was rather amusing to hop down and then to hop up again; but by and by, this skipping about became very tiresome.

Although annoyed by the low bridges, Hall found many items on the canal entertaining or amusing. In Schenectady he found himself greatly interested by "the bustle of stage coaches arriving and departing, and by the numerous canal boats [running] up to the wharf in the very centre of the town; and immediately setting off again, all crowded with passengers; the whole wearing an air of business and dispatch." During his boat ride, he noted:

(Overleaf) *Plan du trace de Canal Erie et du Canal Champlain. Etat de New-York* by Guillaume Tell Poussin (1834). This map shows a detail of the navy facility at Erie, Pennsylvania, and profiles of both the Erie and Champlain canals. The inset drawings on the left show architect Ithiel Town's revolutionary design for a lattice truss bridge. The design was significant because it could be quickly built from common materials and avoided the need for wide piers for stone arches. Town was granted a patent for his design in 1820. The bridge design was so widely used throughout the United States, that Town became wealthy on the royalties. The route of the Great Western Turnpike described by John Duncan (see page 87–90) can be seen crossing New York state just south of the Erie Canal. (*Courtesy of the David Rumsey Map Collection, www.davidrumsey.com*)

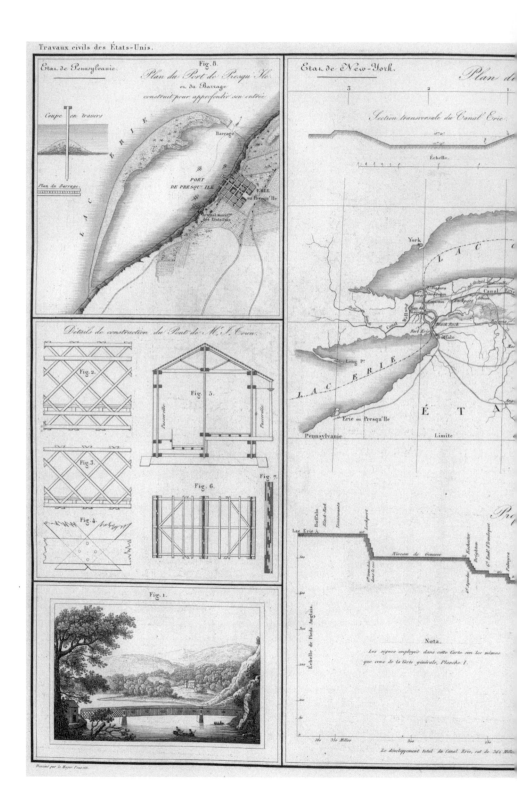

Planche X.

du Canal Erié et du Canal Champlain.

Canal Erié.

Profil du Canal Champlain.

Échelle de Milles Anglais.

There are two cabins in these canal barges; one of which is
for the ladies, with eight beds, and really not very uncomfort-
able-looking. In the gentlemen's cabin there was no appearance of beds, only a line of lockers along each side. After supper, however, about 8 o'clock, I was surprised to see these
lockers folded out into a range of beds. But what struck me as
being extremely ingenious, was a second or higher tier of
sleeping berths, formed by a number of broad shelves, as it
were; little frames with laced sacking bottoms, hinged to the
sides of the cabin midway between the roof or upper deck
and the lower beds.

On the 19th of June we reached the village of Syracuse,
through the very centre of which the Erie Canal passes. . . . [It
has] fine broad streets, large and commodious houses, gay
shops, and stage-coaches, waggons, and gigs flying past, all in
a bustle. In the centre of the village, we could see from our
windows the canal thickly covered with freight boats and
packets, gliding silently past, and shooting like arrows
through the bridges, some of which were of stone, and some
of painted wood. The canal at this place has been made of
double its ordinary width, and being bent into an agreeable
degree of curvature, to suit the turn of the streets, the formal-
ity is removed, as well as the ditch-like appearance which
generally belongs to canals. The water, also, is made to rise
almost level with the towing path, which improves the effect.
I was amused by seeing, amongst the throng of loaded boats,
a gaily-painted vessel lying in state, with the words
"Cleopatra's Barge" painted in large characters on her broadside.[27]

Captain Hall's experience at Syracuse was more pleasant than
Anne Royall's farther down the line:

Having paid my [stagecoach] fare at Utica, to Fink's Ferry,
four miles below Herkimer, I desired the driver to call for me
the second day, but a moment's reflection might have saved
me the trouble of expecting any thing like punctuality from
any stage proprietor in Utica, and I took the first freight-boat

Excavation of the Deep Cut near Lockport, New York. (*Colden, Memoir, 1825*)

that passed to Fink's Ferry. . . . The freight boats are very similar to the packet boats and are of different sizes; passengers
may travel in them for one cent and a half per mile, same
price [as] freight.

Like Hall, however, she was struck by the pairs of locks at
Lockport and by the rock-walled canyon called the Deep Cut. As
she described it:

[T]he excavation begins through solid rock for three miles, in
many places thirty-one feet and upwards, in height. It was
growing dark when we entered this excavation, and [with]
the passage so deep from the surface of the earth, it was ter-
rific, and not long since caused a lady to faint. It staggers
belief; and nothing but reality; the huge machines yet standing on the margin of the canal, with which the stone was
removed out of it; the mountains of stone, heaped up on each
side; and the certainty that you are actually sailing through a
mountain, could [defy the truth] that this stupendous work
was performed by man.
    At the end of the excavation is Lockport, which takes its
name from five double locks combined together, each twelve

feet and a quarter rise. If astonishment was not already wrought up to the highest pitch at seeing this deep cut, through a solid rock of three miles, it would certainly be so at the sight of those locks. . . [They] are the greatest piece of masonry, perhaps, in the United States. Taking the beauty, symmetry, and the style in which it is executed into view, it is not exceeded by the capitol of the United States. The locks are ten in all; a row of five [beside] five others, and empty from one to the other. There are three rows of steps from the first lock to the lowest. Here, the passengers mostly get out and run down the steps. These steps, with the neatness of the whole architecture; the great depth to which the boats descend, looking as if they were sinking down to the bottomless pit, strikes the traveller with nearly the same awe and admiration he feels at the grandeur of the great [Niagara] falls.[28]

Hall spoke of Lockport as "a straggling, busy, wooden village, with the Erie Canal cutting it in two, and hundreds of pigs, stage-coaches, and waggons occupying the crowded streets. . . . Lockport is celebrated over the United States as the site of a double set of canal locks, admirably executed, side by side, five in each, one for boats going up, the other for those coming down the canal."

He further explained one reason for the Deep Cut:

In order to obtain the advantage of having such an inexhaustible reservoir as Lake Erie for a feeder to the canal, it became necessary to cut down the top of the ridge on which Lockport stands, [and for] this purpose, a magnificent excavation, called the Deep Cutting, several miles in length, with an average depth of twenty-five feet, was made through a compact, horizontal limestone stratum–a work of great expense and labour, and highly creditable to all parties concerned.[29]

William Bullock, traveling west to east at the same time (and probably passing Hall and his family in so doing), was equally impressed with the work:

We arrived at Lockport [by stagecoach] some hours before the canal boat, which left Buffalo this morning, and spent some time in examining the stupendous excavations through the solid rock, which were required to complete the navigation here. This great work extends from Albany to Buffalo, a distance of 362 miles, with 83 locks . . . its whole line [is] crowded with boats of considerable size, laden with the various produce of the western and northern states, and returning with numerous emigrants, moving westward with their families and effects; 1500 boats, from 60 to 70 feet long, are stated to be thus employed. It was really surprising to see the numbers of poor emigrants, thus proceeding to their destination (many of them were Irish, and on their way to the Ohio), induced to try their fortune with their countrymen, already established in that prosperous state.[30]

IN DRAWING THE DISTANT POINTS of the country closer together, the Erie Canal was an essential component, but it was not the only one needed. In December 1824, with the canal not quite finished, Secretary of War John C. Calhoun wrote:

The United States may be considered, in a geographical point of view, as consisting of three distinct parts; of which the portion extending along the shores of the Atlantic, and back to the Allegheny mountains, constitute one; that lying on the lakes and the St. Lawrence, another; and that watered by the Mississippi, including its various branches, the [third]. These several portions are very distinctly marked by well defined lines, and have naturally but little connexion, particularly in a commercial point of view. It is only by artificial means of communication, that this natural separation can be overcome; to effect which much has already been done.

The great canal of New York firmly unites the country of the lakes with the Atlantic, through the channel of the [Hudson] river; and the national road from Cumberland to Wheeling, commenced under the administration of Mr.

Jefferson, unites, but more imperfectly, the Western with the
Atlantic states. But the complete union of these separate
parts, which geographically constitute our country, can only
be effected by the completion of the projected canal to the
Ohio [from] Lake Erie, by means of which the country lying
on the lakes will be firmly united to that on the western
waters, and both with the Atlantic states, and the whole inti-
mately connected with the centre.[31]

For the "projected canal to the Ohio," planners could choose
from a multiplicity of routes. A pamphlet on the Erie Canal printed in 1818 had suggested some of them; one was "by means of the
Sandusky and Sciota rivers. The former which empties into the
Lake, and the latter into the Ohio, have their waters from the same
swamp. Their junction would hardly cost an effort. The second
would be by uniting the Muskingum and the Cayuga rivers. The
former empties into the Ohio, one hundred and seventy miles
below Pittsburg, and the latter turns its waters into Lake Erie. Six
miles of Canal would unite them."[32]

Men of vision had seen the possibilities of these connections
well before that time. The 1808 edition of *The Navigator* noted particularly that the Muskingum was

navigable without any obstructions to the Three Legs, 110
miles up, with large batteaux, and to a little lake at its head 45
miles further, with smaller ones; from thence by a portage of
about one mile, a communication is opened to lake Erie,
through Cuyahoga, which at its mouth is wide and deep
enough to receive large sloops from the lake.–The legislature
of Ohio has passed a law to raise by way of lottery the sum of
12,000 dollars for improving the navigation of these two
rivers.[33]

Either the Cuyahoga-Muskingum or the Sandusky-Scioto route
would have served the purpose–too well, in fact. By following relatively short or straight lines from Lake Erie to the Ohio, they
bypassed too many cities that wanted ready access to the canal.

So state officials reached a compromise; there would be two
canals instead of one. The longer and more important of the two–

the Ohio & Erie–would drop south from Cleveland along the Cuyahoga River, swing west along the Tuscarawas and Licking rivers to the vicinity of Columbus, then drop south again along the Scioto to the Ohio. This roundabout route, more than three hundred miles long, would allow it to serve the northeastern and south central parts of the state. The shorter canal–the Miami & Ohio–would extend about sixty miles from Cincinnati to Dayton along the Great Miami River, and thus serve the southwest. Eventually this canal was to make its way north-east, to the western end of Lake Erie.[34]

As a compromise, the measure left much to be desired. But more important, Ohio officials reached a

MIAMI CANAL.
Daily Line of NEW PACKETS.

THE undersigned, thankful for past favors, beg leave to announce to their
friends and the public, that they have formed a
DAILY LINE of NEW PACKET BOATS
On the Miami Canal—the LAUREL and
BANNER. They will leave Cincinnati every, morning at 9 o'clock, and Dayton at 8
o'clock. Their accommodations and speed
will not be surpassed by any boats on the
Canal. Their object will be to please, and
they respectfully solicit a continuance of
patronage.
    DOUGLASS, BUCHANAN & OWEN.
    Dayton, Dec. 3, 1831.   [21-1y]

The Miami & Ohio Canal original-ly connected Cincinnati on the Ohio River with Dayton. The canal became the Miami & Erie Canal when it was extended to Lake Erie. *Western Pioneer* (Springfield), February 1832.

decision and acted on it, avoiding the endless temporizing and delays that doomed many other such projects. Late in 1825, a New Yorker raised his glass to them in tribute and called out, "The way to make a Canal–Stop talking, and like Ohio, go to digging."[35]

According to one newspaper, some eight thousand people flocked to the groundbreaking ceremonies for the Ohio & Erie, and "all the roads leading to the point selected for the celebration were crowded with people on foot, on horseback, and in every description of vehicle, hastening to witness the scene." In September 1825, a newspaper reported that 1,200 laborers were working at the Portage and the Licking Summits (with more on the Miami route near Hamilton), and that contracts had been writ-ten "to the amount of near one million of dollars."[36]

Work continued without letup. In November 1828, the *Ohio Monitor* announced, "Proposals will be received on the 14th day of November next, at Lancaster, for the construction of *forty three miles of Canal*, lying between the Licking summit and Circleville. Twenty eight to thirty Locks, with two Aqueducts and a Dam across Walnut creek, are included in the work to be let."[37]

If Ohio canal workers needed any encouragement, they could find it in an item published by the *Washington (DC) National Journal* in 1829, regarding a just-completed stretch of a new Pennsylvania Canal:

> October 2.–On Wednesday evening, before sunset, a small keel boat, with seventy barrels of salt, towed by one small horse, arrived at Alleghany town, from Freeport, which place she left that morning. To have conveyed this salt by land, would have required six wagons, with five horses and a driver each, and one day and a half travelling. Thus, on the Canal, one horse and two men have performed the work in one day, which, by a turnpike road, would have employed thirty horses and six men for one day and a half each.[38]

In August 1831, Swiss emigrant Joseph Suppiger and his party, after traveling the Erie Canal, steamed across Lake Erie to Cleveland. Once there, he learned that

> prices on [the Ohio] canal are higher than on the New York canal. By the mile one and a half to two cents fare was demanded, for food one-half dollar per day, and freight for [our] effects, one half dollar per hundredweight. This canal is not yet finished, so far only something over 168 miles. There is so little competition here that we could find only one good arrangement. For freight, passage, and food for eleven persons, it was $50 to Dresden, 151 miles from here; then we must detour toward Zanesville. At three o'clock at night all our possessions were loaded and we lay down to sleep in our new quarters. Our canal boat belonged to the Farmers Line and was named "Citizen," with Captain Timothy Capen.

The next morning Suppiger got a look at Cleveland and jotted down his impressions:

> Only small warehouses stand along the water. The city, already laid out regularly, has a magnificent view over the

Lake. It has only one, important, wide, main street bordered on both sides with brick houses. On the adjoining streets already laid out there are only a few buildings. There is a population of 1000. After the completion of the Ohio Canal business will boom. So far there are only 60 canal boats. When we came back to the boat our goods had to be unloaded and weighed for the assessment of tolls. At first everything was carefully brought to the scales, but whenever the Inspector turned away, much was shoved back in the hold and the Captain had to pay tolls on less than half the goods.

We left during breakfast. No attendant has yet been placed at the lock and the boat people have to operate the gates. All day we went through a wooded region, with only a log cabin to be seen here and there. . . . It may have looked just as lonely only four or five years ago on the New York Canal. Commerce will also come to these regions with the development of the canal. The lowest lock at Cleveland is No. 44. Lock No. 1 is on the hilltop at Akron, 31 miles away.

The next day, after getting little sleep, he noted: "We must have been climbing all night. Jolts in the locks woke us often as the boat rose in the swirling water. On rising we were at the 13th lock. The canal led through a rough and steeply rising valley . . . [and now the] little town of Akron lies on the hill. Just above the upper lock the canal leads into a small lake that furnishes the water for the lock. This is the reason why the canal was brought through here."[39]

The major object of the canal, of course, was to provide waterborne travel from Lake Erie to the Ohio River, and by the autumn of 1831, although not yet completed, it allowed such travel by one of two routes: the Muskingum River to the east and the Scioto to the south.

The short cut to the Ohio via the Muskingum–called variously the "Muskingum Side Cut" or the "Dresden Side Cut"–had been publicized by local newspapers as early as 1828. In July of that year, this notice appeared in the Ohio Monitor:

PROPOSALS will be received at Dresden on the 23rd day of July next, for the construction of a SIDE CUT, or LATERAL CANAL, to connect the Ohio canal at or near the residence of

Benjamin Webb, jr. with the Muskingum river at the Old town landing, near the town of Dresden. The work to be let, consists of about two and a half miles of plain excavation and embankment—an Aqueduct over the Tomika creek, near Silliman's mills; and three Lift Locks at the river.[40]

Most of the digging was finished by the close of 1830, and the canal commissioners thought that the entire three-mile stretch would be complete, with locks in operation, by early summer of 1831.

As usual, the estimate was a trifle optimistic. Joseph Suppiger mentioned this fact during his travels down the canal in August 1831: "In the morning we passed Bolivar and in the afternoon, Soir or Zoar, lying on the right side of the canal. Here there are many Germans and Swiss, and vineyards from which wine is sold at forty cents a bottle. . . . As we approached Dresden we left the main canal through a two mile branch that led into the Muskingum River. Here the descending locks are still under construction."

Once in Dresden, Suppiger and his party met John Jacobson, the founder of the town, who

advised us to take a waterway of which we had not heard; we had wanted to go to Dayton overland, in order to get to Cincinnati through the canal starting from Dayton. He assured us that with so much freight 160 miles of land travel would cost us more and be much more uncomfortable. He said that with the high water level of this year the boats could go all the way and he did not doubt that in Zanesville we could find transport [down the Muskingum] to Marietta and from there [board] steamboats to Cincinnati. . . . The keel boat had left for Zanesville just before our arrival, but this morning there was still expected [a] steamer, new since the connection between Dresden and Zanesville was completed fourteen days ago.

Once in Zanesville, Suppiger commented that the place "is already very important because of its many industries and manufactures, such as iron foundries, nail machines, glass works, weavers, saw and flour mills, etc. The great national highway from

Pittsburgh and Wheeling goes through here." To make the seven-
ty-mile voyage to Marietta, he found "something like a fishing boat
of the type in which American families usually make their migra-
tions on the Ohio . . . scarcely 20 feet long and some eight feet
wide." He and his party started downriver the same day; the next
day, about noon, they met "a real keelboat coming up from
Marietta," and the day following arrived at their destination:
"Marietta lies on the left bank where the Muskingum flows into the
Ohio. The former here has taken on such a width that we were at
first deceived into thinking the Ohio the smaller."

The situation that Suppiger encountered at Dresden occurred
again near Circleville two months later: a journey to the city by
canal, a short shift overland, and then a river voyage–in this case
the Scioto River–to the Ohio. As Zadok Cramer had written nearly twenty years earlier in the eighth edition of his *Navigator*, "The
big Sciota . . . is generally gentle in its current [and is] navigable to
Franklinton [above Circleville] with keel boats, of ten tons." The
canal reached the Scioto at Circleville early in October 1831, at
about the same time that the feeder to Columbus opened, and
before the month was out it made its way to Chillicothe. The
arrival here gave rise to the usual celebrations:

> At sunrise a National salute was fired by the Artillery under
> the command of Col. Worthington, at the Northern termina-
> tion of Paint-street on the Canal–At eight the Cavalry, under
> the command of Capt. M'Arthur, and the Chillicothe
> Independent Blues, under the command of Capt. Allan,
> paraded in front of the public square. . . . At nine the arrival
> of His Excellency [the governor] at the head of Second-street
> was announced by the firing of cannon. . . . This mingled mil-
> itary and civic ceremony was conducted with much elegance
> and etiquette, & as the venerable chief magistrate passed
> through the lines there seemed to be but one universal
> expression of *welcome*! from the vast crowd of respectable
> people who filled the streets and the windows and doors of
> the adjacent houses to witness it.

By November 1831, the local paper was referring proudly to the
"Port of Chillicothe!" and listing the daily arrivals and departures of

canal boats by name: the *Victory* and the *Athenian* from Cleveland, for example, or the *Dolphin* and *Governor Worthington* from Columbus.[41]

With the Scioto River now easily accessible from the canal, the drive to complete it could have lessened–but, in fact, efforts actually seemed to increase in the spring of 1832, with contractors calling for even more hands. In April, this ad appeared in the Chillicothe *(OH) Scioto Gazette*: "1500 LABORERS may find employment for 3 or 4 months by applying soon, to the Contractors on the Ohio Canal between Chillicothe and Portsmouth–They may expect healthy situations, comfortable fare, and prompt pay. The rate of wages is at present $14 per month."[42]

Through the spring and summer, the digging and building continued briskly. In August 1832, a breach in a canal dam caused delays, but nonetheless the line was fully open to Waverly by September, and in October–just over seven years after the initial groundbreaking–it finally reached the Ohio River at Portsmouth.[43]

A journalist left a description of a scene which, although written about a canal elsewhere, could have applied just as well to the now-completed Ohio & Erie: "It was a glorious sight to see the numerous boats as they lay in the basin by night, each illuminated by a glowing coal fire, which cast a long level of light across the water; and the silence of night was not unpleasantly interrupted by the cries of the hoarse boatmen, as they were disturbed from their moorings by new arrivals, and driven to closer contact with their neighbors."[44]

The Ohio River itself had been friendlier to navigation since the close of 1830, with completion of the long-discussed Louisville & Portland Canal past the falls of the Ohio. Duke Bernhard watched it taking shape in 1826:

> The length of the canal amounts to nearly two miles. It commences below Louisville in a small bay, goes behind Shippingport, and joins the Ohio between that place and Portland. . . . Three locks, each at a distance of one hundred and ninety feet from each other, will be located not far from the mouth near Shippingport, and the difference of level in each will be eight feet. The breadth of the locks was fixed at fifty feet, to admit of the passage of the broadest steamboat,

The Ohio & Erie Canal reached Waverly, Ohio, in September 1832. (*Courtesy waverlyinfo.com*)

on which account also the interval from one lock to the other was made one hundred and ninety feet. . . . To dig this canal out, twenty-seven feet of yellow clay at its thickest part, then seven feet thick of yellow sand; from here fifteen feet thick of blue clay, must be passed through before you come to the rock, where there are ten feet thickness still to be dug away. . . . The soil intended to be dug out, was first ploughed by a heavy plough, drawn by six oxen. Afterwards a sort of scoop drawn by two horses was filled with earth, (and it contained three times as much as an ordinary wheel-barrow,) it was then carried up the slope, where it was deposited, and the scoop was brought back to be filled anew. In this manner much time and manual labour was saved.[45]

A high percentage of the traffic on the Ohio River had first passed through New York's Erie Canal, which carried westbound emigrants at an ever-increasing rate. In 1832, an observer in Buffalo wrote:

Canal boats filled with emigrants, and covered with goods and furniture, are almost hourly arriving. The boats are discharged of their motley freight, and for the time being, natives

of all climates and countries patrol our streets, either to gratify curiosity, purchase necessaries, or to inquire [about] the
most favorable points for their future location. Several steamboats and vessels daily depart for the far west, literally
crammed with masses of living beings to people those
regions. Some days, near a thousand thus depart.[46]

Other canals followed the Erie, as well as the Ohio & Erie, but
none of the newcomers had the same effect on the westward
movement. Ohioans and New Yorkers had heeded the words "stop
talking, and go to digging." Others did not or could not; their
canals reached completion too late in the game, and had to deal
with competition not only from the originals in New York and
Ohio, but also from a growing number of turnpikes, and a still
newer system of travel: the railroad.

There was one exception, the Pennsylvania canal system, which,
because of the terrain, was not fully operational until 1834. In the
Pennsylvania system, a canal and a railroad worked in concert.

RAILROADS

EVEN BEFORE THE FIRST SHOVELFUL OF EARTH flew from the Erie Canal's route, far-thinking men were proposing an alternative form of transport. Albert Gallatin's report of 1808 included a letter by the eminent Robert Fulton, which said in part:

> It has . . . occurred to me that a few remarks about railroads might not be unacceptable to you, especially as the public attention has been often called to this sort of improvement . . . . [T]he rails are of cast iron, and consist of a tread and a flanch, forming in their section the letter L. . . . [T]hey may be cast in lengths of five to six feet [and should] be laid at the distance of from three and a half to five feet [apart] according to the carriage that is to run upon them. . . . The principle upon which such astonishing loads may be drawn on [these] ways by a single horse, is the diminution of friction in the greatest possible degree. On a good railroad, descending under an angle of only one degree, one horse may draw eight tons in four wagons of two tons each without difficulty. [In contrast,] on a road of the best kind, four horses, and sometimes five, are necessary to transport only three tons.[1]

Primitive railways had been in use for at least two hundred years before Fulton wrote his letter. In 1603–04, for example, Englishman Huntington Beaumont built the Wollaton Wagonway, a two-mile stretch of wooden rails that carried horse-drawn, coal-bearing wagons. An account of 1676 specifically described the practice: "the manner of the carriage is by laying rails of timber from the colliery to the river, exactly straight and parallel; and bulky carts are made, with four rollers, fitting those rails, whereby the carriage is so easy, that one horse will draw down four or five chaldron [144 or 180 bushels] of coal." The wooden-rail technique steadily spread to other parts of England; one element in this expansion was the Middleton Railway, first chartered as a wagonway in 1758, and still in business more than two hundred years later. By the time the Middleton's charter was granted, flanged wheels of cast iron were known, and the rails themselves were sometimes reinforced with strap iron. By 1780, rails made entirely of cast iron were coming into use; one notable example of an English cast-iron plateway was the Little Eaton Gangway–officially the Derby Canal Railway–laid out by Benjamin Outram about 1793. When completed in 1795, Outram's railway extended for about five miles between the Derby Canal and the nearest coal mines. The horse-drawn wagons that rolled over it were basically little flatcars on cast-iron wheels, carrying separate coal-bearing containers. With this arrangement, the containers could be shifted bodily from the cars to canal boats, the transfer taking comparatively little time. (This was an early example of containerization, and in theory these containers, like their counterparts in the twentieth century, could have traveled thousands of miles by water, because as Outram's railway led to the Derby Canal, so did the Derby Canal lead to England's ninety-four-mile Trent & Mersey Canal, which linked the port of Hull on the North Sea to the port of Liverpool on the Irish Sea.)[2]

Originally, Outram had planned to use iron-shod oak rails for his project, but he finally chose solid cast iron instead. Another user of such rails was the Surrey Iron Railway of 1803, a horse-powered, freight-hauling enterprise near London that, unlike Outram's railway, made its services available to the general public. Four years later, a rail service for passengers, the five-mile-long Swansea and Mumbles, began operation in Wales.

Again, horses did the pulling, but an alternative form of power was already within reach. In 1804, after years of experiments, a steam-powered locomotive built by Richard Trevithick in Wales managed to pull ten tons (and seventy men) nearly ten miles. Its speed over the rails was just under five miles an hour–but it worked.

At first glance, Trevithick's engine, the "Pen-y-darren" looked fairly simple: a horizontal boiler, vertical smokestack at the front, and four driving wheels, without the smaller leading and trailing wheels used in later designs. Closer study, however, revealed some interesting features, among which was the flywheel needed to smooth out the operation of the engine's single long-stroke cylinder. In 1808, Trevithick built another engine, named the *Catch Me Who Can*, and used it in a "Steam Circus" in London to give rides to adventurous onlookers for one shilling each.[3]

No doubt ROBERT FULTON, who from the 1780s had spent a fair amount of time in England, was aware of these developments. However, his remarks to Gallatin on railroads made no mention of locomotives. Instead, he confined himself to the proper choice of rails: "Railroads may be constructed of iron or of timber. The most durable (but also the most expensive) railroads consist of cast iron rails let down on stone foundations; such roads will last for ages. Cast iron rails secured on beds of timber are sufficiently durable for our country, and of moderate expense. Railroads, entirely of timber, are fit only for temporary purposes."[4]

To other Americans of the time, steam locomotives were a subject of special interest. In 1812, John Stevens, a prosperous inventor who already held several patents, published the thirty-six-page booklet *Documents Tending to Prove the Superior Advantages of Railways and Steam Carriages Over Canal Navigation*. Stevens made a good case, based partly on his years of work with steamboats, and much of what he predicted later came true–including the astonishing statement that locomotives could eventually reach speeds of one hundred miles per hour.[5]

More conservatively, visionary inventor and entrepreneur Oliver Evans declared in 1813:

> The time will come when people will travel in stages moved by steam carriages from one city to another, almost as fast as birds can fly, 15 or 20 miles an hour. . . . A carriage will start

from Washington in the Morning, the passengers will breakfast at Baltimore, dine at Philadelphia, and sup in New York
the same day. . . . To accomplish this, two sets of railways will
be laid so nearly level as not in any place to deviate more than
two degrees from a horizontal line, made of wood or iron, on
smooth paths of broken stone or gravel, with a rail to guide
the carriages so that they may pass each other in different
directions and travel by night as well as by day.[6]

But the early locomotives had their disadvantages as well. They
were expensive, they were heavy—so heavy that they sometimes
broke the track they rode on—and, if carelessly handled, they were
dangerous. In 1815, the *Mechanical Traveller*, an engine designed by
William Brunton, exploded and killed at least twelve of the spectators watching its maiden run. Other accidents would follow.

Anyone interested in building a railroad still had the option of
using horsepower, of course, but thanks largely to the ever-growing promise of the Erie project, American businessmen tended to
overlook railroads in favor of canals. As an example, a detailed
twenty-three-page article on internal improvements in the *North
American Review* in January 1827 spoke only of roads and canals,
with no mention of railways.[7]

However, this situation was about to change, and the men
largely responsible for it were Baltimore entrepreneurs. Prior to
1820, Baltimore had been as prosperous as any other major city on
the Atlantic Coast—perhaps more so, because it was closest to the
eastern terminus of the National Road. But with the completion of
the Erie Canal in 1825, more and more of Baltimore's trade shifted to New York. And with a new canal, the Chesapeake & Ohio,
soon to start west along the Potomac from the nation's capital,
Baltimore could expect to lose even more. The topography west of
the city did not favor a canal, and thus the men of commerce, left
with few alternatives, concluded that a railroad gave them the best
chance to recoup their losses.

As early as February 1825, a newspaper in far-off Vincennes,
Indiana, predicted such a move. In a piece titled "Steam Carriages,"
the *Western Sun* first noted that a railroad worked by a "locomotive
steam engine" was far superior to either a canal or a horse-drawn

railroad, then concluded that in such an enterprise "Baltimore would have some decided advantages [over Boston or Philadelphia], as it is much nearer to the great Western Country, and there couldn't be an insurmountable objection to a rail road, connecting that city with the nearest navigable point of the Ohio."[8]

Baltimore papers added fuel to the fire. In February 1826, the *Baltimore Patriot* printed an editorial about the efforts to establish a railroad between the Mohawk and Hudson rivers:

> New York, the first in Canals, is about to be the first in Rail Roads, among the States of the Union. [Two gentlemen] have petitioned the Legislature of New York for the charter of a company to erect a rail road between the Mohawk and Hudson rivers, between which the great Erie Canal now extends, to obviate the difficulty and loss of time in passing the canal from Schenectady to Albany [due to] the great number of locks and circuitous route. The time taken in passing on the canal between the two places is stated to be frequently two days, while on the rail-road, passengers and goods may be carried in a few hours. . . .
>
> We have frequently thought, that a rail road between Washington and Baltimore would be the most profitable investment of capital, and the most beneficial to the public, of any item of improvement now in operation or in contemplation.–Goods from Baltimore are now carried to Washington and Georgetown by way of the Chesapeake and Potomac, occupying several days, frequently a week in the passage. If a rail road was constructed, goods could be carried in a few hours; and the expense would not be greater than the present freights. . . . These are hints merely thrown out to attract public attention to the subject; whether they are of any value the public must decide.

Less than three months later the paper, with an additional hint to "attract public attention to the subject," published a well-illustrated piece about the Hetton Railroad in England. Such articles undoubtedly caused comment and discussion.[9]

Discussion was one thing, decision another. The principals who actually made and acted on a decision to launch a Baltimore railroad were Alexander Brown and his son George, bankers and linen merchants who also happened to be major players in the overseas trade between Baltimore and Liverpool. Working with them were brothers Philip and Evan Thomas, successful hardware merchants who had edged into the banking business. After two meetings in February 1827 with other business leaders, the group, spurred by "the immense commerce which lies within our grasp to the West," agreed to build a railroad to capture it. But the gamble involved was a big one, because this would be no short-line road: its rails would reach all the way to the Ohio River.

In theory, the gamble would pay off handsomely. Federal engineers had recently completed their survey of the route for the Chesapeake & Ohio Canal from Washington to Pittsburgh, a distance of 340 miles. Because it had to cross the Allegheny summit, the canal would require nearly four hundred locks, in addition to a four-mile tunnel. The dollar estimate for such an undertaking came to a knee-buckling $22.5 million, or about $59,000 per mile. Promoters of the canal argued vigorously that this estimate was excessive; the 180-mile stretch following the Potomac from Washington to Cumberland, they claimed, would cost only $4 million instead of the estimated $8 million. But even with the numbers revised downward, the bill for the canal would still be in excess of $50,000 per mile. The Baltimore men, using all the information at hand, concluded that their railroad would cost less than half of that.

Events followed in rapid succession. Thanks partly to political influence, Maryland granted the railroad's charter in late February 1827–less than three weeks after the organizers first met–and in March, when 15,000 shares of stock went up for sale at a dollar a share, eager buyers snatched up almost all of them within four hours. At that point not even a preliminary survey of possible routes had been made.

To correct that situation, Philip Thomas and two other directors paid a call on President John Quincy Adams, a man friendly to internal improvements. Adams's secretary of war, a man of like mind, assigned three of the army's topographical engineers to the task.[10]

There was good reason for giving such a job to army engineers: at the time, the U.S. Military Academy at West Point housed what was probably the finest engineering school in the country. After William Blane toured the school in 1822, he wrote:

> [F]or severity of study, for order, regularity, and quiet, this institution very far exceeds any place of either military or civil education I have ever visited or even heard of. . . . [I]t is the only place where the higher branches of mathematics are attended to, and the education which the cadets receive is such, that if they prosecute their studies, they may vie with the scientific men in any part of the world. Many, after entering the army, remain in it but a short time, and are appointed civil engineers to different States, or are employed in superintending public works and topographical surveys.[11]

Of the three engineers assigned to the Baltimore & Ohio project, one was already nationally known: Lt. Col. Stephen H. Long, who knew the West about as well as any man alive. Early in 1817, for example, he had surveyed the country beyond Lake Michigan and reported that a canal built on the Illinois River would, at minimal expense, provide a waterborne connection between the Great Lakes and the Mississippi. Two years later, as a leader of the army's Yellowstone Expedition of 1819–20, Long had traveled up the Missouri River by steamboat to Council Bluffs, then journeyed west along the Platte to the Rocky Mountains, following the Front Range south to the Canadian River in New Mexico before finally turning back toward civilization.

The two other engineers, Capt. William McNeill and William Howard, had already conducted surveys for the Chesapeake & Ohio Canal, and so were well familiar with the terrain between Baltimore and the Ohio.[12]

So, in July 1827, only six months after publishing its lengthy piece on internal improvements that ignored railroads completely, the *North American Review* presented this report:

> Baltimore was naturally concerned to draw back the gainful trade, which had been diverted from her, and the late publications in England on the subject of railways, led some of her intelligent citizens to the idea, that a connexion of this sort might be advantageously substituted for a canal. . . . Little

known as railroads are in America, and their more extended use not yet fully proved in England, the scheme is certainly a bold one, of constructing a road of this sort, not less than two hundred and fifty miles in length, and surmounting an elevation of three thousand feet.[13]

A bold scheme it was indeed, because the longest railroad in existence at the time, England's Stockton & Darlington, ran for only twenty-five miles, a tenth of the distance proposed for the Baltimore & Ohio, which, in the bargain, would have to thread its way through much more difficult terrain. In other words, the decision to build the B&O was every bit as daring as that to build the Erie Canal.

The *North American Review* mention of English railroads indicated how closely certain Americans had watched developments there. In 1825, for instance, Pennsylvania's Society for the Promotion of Internal Improvement had sent architect and engineer William Strickland to England specifically to study the country's advances in transportation. Strickland returned not only with written reports of his observations but also with a stack of printed matter, including books and pamphlets on railroads. Among them were Thomas Gray's *Observations on a General Iron Railway* and Thomas Tredgold's *Practical Treatise on Rail-roads and Carriages.*[14]

The author of another such treatise was Nicholas Wood, a prominent figure in the planning of the Stockton & Darlington, which for a brief period was the world's best-known railway. In 1821, Parliament, acting on the request of wealthy retired merchant Edward Pease, authorized a horse-drawn plateway between Darlington and the port of Stockton-on-Tees, near the North Sea. Shortly afterward, two visitors from nearby Killingworth Colliery appeared at Pease's door. One of them was Nicholas Wood and the other a co-worker, George Stephenson, a designer and builder of locomotives. When Pease commented that "a horse on an iron road would draw ten tons for one ton on a common road," Stephenson declared that one of his locomotives was "worth fifty horses," and that engines built like it would "entirely supersede all horse power upon railroads." To prove his point, Stephenson invited Pease to visit Killingworth and inspect the engines for himself. Pease did so, and the visit convinced him.[15]

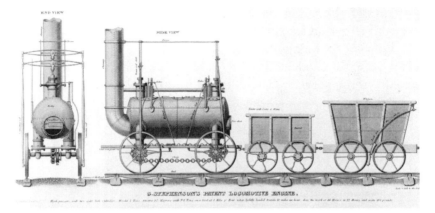

An 1826 engraving of George Stephenson's *Locomotion No. 1* which pulled cars along the Stockton & Darlington Railroad in September 1825. The event was an international sensation and helped affirm American interests in the practicality of horseless railroads. (*Library of Congress*)

So in September 1825, amid much fanfare and numerous spectators, Stephenson's engine *Locomotion No. 1* pulled a train of more than thirty cars from Darlington to Stockton. A newspaper reporter in the crowd wrote breathlessly: "The scene, on the moving of the engine, sets description at defiance. Astonishment was not confined to the human species, for the beasts of the fields and the fowls of the air seemed to view with wonder and awe the machine, which now moved onward at a rate of 10 or 12 mph with a weight of not less than 80 tons attached to it." Another reporter described an incident that would occur again on the American frontier: "The passengers [near] the locomotive engine had the pleasure of . . . cheering their brother passengers [on a] stage coach which passed alongside, and observing the striking contrast exhibited by the power of the engine and the horse–the engine with her 600 passengers and load and the coach with four horses and only 16 passengers."

These events were well known by the time Baltimore's leaders opted for a railroad. American journals were carrying stories about the Stockton & Darlington as early as November 1825, and in the summer of 1826, Evan Thomas, Philip's younger brother, sailed to England to watch the railroad's operation firsthand. He brought back glowing tales of its performance.[16]

Through the summer and fall of 1827, McNeill and Howard traversed the ground west of Baltimore, looking for a suitable path for the railroad to follow. Stephen Long would have been heavily involved in this exercise, but he fell ill and remained so for the better part of the year. In November, while not yet fully committed to a specific route, the engineers declared a railroad to the Ohio River "practicable," requiring no more than "a reasonable expenditure of time and money."[17]

Within the month, the *Baltimore Patriot* published notices requesting proposals to supply "Stone, Timber, and Iron of the following dimensions, to wit: White Oak or yellow pine scantling 7, [8, and 9] inches square, in pieces of 12 to 18 feet long. . . . Locust posts 8 feet long, 6, [7, and 8] inches diameter at the small end. . . . Rolled iron bars, 2-1/2 or 2-3/4 inches wide, 3/8 inches thick and 15 feet long. The foregoing to be delivered in the City of Baltimore on or before the first day of July 1828."[18]

In April 1828, Stephen Long, now recovered, completed his final report regarding the railroad's best route to the Potomac, which the company's president, Philip Thomas, presented to the stockholders: first a jog southwest from the city across Gwynn's Falls to the Patapsco River; thence generally west-northwest along the river valley to the settlement of Ellicott's Mills. This stretch, about thirteen miles long, was declared the "1st Division." From Ellicott's, where it crossed the Baltimore-Frederick Turnpike, the route continued its west-northwesterly direction to the forks of the Patapsco, a stretch comprising the "2nd Division." At the forks, the route turned west and generally maintained that course toward Parr's Spring Ridge, the highest point the railroad would encounter between Baltimore and the Potomac River. Just east of the ridge line, the route met the turnpike again, and they crossed it alongside each other–this extent labeled the "3rd Division." Once over the ridge (about forty railroad miles from Baltimore), the route paralleled the turnpike closely for several miles before gradually diverging, holding a westerly direction until it reached the Monocacy River, almost due south of Frederick. This length constituted the "4th Division." At the Monocacy, the route swung to the southwest, meeting the north bank of the Potomac at Point of Rocks, at the south end of Catoctin Mountain, a well-know land-

mark. The entire distance from Baltimore to the Potomac, following the railroad's path, was sixty-plus miles.[19]

By the time Long completed his report, encouragement for the
B&O was coming even from the far West. In April 1828, the
Missouri Intelligencer, after quoting an item about the Liverpool and
Manchester Railway, presented a letter from "a member of
Congress":

> I have just received letters from two of ten or fifteen other
> merchants at Wheeling, who state that they alone have for-
> warded by waggons to Baltimore, on the Cumberland road,
> during the last year, 3,500,000 lbs of country produce, tobac-
> co, & c. equal to about 1,750 tons, loading perhaps 900 or
> 1000 waggons; and one of the gentlemen expresses the confi-
> dent opinion, that if the cost of transportation were reduced
> one third or one half there would be forwarded from that
> place alone & the neighborhood . . . at least 200,000,000 lbs.
> or 100,000 tons of produce annually. Such has been the effects
> of the *Cumberland road,* and such would be the effects of a *rail
> road from Baltimore to the Ohio, at Wheeling or Pittsburg.*[20]

The Brown and Thomas men were losing no time in pursuing
their project. More requests for proposals appeared in June, this
time for excavation and construction, and on the Fourth of July,
with the proposals coming in, the actual groundbreaking ceremonies took place. One dignitary handling the shovel was Charles
Carroll of Carrollton, the last living signer of the Declaration of
Independence, who said that his part in the groundbreaking was
second in importance only to his signing of the Declaration—if,
indeed, it was not equally important.[21]

Later in July, Baltimore papers began printing requests for proposals for the twelve miles of work required from the "First Stone"
laid to Ellicott's. Costs of construction were lessened somewhat by
the fact that some of the landowners along the right-of-way, real-
izing the benefits that the railroad would bring them, donated the
needed land rather than selling it.[22]

But trouble was shaping up in different quarters. It was well
known that the initial stages of construction would be difficult: first
a bridge over Gwynn's Falls, just beyond the city, and then a "Deep

Cut" through the ridge dividing the falls from the Patapsco River valley. Beyond that, lowlands at Gadsby's Run had to be filled in, then a bridge built over the Patapsco itself. The terrain along the river would pose its own challenge. As a local paper described it, "Indeed the valley of the Patapsco is sometimes quite Alpine in its features, the cliffs which enclose it being the faces of hills between eight and nine hundred feet high, and consisting of granite rock, the fragments of which fill the bed of the river, and add to the vivacity of its current."[23]

Still another problem arose at the far end of the line, near Point of Rocks. Between the rocks and the north bank of the Potomac, only a narrow neck of land remained, which the railroad needed to get farther west. But the Chesapeake & Ohio Canal needed access to it as well. So in November 1828, when the railroad requested proposals for the "Graduation of about eight and a half miles of this Road . . . to the western base of the Catoctin Mountain, comprehending the 'Point of Rocks,' on the northern margin of the Potomac River," the canal's attorneys got an injunction prohibiting railroad construction anywhere in that area. This was not the last time the railroad and the canal would clash.[24]

The bridges were no less troublesome. In April 1828, the company hired two veterans of the National Road, Jonathan Knight and Caspar Wever, to help superintend the work. Wever, in fact, had supervised most of the National Road's construction in eastern Ohio. At first the relations between the four principals in the field–Knight, Wever, Stephen Long, and William McNeill–were cordial enough. But gradually friction developed over procedural matters, and worsened over the matter of bridges. Long, wanting to minimize costs, stated emphatically that wooden bridges, properly designed and built, would handle any stress required. Wever, thoroughly familiar with the now-famous stone bridges on the National Road, insisted on such structures for the railroad. The Board of Directors first sided with Long, but then agreed with Wever, and soon saw a steady rise in costs.[25]

The rails themselves caused another problem. The original requirement, publicized even before 1828, called for strap iron three-eighths of an inch thick, up to two-and-three-quarters inches wide, and fifteen feet long, to be laid on wood stringers. As it turned out, however, few American ironworks could supply such an item, and those that could warned that the price would be steep. So Philip Thomas turned to England, where iron rails were already standard production pieces. Again the matter of costs intervened, this time because of the tariffs the United States imposed on imported goods. But Thomas and company learned that if the iron was made and finished specifically as a railroad rail, instead of merely bar (or strap) iron, it could be brought in as "manufactured iron" at a significantly lower rate.

So in the fall of 1828, Thomas wrote to Brown & Company of Liverpool, ordering 50 tons of rails, with 450 more tons to follow. Details of manufacture were to be specified by three B&O engineers–William McNeill, Jonathan Knight, and George Whistler–who sailed to England at that time to observe the latest railroad developments there.[26]

These developments centered on a new railway, the Liverpool and Manchester, whose activities would have far-reaching effects on railroads everywhere. Almost from the first, its backers had insisted on using locomotives, rather than horses or stationary steam engines, to draw its cars, a position so controversial that in 1825 Parliament vetoed the whole operation. After all, locomotives traveled too fast for safety, frightened horses, and might well explode. Nevertheless the evidence in favor of the locomotive continued to mount, a fact observed by the three B&O engineers in December 1828 when they toured the Newcastle area. While there, they met one of the great figures of early railroading, George Stephenson, whose engine *Locomotion No. 1* had made history on the Stockton & Darlington. With George was his son, Robert, already a skilled engineer. Father and son escorted the B&O men around Newcastle, showing them stationary engines at work, and riding with them over hill and dale on locomotive-drawn cars. Work on the Liverpool and Manchester was intense, even continuing at night by torchlight. Stephenson had designed the road exclusively for locomotives, so, since no steep grades were allowed, the number of cuts and fills were staggering, with a breathtaking cost of some $60,000 per mile. Altogether, what the B&O men saw encouraged them: their railroad could indeed reach a successful completion, and at less cost. In the bargain, locomotives might be "advantageously introduced" on it.[27]

Meanwhile, work on the B&O progressed, but slowly and painstakingly. For one thing, the winter of 1828–29 was unexpectedly severe. The road's first fatalities occurred in February 1829, when falling earth buried four Irish laborers. By May, when the three B&O engineers returned from England, workers were still only halfway through the Deep Cut, so the company doubled its labor force, to two thousand men, accompanied by numerous horses and carts. Perhaps taking a leaf from the Liverpool and Manchester book, work continued even at night, with torches, using blasting powder or plows drawn by oxen–and plenty of them. A newspaperman watching the work wrote: "The digging at the deep cut is equal to the grading of thirty or forty miles of ordinary turnpike.–The soil through which it passes is of so tough a nature that fourteen oxen have to be used to draw a single plough in it." The earth forming the ridge through which the cut had to pass was called "indurated clay," and according to the contractors was almost as resistant to removal as rock itself. Consequently, the excavation work fell far behind schedule.

One reporter noted:

> In other countries, communications of this sort lead principally through populous districts; here the eye rests on lonely hills, covered with interminable forests, and all would be solitude but for the singular contrast of activity displayed along the rail-road . . . where some hundreds of labourers, with their various vehicles and implements of labour, present all the bustle of a city. . . . [I]n many cases greater difficulties have occurred in this first section, than will be found higher up the country, even in the passes of the Alleghany, where it conforms for the most part to the direction of the river valleys. The works rendered necessary by this circumstance in the very outset, are highly worth seeing. The bridge or viaduct over Gwinn's Falls will, from its span and elevation, be striking and beautiful. The "Deep Cut" is a stupendous undertaking, not only from the quantity of the excavation, but from the unpracticableness of the soil, a stiff, tenacious clay, more difficult to manage than the living rock itself. . . . At this moment, when the freshly removed earth lies in great masses beside

the excavations, or is brought together in rough mounds, bare and brown, to connect the sides of opposite hills, the scene is [more] astonishing than agreeable.

Additional difficulties lay ahead:

On reaching [the Patapsco], the road is carried along the face of the cliffs which border it, and which sometimes reach a height of many hundred feet. Here the operations, if not actually greater than on previous parts of the route, have left more striking evidences to the eye of the spectator. The debris of the cliff cover the descent, and line the side of the ordinary [wagon] road, which runs at its base, in masses of every size, some of them seemingly too vast to have been thrown thither by gunpowder. The clank of boring, and an occasional distant explosion, serve to show that the scene is not without its dangers.

But by September, the Baltimore papers could report:

Of the first thirteen miles, that is, to Ellicott's Mills, there are ten miles which are in a situation to receive the rails, and of the twelve miles above the mills, there are nine miles which are also ready for the rails;–of the remainder, including the deep cut, the bridge at Gwinn's falls, the bridge over the Patapsco, the filling at Gadsby's run, and the other unfinished parts, there is, on a general average, three fourths of the work done. . . . At the deep cut, the recent excavation has been immense.

A few weeks later another correspondent remarked, "The work done and the difficulties overcome on the first division, considering that the general operations commenced little more than a year ago, is truly a matter of astonishment, and any one who personally inspects the route can scarcely realise the fact that so much could be done by human agency in so limited a period."[28]

The company began laying its English-made rails in October. Half an inch thick and two-and-a-quarter inches wide, the rails had holes punched every eighteen inches and ends specially trimmed to match one another, thus qualifying as manufactured iron, with a lower import rate. They rested on either wood or stone stringers, depending on where they were along the line, and were kept parallel by "sleepers," or crossties.[29]

By late December 1829, with the Deep Cut finally finished and the bridges at Gwynn's Falls and the Patapsco officially open, the company could regard all the major construction work to Ellicott's as completed. Moreover, rails were in place between city's edge and the falls, allowing brief excursions in horse-drawn cars.[30]

After James Boardman toured the site at the time, he wrote:

> The great object of attraction at the period of our visit to Baltimore was the railroad, which, when completed, will communicate with Pittsburgh, on the River Ohio, the Birmingham of America. The distance between the two cities is about three hundred miles; and although eighteen months had scarcely elapsed from the commencement of this magnificent undertaking, the line for the first ten miles was about to be opened. The rails of this road are constructed of timber, the upper edges of which are plated with flat bar-iron, and they are strongly fastened to the sleepers, as the transverse logs upon which the rails rest are called. The viaducts already finished are either of freestone or granite.[31]

But getting the thirteen miles to Ellicott's had been an expensive proposition, with a cost per mile exceeding $37,500–nearly twice the original estimate. Expenses for the Deep Cut alone amounted to more than $120,000, and the cost of the Gwynn's Falls Bridge had swollen to four times its original $15,000 estimate.[32]

Faced with such numbers, railroad officials petitioned the federal government for assistance, but no money materialized. At this time the White House was occupied by Andrew Jackson, a man not always friendly to internal improvements, and the lack of financial support brought forth a pointed response in the *Baltimore Patriot*:

> *Benefits of Jacksonism.*—The Jackson nullifiers oppose measures of Internal Improvement—such as the Baltimore and Ohio Rail Road––the Maysville Turnpike––the Louisville

Two of the most impressive and significant railroad structures in the United States can still be seen today, the Baltimore & Ohio Railroad's Patterson Viaduct, top, that spanned the Patapsco River at Ilchester, Maryland, and the Carrollton Viaduct, below, that spans Gwynns Falls, both built in 1829. The Patterson Viaduct was severely damaged by flooding in 1866 and another bridge was built to replace it, but the Carrollton Viaduct is still in use today supporting railroad traffic. (*Historical American Building Survey/Library of Congress*)

and Portland Canal—involving an expense of a few hundred thousand dollars—because they pretend them to be inexpedient and unconstitutional. But they think it to be both expedient and constitutional to spend *twenty four millions* of the people's money, in coercing the Indians out of two or three of the Southern States, and removing them beyond the Mississippi. If there is no national utility in such a work as the Baltimore and Ohio Rail Road—where is the national utility in buying some millions worth of Indian farms and bestowing them on the people of Georgia?

Even with the railroad's difficulties, a Cincinnati paper made a surprising prediction: "In twenty years, the many hundred miles of Canals made, and now making in the United States, at an expense of about thirty millions of dollars, will all be filled up or drained, to make foundations for Rail Roads."[33]

The money needed to continue the operation came from a "corporation of the city of Baltimore, with its characteristic liberality and public spirit," backed by notes signed by the directors themselves. And despite the winter cold, there was no letup in the work. In February of 1830 company officials called for contractors to lay down

> a single track of Rail Road (exclusive of horse path) on the surface graduated for that purpose, between [Baltimore] and Ellicott's Mills on the Patapsco, a distance of about thirteen miles. The line will be considered as divided into twenty-seven sections, named, numbered, and marked identically as they were for the grading. The necessary Wood and Iron for the construction will be delivered on the Section by the Company, clear of any charge to the Contractor.[34]

By mid-May 1830, the rails were in place all the way to Ellicott's, and late that month the B&O announced the start of regular service. For the inaugural trip, the dignitaries who gathered at the Pratt Street Depot included B&O officials, the mayor and city council, various editors,

> and several strangers, among whom we noticed Major Shannon, representative in Congress from Kentucky . . . Messrs. Stevens and Sloan of the Camden and Amboy Railroad Company, Mr. Winter, President of the Lexington and Ohio Rail-road Company, and Mr. Townshend Wood, of Liverpool. . . .

The Mount Clare Station is home to the B&O Railroad museum on Pratt Street in Baltimore. This nineteenth-century building is at the site of the Pratt Street Depot where the B&O first began service. It is also the site where the first telegraph message was sent in May 1844, using Samuel F. B. Morse's invention. (*Historical American Building Survey/Library of Congress*)

Four carriages, to each of which a single horse only was attached, were in readiness to receive the company, which numbered between ninety and one hundred persons.–The Pioneer, a beautiful coach built by Imlay, was in front, containing the members of the Board and several of the strangers. . . . Precisely at nine the carriages left the depot, amidst the salutes and cheers of the spectators and the enlivening notes of the kent bugle, the horses travelling only at a moderate speed for the purpose of affording a more satisfactory view of the various points along the line.

These points included the Gwynn's Falls Bridge–now called the Carrollton Viaduct–the Deep Cut, and the "extensive embankment at Gadsby's Run Valley with its granite road-way and bridge." After six and a half miles of travel and a change of horses, the train

entered the romantic valley of the Patapsco. The road, which is here about sixty feet above the bed of the river, pursues a winding course along the side of the elevated hill which rises

far above it, laying open to the view the numerous masses of
rock which form the projecting spurs through which it passes. The country now assumed a different aspect, presenting .
. . works of nature in their more rugged and imposing character. Immediately after entering this part of the Road, the
crosswise wooden sleepers used thus far in its construction
terminated, and in their stead the more solid and durable
material of granite blocks was found to be employed for the
remaining part of the line to Ellicott's Mills. The train continued its progress [until] it reached the Patterson Viaduct, the
immense structure of granite by which the Road is carried
across the Patapsco.–Here the party alighted, and having
spent some time in the examination of the viaduct, resumed
their seats, and soon after reached the village of Ellicott's
Mills. . . . At noon the "Pioneer" and one of the other carriages
started from the Mills on their return to the city. . . . The trip
back to the depot, according to an accurate observation of the
time, was performed in the short space of one hour and five
minutes!

Moreover, "The graduation and masonry of the Second
Division, comprehending a distance of twelve miles [to the Forks
of the Patapsco], are finished, and the Road is ready for the reception of the rails at any time."[35]

In June the company requested proposals for "the graduation of
the Third Division of the Rail road, extending from the Forks of
the Patapsco River to a point on the Fredericktown Turnpike
Road, near Ridgeville, and embracing a distance of about fifteen
miles; and also for the necessary masonry thereon." Two months
later came a happy announcement:

Experience, with regard to the celerity of the conveyance of
passengers during the preceding four months on the first 13
miles of the Baltimore & Ohio Railroad, is of the most cheerful and convincing character. The practicability of maintaining a speed of 10 miles per hour with horses has been exhibited. With proper relays, this rate of traveling may be continued through any length of railway, the ascents and descents
of which shall not exceed about 30 feet per mile.[36]

An important factor in easing the strain on the horses was the reduction of rolling resistance, or rolling friction, in the cars. In part, this reduction was inherent in the railroad itself; a hard cast-iron or wrought-iron wheel, resting on a smooth, well-laid iron track, required comparatively little effort to move. But another element to consider was the lessening of friction between the wheel and its axle. Several English patents dating from the early 1820s had addressed this problem, but, closer to home, New Jersey farmer-turned-inventor Ross Winans patented a similar idea in October 1828, bringing it to the B&O two months later. Basically, Winans's plan (titled a "Car Truck" in his patent) embodied what amounted to a simple roller bearing. Compared with other rail cars,

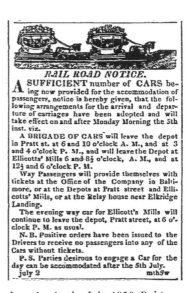

RAIL ROAD NOTICE.

A SUFFICIENT number of CARS being now provided for the accommodation of passengers, notice is hereby given, that the following arrangements for the arrival and departure of carriages have been adopted and will take effect on and after Monday Morning the 5th inst. viz.

A BRIGADE OF CARS will leave the depot in Pratt st. at 6 and 10 o'clock A. M., and at 3 and 4 o'clock P. M., and will leave the Depot at Ellicotts' Mills 6 and 8½ o'clock, A. M., and at 12½ and 6 o'clock P. M.

Way Passengers will provide themselves with tickets at the Office of the Company in Baltimore, or at the Depots at Pratt street and Ellicotts' Mills, or at the Relay house near Elkridge Landing.

The evening way car for Ellicott's Mills will continue to leave the depot, Pratt street, at 6 o'clock P. M. as usual.

N. B. Positive orders have been issued to the Drivers to receive no passengers into any of the Cars without tickets.

P. S. Parties desirous to engage a Car for the day can be accommodated after the 5th July.

july 2   mth3w

A notice in the July 1830 *Baltimore Patriot* announcing passenger service along the Baltimore & Ohio Railroad. As the accompanying drawing illustrates, the first service on the line used horse-drawn cars.

Winans's was noticeably free-wheeling, and as banker Alexander Brown noted enthusiastically, "A man can easily push along 5 or 6 tons on a level road, and we really believe that a horse will draw 30 or 40 with ease." The thirty-ton theory was later proved, at least for short distances, but over time the Winans design showed excessive wear, and more refined wheel bearings eventually replaced it. However, Winans was just beginning a long and profitable relationship with the B&O, one that would go far beyond car wheels.[37]

Even though the line was running only as far as Ellicott's Mills, business was brisk. In September 1830, Stockton & Stokes, the local stagecoach kings, announced, "For the better accommodation of the Frederick and Hagerstown travelers the subscribers have doubled their Accommodation Line connecting at Ellicott's mills with the Rail road."[38]

Then, late in November, "A Gentleman of Lexington" wrote the president of the newly organized Lexington & Ohio Railroad about the progress on the B&O:

> I reached Ellicott's mills on the Patapsco river, last Monday evening, to which point (13 miles) the magnificent Baltimore and Ohio Rail Road, with a double track, is nearly finished, at a cost of $43,006 per mile, on an average. . . . Anxious to obtain minute information as to the general topography of the country above this point–the cost of grading–furnishing the granite sills and rails, and finishing the work, I proceeded on horseback next day for several hours up the river along the road, examining every thing and seeing the work in almost every stage towards completion.–I conversed with laborers, masons, superintendants, engineers–every one from whom I hoped to obtain any information. Any one taking the same course I have done to obtain precise information on the subject, will not hesitate, I think, to say, that this grand enterprise must inevitably succeed.[39]

While the Gentleman of Lexington was making his inspection tour, another enterprise more than three hundred miles to the north was also taking shape and counting on inevitable success: the Mohawk & Hudson Railroad, designed to span the sixteen miles from Albany to Schenectady and so bypass the Erie Canal's multiple locks in that stretch. The road had been chartered as early as 1826 (as noted by the *Baltimore Patriot* at the time), and although this predated the B&O's charter by a year, the New York road did not begin serious construction until 1830. Still, based on the distance involved, company officials expected the project to be completed within a year.[40]

B&O officials had a far greater distance to cover and were well aware of it. By December 1830, the company was requesting proposals for "the graduation of parts of the 4th, and of the 5th Divisions of the Rail road and of a lateral road to Fredericktown, together embracing a distance of about 20 miles. . . . The lateral road commences near the crossing of the Monocacy and extend[s] to the city of Frederick." A warning followed:

A promotional drawing from the 1870s of the Mohawk & Hudson Railroad, the first chartered railroad in New York and the first railroad designed to use locomotives to pull the cars rather than horses or gravity. The locomotive pictured is the *DeWitt Clinton*. (*Library of Congress*)

Proposers are invited to devote more attention to an examination into the situation and character of the earth to be removed, and the Stone Quarries to be used, than has usually been done. Proper attention to this matter may prevent much difficulty and embarrassment, if not loss, in the progress of the work.–The line will be divided into convenient Sections. Recommendations for temperance, capacity, and integrity will be expected to accompany all Proposals.

Below this note was a request for proposals to build "a bridge across the Monocacy river. The Stream will require a vent of about 300 feet. Proposals will be taken 1st, for a bridge of Stone, 2d for one of Stone abutment and piers and brick arches, and 3d, for one of Stone abutment and piers, and superstructure of wood." (When the bridge was completed months later, it had a wood superstructure.) [41]

In February 1831 the company could state, optimistically:

By the reports received from the Engineers of this Company, the Board are warranted in the confident expectation that the road will be in operation as far as to the city of Frederick, and probably to the Point of Rocks, by the latter part of the current year. . . . [A]ll the obstacles which opposed the execution of this work between Baltimore and the Valley of the Potomac have been subdued, and . . . the labor now to be performed is comparatively light and of easy accomplishment.

Six weeks later, an observer near Frederick could report that "we visited the line of the rail road, near the Monocacy bridge, on the road to George Town, and were greatly surprised to find the work progressing with such spirit. Laborers are at work on all the sections, and in many places they will soon be ready for grading."

Officials continued to press the work. In May, company advertisements called for contractors to submit, by June, proposals "for laying a single track of Wooden Rails upon the 4th Division of the Baltimore & Ohio Rail Road, extending from the summit of Parr's Ridge to the Monocacy River, a distance of about fourteen and a half miles . . . and for laying a single track of Wooden Rails upon the lateral road to Frederick City, a distance of about three and a half miles." [42]

At about the same time, newspapers printed reminders of how efficient a railroad could be:

> Our country friends, who are in the habit of employing a driver and team of five or six horses in sending a wagon load of sixteen barrels of flour to market, at the rate of about twenty miles a day over the best turnpike roads, will perhaps be a little surprised when we inform them that on the Rail-road, last week, loads of seventy-five barrels of flour were repeatedly brought from Ellicott's Mills to Baltimore, by a single horse only. The distance was traveled with ease in two hours, being at the rate of six and a half miles an hour. Much greater loads than these have been heretofore drawn by one horse, but the fact we have just stated will nevertheless be deemed sufficiently striking to illustrate the utility and value of Rail-roads. [43]

But—abruptly—the work slowed down. In June 1831, one of the contractors working on the third division between the forks of the Patapsco and Parr's Spring Ridge shortchanged his Irish laborers. Finally, their complaints unanswered, the Irishmen began tearing up the road. The local sheriff then called out the militia, which, after an all-night train ride and seven-mile march, arrested the Irish at their shanties near Sykes's Mill, some eight miles west of the river fork. Most of the laborers were released shortly afterward. But more trouble erupted in August, on the fourth division, when the

Irish clashed with black workers near New Market. Twenty Irishmen were arrested, whereupon four hundred of their brethren gathered to release them by force. While company officials and a Catholic priest tried to dissuade them, militiamen rushed east from Frederick to keep order.[44]

Laying rails to Frederick meant getting over Parr's Ridge, and the plan to do so centered on four inclined planes, two of them side by side on each slope, with stationary steam engines at the top to do the pulling. As it turned out, the engines were not really necessary; the grades ranged from slightly over 3 percent on the eastern slope to 5 percent on the western–steep by railroad standards, but easily negotiated by good horses, and significantly less than the gradients found on most turnpikes, including the National Road. With smooth-rolling rail cars, in fact, a problem could arise not in the ascent but in the descent: an unattached car could roll downhill at breathtaking speeds, badly frightening–if not maiming or killing–passengers. Such accidents had already occurred on a number of English railroads, and Hezekiah Niles, owner-editor of the widely read *Niles Register*, later confessed that he never traversed such planes without a certain degree of apprehension.

In mid-November, a large party from Baltimore rode the cars to the ridge, finding the rails laid over almost all of it. And on the first of December, attended by the usual ruffles and flourishes, the first railroad car rolled into Frederick.[45]

A correspondent for the *Virginia Free Press* reached the place too late for the ceremonies, but had a chance to ride the rails shortly afterward:

> [A]fter a little bustle to get the baggage safely transferred, fifteen of us were snugly stowed away, while as many more were mounted on the top, or hung upon the sides. A single horse started off in his best trot, at the rate of ten miles an hour, and soon performed his allotted task of whirling us, with very little motion, over the first five miles, and apparently without fatigue. The biting blast [of winter] compelled us to "look out" rather shyly upon the scenery around, so that I can give no description of it, [but] in forty minutes, we reached Sykesville, nine miles from the starting point, where

a savoury dinner was smoking upon the board. This dispatched, a fresh horse moved off to the measure of "twelve knots" an hour, and in four hours, we had traversed forty miles, without jolt or jar. . . . As a traveller upon [such] a flying journey, I have no time even to think; so I must give you this scrawl without revision. I am now confident of the entire success of the scheme; its benefits and its conveniences will be incalculable; [so all] I can now say, is–Success to the enterprising Baltimoreans; may they reap a rich reward of profit and glory![46]

The profits and the glory were already materializing. From January through September 1831, "the number of passengers on the portion of the rail-road from Baltimore to Ellicott's Mills (13 miles) was 81,905; and within the same period 5,931 tons were transported upon it, yielding an income of $31,405, and involving an expense of $10,994."[47]

Not long afterward, in the spring of 1832, Nathaniel Wyeth and his party arrived in Baltimore. They were bound for a far-off destination: the Oregon country. Young John Wyeth noted that

our whole company was an object of no small curiosity and respect. This, said they, is "Yankee all over!"–bold enterprise, neatness, and good contrivance. [To avoid] the expense of inns and taverns, we marched two miles out of Baltimore, and there encamped during four days; and then we put our wagons into the cars on the rail-road; which extends from thence sixty miles, which brought us to the foot of the Alleghany mountains.[48]

Thousands more would follow them.

Part Three
1832-1843

AFTER TRAVELING THROUGH NEW YORK state on the Erie Canal in 1834, A. A. Parker wrote:

> New-York, I believe, possesses more of the sublime and beautiful, than all the remainder of the United States. It has its mountains, lakes, springs, rivers, water-falls, canals, railroads, and edifices. . . . But notwithstanding its attractive scenery and rich lands, the "western fever" rages here as violent as on the sterile hills of New-Hampshire. I found more families from New-York at the West and moving thither, than from all the New-England states. . . . [J]ust the same feeling is manifested in Kentucky, Ohio, and Indiana. And even in Illinois itself, some I found, seeking a better country farther west![1]

And the westbound emigrants kept coming. In 1835, a correspondent for the *Baltimore American* sent this observation to his paper: "The flood of Westward emigration, great as it has been in former years, is, this year, altogether unprecedented. . . . [The road] seemed constantly thronged with travelers on foot and horseback, going on to explore the 'Great West'. . . . The time is close at hand when the region west of the Alleghany mountains will sway the destinies of the nation."[2]

John Mason Peck's *A New Guide for Emigrants to the West,* published in 1836, had this to say: "Such an extent of forest was never before cleared,–such a vast field of prairie was never before subdued and cultivated by the hand of man, in the same short period of time. [As Isaiah said in the Old Testament:] 'Who hath heard such a thing? Who hath seen such things? . . . . [S]hall a nation be born at once?'"[3]

(Overleaf) *Mitchell's National Map of the American Republic or United States of North America*. Drawn by J. H. Young (1843). The 1830s saw only two states admitted to the Union: Arkansas and Michigan. Not until 1845 did the next states, Florida and Texas, join the Union. The west was still in flux, with Iowa and Wisconsin indicated alongside territory dominated by American Indians. Note the location west of Missouri and Arkansas of the Delaware, Shawnee, Seneca, Cherokee, Creeks, and Choctaws who were among the many American Indian groups displaced from their original homelands in the east. The northern boundary of Maine was settled by treaty in 1842 and is shown in an inset. Young's map also includes a table of the population of each county in the states and American territories. (*Courtesy of the David Rumsey Map Collection, www.davidrumsey.com*)

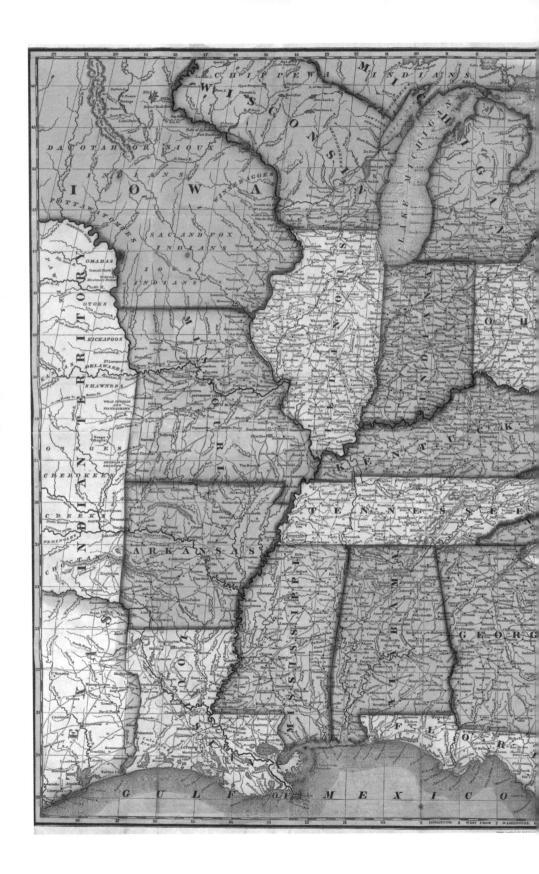

MITCHELL'S
National Map of the
AMERICAN REPUBLIC
OR
UNITED STATES of NORTH AMERICA:
Together with Maps
of the Vicinities
OF THIRTY-TWO OF THE PRINCIPAL CITIES AND TOWNS
in the Union.

Published by S. AUGUSTUS MITCHELL Philadelphia.
No 8¼ South ——1843—— Seventh Street.
Drawn by J.H.Young.   Engraved by J.H.Brightly.

POPULATION OF EACH COUNTY, &c., IN THE DIFFERENT STATES AND TERRITORIES OF THE UNITED STATES, IN 1840.

MAP OF THE
NORTH-EASTERN BOUNDARY
OF THE UNITED STATES,
According to the Treaty of 1842.

MAP OF THE
SOUTHERN PART
OF
FLORIDA.

Captain Henry Miller Shreve clearing the Great Raft from Red River, 1833–1838, by Lloyd Hawthorne (1924–2003). Captain Shreve was instrumental in clearing the massive centuries-old log jam in the Red River. In 1838, he received a patent for his "snag boat," a twin-hulled steamer that could straddle and lift logs from the surface. (*Courtesy of the R. W. Norton Art Gallery, Shreveport, Louisiana*)

9

WATERWAYS

Despite all the attention devoted to canals and railroads, a passageway by river did have a major advantage, as a young rail-splitter from Illinois named Abraham Lincoln explained in March 1832:

> There cannot justly be any objection to having rail roads and canals, any more than to other good things, provided they cost nothing. The only objection is to paying for them. . . . A meeting has been held [by local citizens for the purpose of constructing a rail road from some eligible point on the Illinois river through their town] in Sangamo[n] county. This is, indeed, a very desirable object. No other improvement that reason will justify us in hoping for, can equal in utility the rail road. It is a never failing source of communication between places of business remotely situated from each other. Upon the rail road the regular progress of commercial intercourse is not interrupted by either high or low water, or freezing weather, which are the principal difficulties that render our future hopes of water communication precarious and uncertain. Yet, however desirable an object the construction of a rail road through our country may be; however high our imaginations may be heated at thoughts of it–there is always a heart appalling shock accompanying the account of its cost . . . the bare statement of which, in my opinion, is sufficient to justify the belief, that the improvement of the Sangamo[n] river is an object much better suited to our infant resources.[1]

For army engineers, in fact, improving river travel had been an ongoing task for years, especially along the Ohio and the Mississippi. Now they were taking on a major job along one of the Mississippi's more important western tributaries, the Red River: breaking up the "Great Raft," the series of massive log jams spread out over some 150 miles of river above Natchitoches that blocked upstream travel by vessels of any appreciable size. In November 1832, the army's chief engineer reported:

> Instead of deepening the bayous and connecting them by short canals, and thus opening a communication around the raft, it is the opinion of persons who have had opportunities of judging, that the raft itself might be removed through the agency of one or two of the steamboats at present employed in improving the navigation of the Mississippi and Ohio rivers. . . . In addition to the benefit which the removal of the raft would confer upon the navigation of the river, it would reclaim by drainage an immense tract of valuable land.

A year later, the officer could report, "The removal of the Great Raft from the bed of [the Red] river has been shown, by the operations of Captain H. M. Shreve, during the last summer, to be perfectly practicable . . . and his success leaves the most ample testimony of his great zeal and ability."[2]

At the time of this report, Henry Shreve was a near-legend on the rivers. Late in 1814, he had brought the steamboat *Enterprise* from Pittsburgh down to New Orleans, carrying needed supplies to Gen. Andrew Jackson's force there, and then shuttling reinforcements wherever required just before the climactic battle in January 1815, where he served as a captain of artillery. Turning north after the smoke cleared, he piloted the vessel on an impressive, 2,200-mile voyage up the Mississippi and the Ohio, past Louisville and Pittsburgh to Brownsville on the Monongahela. Always interested in river travel, Shreve engaged himself in steamboat design, and in the 1820s worked out various plans for a "snag boat" that could clear the major waterways of countless submerged tree trunks, called planters or sawyers depending on whether they were nearly vertical or nearly horizontal. Whatever their position, they could easily rip out a boat's bottom, and did so on numerous occasions.[3]

As finally patented in September 1838, Shreve's design comprised twin hulls, sheathed in iron, between which the log was snagged, pulled aboard by a steam-powered windlass, and cut up by a sawmill. Between the start of the task in 1832 and the issue of his patent six years later, Shreve's men and his vessels—the *Archimedes, Java,* and others—battling the logs, the alligators, clouds of mosquitoes, and the attendant illness, whittled almost all of the Great Raft away. Considering the gigantic mass of timber involved, it was an astonishing feat. Its accomplishment opened the river to steamboats all the way to Fort Towson (in present-day Oklahoma), more than seven hundred miles above its juncture with the Mississippi. In Shreve's words, written shortly before the job was finished, the removal of the blockage "will open a safe and easy steamboat navigation to the heart of the Indian settlements on the west side of the Mississippi river, as well as to an extensive line of the Texas frontier. The country above the raft is also populating with great rapidity. Its settlers are now shut in from market, which will be of easy access [when] the remainder of the raft can be removed."

As indeed it was.

The same techniques were used on the Arkansas River. Serious clearing work had started there in 1834, and by the fall of 1837, Shreve could report that, with the help of his well-named snag boat *Eradicator,* he had removed most of the major obstructions as far as Little Rock, 250 miles from the river's mouth.[4]

These efforts resulted in greater numbers of steamboats on the western waters, and greater numbers of emigrants aboard them. When Thomas Hamilton arrived in Wheeling, for example, he saw that "Steam-boats, of all sizes, were ranged along the quays; and the loud hissing of the engines gave notice of numerous preparations for departure."[5]

Even more colorful were the *Cincinnati Gazette's* comments in 1843:

It is curious to see our steamers sometimes when full. They appear often as if they were made for the same purpose as Noah's Ark. The Goddess of Liberty, in a late trip to St. Louis, looked like one. She was literally covered and crammed with

"New Orleans, sketched from the opposite side of the river upon a mast of a vessel during a very low water/sketched in October 1839 by S. Pinistri, arch't. and civl engr." This fascinating and detailed drawing shows both ocean-going sailing ships and a wide variety of steam- and wind-powered vessels used on the Mississippi River at this time. Two ferries looking like two-story houseboats, one with a single stack and the other with two, are shown on either side of the three sailing vessels in the center. Several twin-stacked side-wheel steamers are also shown. In the 1840 census, New Orleans was the third largest city in the United States, behind New York City and Baltimore. (*Library of Congress*)

passengers, horses, cattle, hogs, dogs, furniture and freight, having on board upwards of 400 men, women and children, more than 60 horses and hogs, about 170 dozen chairs, 40 wagons and carriages, about 400 tons of freight in the steamboat, and a freighted keel boat in tow. A child was born on the passage, [along with] seven pigs, and a calf. So much for emigrating West.[6]

Bᴜᴛ ᴡᴇʟʟ ᴀꜰᴛᴇʀ 1830, ᴡɪᴛʜ sᴛᴇᴀᴍʙᴏᴀᴛs a common sight, keelboats continued to work the rivers. They cost much less to build
than steamboats, served well and cheaply for downstream work,
and were better suited for use in shallow waters, which could pose
a real problem by late summer. And when the waters were too
shallow for keelboats, it was time to take to the road. In August
1834, the *Baltimore Patriot* reported smugly:

> We have learnt yesterday that a large Keel Boat, full of Dry
> Goods, was sunk at Racoon Shoals 34 miles below Pittsburg.
> Particulars have not reached us, but it is said the boat swung
> over the bar and filled in deep water. The cargo must be prin-
> cipally wet. We hope for the sake of our Western friends, that
> the damage will not be heavy. It is quite certain, however, that
> if these goods had been sent by our Baltimore and Wheeling
> route, they would have escaped injury on these Shoals, or on
> any other of the numerous impediments to free and safe nav-
> igation which exists at this season between Pittsburg and this
> place.[7]

During the same year, in Indiana, a paper noted:

> The [Ohio] river has been rising slowly for a few days past,
> and is now 18 inches or 2 feet above low water mark. The
> swell, though of considerable benefit to the small craft, is not
> sufficient, however, to give any thing like activity to steam
> boat business: as none of them, excepting the smallest, are yet
> enabled to pass the bars and shoals between Louisville and
> Maysville; and above the latter place, it is, or was a few days
> ago, even difficult to get along with a keel boat.[8]

Charles Augustus Murray observed while on the Mississippi
that year, "This village of Keokuk is the lowest and most black-
guard place that I have yet visited: its population is composed
chiefly of the watermen who assist in loading and unloading the
keelboats, and in towing them up when the rapids are too strong
for the steam-engines."[9]

Five years later, in 1839, the *Wheeling Times* commented,
"Business is dull, money scarce in people's pockets, and water

'mighty scarce' in the river, so that the steamboats cannot run, and the goods from the east have to be shipped in keel boats."[10]

Water was also "mighty scarce" in a locale far to the west, the Republic of Texas, so keelboats were much in evidence there. In March 1838, the *Houston Telegraph* mentioned that a keelboat had wrecked itself at the Rocky Rapids on the Brazos; but nevertheless, a month later, the paper announced that Daniel Brock "intends running a keel boat regular in the Trinity River." In April 1840, the *Hudson River Chronicle* noted, "Several keel boats are running between San Jacinto and Houston." One of Houston's major advantages was the fact that it was easily accessible from the Gulf of Mexico (and thus from New Orleans) by way of Galveston Bay and the port of like name at its mouth. Galveston, incidentally, proved to be the point of entry for increasing numbers of German emigrants, driven from the fatherland by harsh conditions there and lured to Texas by the prospect of free land.[11]

Doubtless there were other German immigrants riding the great numbers of keelboats, flatboats, and steamboats that continued to ply the Ohio River. During the entire period of western expansion, in fact, the Ohio never lost its importance. The second edition of Robert Baird's *View of the Valley of the Mississippi*, published in 1834, and John Mason Peck's *A New Guide for Emigrants to the West*, published in 1836, laid down any number of routes for those headed west, and in most of them the mighty Ohio was a major element. Peck's routes, one "northern" and three "southern," were also cited by later guidebooks, but whether northern or southern, the Ohio figured prominently:

> If a person designs to remove to the north part of Ohio, and Indiana, to Chicago and vicinity, or to Michigan, or Greenbay, his course would be by the New York canal, and the lakes. . . . The same route will carry emigrants to Cleveland and by the Ohio canal to Columbus, or to the Ohio river at Portsmouth, from whence by steamboat, direct communications will offer to any river port in the Western States. From Buffalo, steamboats run constantly, (when the lake is open,) to Detroit, stopping at Erie, Ashtabula, Cleveland, Sandusky, and many other ports from whence stages run to

every prominent town. Transportation wagons are employed in forwarding goods. . . .

The most expeditious, pleasant, and direct route for travelers to the southern parts of Ohio and Indiana; to the Illinois river, as far north as Peoria; to the Upper Mississippi, as [at] Quincy, Rock Island, Galena, and Prairie du Chien; to Missouri; and to Kentucky, Tennessee, Arkansas, Natches, and New Orleans is one of the southern routes. These are, 1st, from Philadelphia to Pittsburg by rail-roads and the [new] Pennsylvania canal; 2nd, by Baltimore,–the Baltimore and Ohio rail-road,–and stages to Wheeling [i.e., via the National Road]; or 3dly, for people living to the south of Washington, by stage, via Charlottesville, Va., Staunton, the hot, warm, and white sulphur springs, Lewisburg, Charleston, to Guiandotte [later Huntington], from whence a regular line of steamboats run 3 times a week to Cincinnati. . .

Farmers who remove to the West from the Northern and Middle States will find it advantageous in many instances to remove with their own teams and wagons. These they will need on their arrival.[12]

All these routes had been in use for more than ten years before Peck's work appeared. Nevertheless, the farmers who, on Peck's recommendation, decided to take their own teams and wagons west were wise to first study a map and locate the roads best suited for their move.

ROADWAYS

NOT SURPRISINGLY, THE MAPS PUBLISHED between the late 1820s and mid-1830s showed new roads leading west. Henry Tanner's well-known map of 1829, for example, depicted narrow roads along the Red, Canadian, and Arkansas rivers–also, the Osage Road, which branched off from the Arkansas and ran along the Nesuhetonga (later the Cimarron) River.

A road farther east that saw increasing use in the 1830s started at the foot of Lake Michigan and led southwest across Illinois, generally following the river of that name, to Quincy on the Mississippi. It was used principally by those who came west by sailing through the Great Lakes, all around the Michigan peninsula, to Chicago or a nearby point on Lake Michigan's south shore.[1]

Another road, not fully in use until the late 1830s, lay just to the east and also met the lake's south shore. When finally completed, this route, the so-called "Michgan Road," extended all the way through Indiana, on roughly a north-south axis, from Lake Michigan to the Ohio River. Its southern leg, finished first, led northwest from Madison, a port on the Ohio, to Indianapolis. The northern leg headed south to Indianapolis from Lake Michigan, and for that reason earned its understandable but misleading name.[2]

Yet another road, more heavily traveled in the 1830s than previously, was Virginia's Northwestern Turnpike–a better-planned and better-graded version of the road shown on the old Bradley maps leading west from Winchester through Romney and

Clarksburg to Parkersburg, on the Ohio River just downstream from Marietta.[3]

At the same time, the roads leading to the Ohio through Pennsylvania continued to be well traveled. Tyrone Power, a popular Irish actor of the period (and great-grandfather of the famous film actor of the 1940s), left this description of a group he encountered on Laurel Ridge:

> When very near the top of the mountain,–for the ascent is full four miles,–I encountered one of those groups which appear in constant progress along the great Western line. The extent, however, of the present caravan made it peculiarly interesting. It consisted of five long, well-covered waggons, each drawn by eight or six horses, was attended by three or four led nags, and a number of dogs of various denominations. The occupants of the waggons were women and children: the faces of the chubby rogues were all crowded in front to look upon the passing stranger, with here and there a shining ebony [face] thrust between; the chief freight appeared to consist of household furniture and agricultural implements.
>
> By the side of these waggons first rode four or five horsemen, well mounted, who might be the principals of the party, for they were men past the meridian of life; straggling in the rear, or scattered along the edges of the forest, walked eight or nine younger men, rough-and-ready looking fellows, each with his rifle in his hand. Wild pigeons abounded along the cover-edge, and the sharp crack which every now and then rang through the thin air of morning told that the hunters were dealing upon them.
>
> From the construction of the waggons, as well as because their owners evinced no inclination either to hold communion or exchange civilities with a passing wayfarer, which no Southern ever fails to do, I concluded this to be a party of New England men, who, abandoning their worn-out native fields, were pushing on for the "far West" with the lightness of heart consequent on the surety of reaping a brave harvest from a soil which withholds abundance from none who possess hearts and arms to task it.[4]

Sᴛɪʟʟ ᴀɴᴅ ᴀʟʟ, ɪᴛ ᴡᴀs ᴛʜᴇ Nᴀᴛɪᴏɴᴀʟ Rᴏᴀᴅ that carried the heaviest traffic. During his trip through Ohio in 1834, German explorer Prince Maximilian of Wied, noted, "At sunrise we reached
Hebron, a town . . . on the great national road from Zanesville to
Columbus, which comes from . . . Cumberland, on the Potomac,
and passes through the states of Ohio, Indiana, and Illinois. Many
workmen were employed upon the road, and a quantity of stones
was brought, on the canal, in large square flat boats."[5]

The roadwork that Maximilian saw in Ohio was done according to the MacAdam plan, and, logically, could be expected to hold
up fairly well. But the original road surface east of the river, using
two sizes of stone and subject to the winter weather of the
Alleghenies, needed costly repairs. These repairs fell on the army's
shoulders because of the congressional consent given early in 1831
to acts by the Ohio and Pennsylvania general assemblies, under
which each state would take over that stretch of the road within its
boundaries, keep it in good shape, and charge tolls for doing so.
Early in 1832, Maryland and Virginia passed similar acts, and in
July of that year Congress made this practice the law of the land.
Part of the agreement stipulated that the road would be in proper
condition when the states assumed ownership—hence the army's
unwelcome job.

As army engineers noted, the repairs would be costly even if
they did not follow MacAdam's rules to the letter. One officer who
arrived on the scene in 1832 decided to leave the old roadbed in
place wherever he thought possible instead of ripping it up entirely, noting that a road through the Allegheny Mountains might
have different requirements from a road over the flatlands.

But Gen. Charles Gratiot, the chief engineer, saw things differ-
ently. His report to the secretary of war in November 1832 stated
flatly:

> In the course of my recent inspection of this road [east of the
> Ohio] . . . I ascertained that, in making contracts for the
> repairs, the contractors were, in many instances, permitted to
> use the best of the stone composing the old covering of the
> road when none better could be procured in the neighbor-
> hood; and it is believed that advantage has been taken of the

opportunity thus offered to introduce into the new covering material of inferior quality, and which had been previously condemned. I also found that the stone in general was not broken to the size prescribed by the contracts, and that the side drains had not been sufficiently attended to.

Furthermore, Gratiot explained (quite rightly) that only the best materials and methods for repair would be able to stand up under "the immense travel passing the mountains by this route."[6]

Keeping a national highway in good condition by charging tolls on it continued to cause hot debate. So, while the states began building toll booths, David Crockett of Tennessee, the honorable congressman and now-legendary frontiersman, reportedly thundered:

> What have I to say against Martin Van Buren? . . . He voted against the continuance of the national road through Ohio, Indiana, Illinois, and against appropriations for its preservation. . . . He voted against donations of land to Ohio, to prosecute the Miami canal. . . . He voted in favour of erecting toll gates on the national road; thus demanding a tribute from the west for the right to pass upon her own highways, constructed out of her own money—a thing never heard of before.[7]

But from those who used it, there were no complaints about the road west of the Ohio. Mary Reed Eastman, who traveled it eastward with her husband in June 1833, wrote:

> After we left Granville [Ohio] the road was better & 12 miles farther, we came on the Great National Road, or "the Pike," as the people call it here, which was very smooth & good & we slept sweetly, undisturbed, until we reached Zanesville soon after 12. . . . We took the stage at Zanesville on Wednesday night at 11 o'clock. The road was smooth & excellent, so that we could sleep very quietly, the morning was delightful, the air clear & cool, & the country through which we passed was rich & varied in scenery. . . . I wondered not, that so many told us "it would be very pretty riding on the Pike"–It has been Mc'Adamized & is now perfectly

smooth, the hills have been so nearly leveled, that the horses can trot up with the greatest ease, & there is no need of locking the wheels in descending. The bridges over the numerous creeks are all of stone, & very handsome as well as durable. There is no road in the United States equal to this, extending more than 100 miles, in such perfect order. We reached Wheeling on Thursday at 12 not much fatigued.

Rumors of cholera in Pittsburgh, their intended stop, caused Mary and her husband to change their plans:

[W]e concluded to go directly to Baltimore & proposed to go as far as Washington 32 miles & stop for the night. The Mail Stage was going with no other passengers, & if we would go in that & travel all night and the next day, until we overtook the Accommodation [coach] at Cumberland, we were offered the privilege of resting that night, taking that stage next morn as far as we pleased, & then to enter the Mail again if we preferred.

The Stage was a very comfortable one, & the weather so pleasant, we concluded to go; & at 3 o'clock left Wheeling. . . . Although we were still on the National Road, it was not so good as in Ohio; it has been made many years & was originally formed of large stones, spaces between which, were filled with sandstone, but this is now worn off & the earth around them washed away & we were constantly riding over large rocks. The night was pleasant, & we slept part of the time. At daylight, we crossed the Monongahela at Brownsville in a flat boat, which was "poled across."

About 6 miles before we reached the breakfast house, a gentleman & lady joined us, who were in a stage that broke down the evening before; and soon we began to ascend the Mountains. At the foot of Laurel Hill [Chestnut Ridge], 2 more horses were attached to our team, on one of which sat a little boy to guide us & then we went up, & up & up 3 miles, admiring the hills & forests around & the prospects which were ever varying. . . . From the top of Laurel Hill, we had a view of Union Town, which we had left 6 miles [behind us].

The collection of dwelling houses, the fields cultivated with grain of different kinds, and all distinctly visible by their several colors, formed a most beautiful picture. . . . [Then] we went up & down from morn till night, seeing and admiring something new at every turn. The road was generally good. Many were employed breaking stones to cover it, or repair it, where it was worn—but when we descended, the horses trotted every step as fast as they could go. . . . At one point, our driver told us we had risen to an elevation of 1400 ft. during five miles, & it really seemed as if we were far above all the rest of the world, seeing nothing above us but the sky, & the mountains far below us, completely encircling us. . . . But such an elevated station we could not long occupy, but must descend to the vales below; & now the road became rough, & at one time for 5 miles we were continually on the descent, with the exception of a level of 1/8 of a mile. The horses appeared to fly & we were but just able to keep our seats, while in such rapid motion. The lady with us could not keep still, but would bound from side to side with such force, her husband was obliged to hold her with all his strength; but we reached Cumberland with no other accident, than breaking the iron of the wheel.[8]

The men building the road, however, continued to have their problems. By 1834, with work proceeding simultaneously in Ohio, Indiana, and Illinois, one delay was following another, sometimes due to unexpected causes. In October 1835, Engineer Lt. Henry Brewerton summarized the problems that year while building the road in Ohio. (Later generations would describe one of the problems as "rising fuel costs"):

The whole of this division of the road [between Zanesville and Columbus] would have been completed, so far as regards the first two strata of metal [stone], early in the last month, had not the unusually wet weather experienced this year retarded this branch of our operations from the very commencement of the working season. Much greater difficulties have been encountered, than [were] at first anticipated, in

Above, the first National Road bridge across the Scioto River was the Broad Street Bridge, which opened in 1833. Left, a portion of the National Road near Zanesville, Ohio, showing the fine macadam surface for which it was praised. (*Franklin County [Ohio] Engineer's Office*)

procuring a sufficient quantity of gravel for the covering, having nearly exhausted the whole district of country between the Licking canal feeder and [Columbus] of that material. . . . [Moreover, early] in the spring, and during the greater part of the summer, grain of every description was held at so high a price as to deter most persons owning teams from bringing them on to the road, without the expectation of a considerable advance in our usual rates of hauling. . . . [Another] heavy expenditure, consequent upon this most remarkable season, was the loss of labor in preparing the surface of the road again and again for the reception of the metallic cover; the frequent rains, with the increased amount of travel, having destroyed the graded surface before it could be covered with metal. This has been so great an evil on the division of the road west of [Columbus] as to compel us to prohibit the travel on it until the metal is put on. Sickness, too, has been more than usually prevalent along the line of the road.

Even with all the problems, the lieutenant could claim that "the amount of work done, as is shown by the exposition of the state of our operations, exceeds very considerably that of any former year."[9]

Edmund Flagg, who traveled it by horseback in Illinois in 1836, had no complaints:

> The close of the day found me once more upon the banks of the Kaskaskia; and early on the succeeding morning, fording the stream, I pursued my route along the great national road towards Terre Haute. This road is projected eighty feet in breadth, with a central carriage-path of thirty feet, elevated above all standing water, and in no instance to exceed three degrees from a perfect level. The work has been commenced along the whole line, and is under various stages of advancement; for most of the way it is perfectly direct. The bridges are to be of limestone, and of massive structure. . . . Upon this road I journeyed some miles; and, even in its present unfinished condition, it gives evidence of its enormous character. Compare this grand national work with the crumbling relics of the mound-builders scattered over the land, and remark the contrast. . . . [But now] my route, at length, to my regret, struck off at right angles to the road, and for many a mile wound away among woods and creeks.[10]

To keep other travelers just as happy, an engineer lieutenant warned that

> the expense of keeping [the road] in repair will arise almost wholly from the renewal of the metallic cover, which, from the extent of the transportation over it in heavy coaches and wagons, is subjected to great wear. The vast amount of travel and emigration which follows this national thoroughfare, and the annual increase thereof, is such as to defy any attempt at even a conjectural estimate of the amount which may be [needed] to keep the road in good and sufficient repair.[11]

After Frederick Hall reached the National Road in western Pennsylvania in May 1837, he noted happily, "Traveling on it is indeed a pleasure, after our laborious trudging of the last twenty-four hours. This is, in fact, a magnificent high-way, and everywhere shows proof of having been constructed by the Nation's hand." But at Wheeling, where the road crossed the Ohio River, he found the facilities especially crowded. Because the road passed through it, Hall thought that

> Wheeling must, therefore, ever be one of the great thorough fares for western travellers, and for western merchandise. Even now, the daily arrivals and departures of stages and boats create no inconsiderable activity and confusion. At the stage-houses, quiet may be coveted, but is not always easily obtained. The multitude of river voyagers who stop here, a longer or shorter time, as most of them do, is wonderfully large. The company at our dinner-table to-day, consisted of seventy-four ladies and gentlemen, and the proprietor of the house informed me that his customers this season, are certainly not more than half as numerous as they have been in past years "when times were good."[12]

A fitting summary of the road, and its importance, was written by Engineer Capt. C. A. Ogden in October 1837:

> [D]uring the thaws of the spring and at seasons of heavy rains [the road] is liable to become exceedingly muddy and almost impassable; yet during the greater portion of the year it is a smooth, firm, and delightful highway. Emigrants, travelers, and others, give it a preference over all the other western routes. The travel on it, though immense, is still increasing; and during the summer and fall months of the year the tide of western emigration rolls along this great national thorough-fare in a continued and almost unbroken stream.[13]

Two years later, at the former Illinois state capital of Vandalia, some sixty miles east of St. Louis, construction of the National Road came to a close. Nevertheless, travelers "in a continued and almost unbroken stream," continued using it throughout the 1840s. In his later years, an old wagoner mentioned one of his many memories of it at the time. Outside a tavern on Maryland's Negro Mountain, just west of the Little Youghiogheny,

> thirty six-horse teams [were in] the wagon yard, one hundred Kentucky mules in an adjacent lot, one thousand hogs in other enclosures, and as many fat cattle from Illinois in

The first cast-iron bridge in the United States was built in 1839 where the National Road at Brownsville, Pennsylvania, crosses Dunlap's Creek. The bridge has been reinforced and still regularly bears the weight of 18-wheel tractor-trailers despite being more than 170 years old. (*Historical American Building Survey/Library of Congress*)

adjoining fields. The music made by this large number of hogs, in eating corn on a frosty night, I will never forget. After supper and attention to the teams, the wagoners would gather in the bar room and listen to music on the violin, furnished by one of their fellows, have a "Virginia hoe-down," sing songs, tell anecdotes, and hear the experience of drivers and drovers from all points on the road.[14]

And this was only one of many taverns along the way.

The construction of the road ended in a fitting manner. It had long been famous for its bridges: the single-arch span over the Little Youghiogheny, the triple-arch bridge over the Big Youghiogheny, and the smaller "S" bridges in western Pennsylvania and Ohio. Now it was to acquire another one of note: in 1839, after three years of effort, a bridge made of cast iron fell into place across Dunlap's Creek in Brownsville—the first of its kind in the United States. This bridge was to stand indefinitely, carrying untold numbers of pedestrians, horses, wagons, and coaches.[15]

STAGECOACH LINES

A SINGLE ADVERTISEMENT IN THE *Washington (DC) National Intelligencer* in January 1832 presented readers with the names of the two major firms in western stagecoaching: "The United States Mail Coach, through to Wheeling in 2-1/2 days, to Maysville and Cincinnati in 5-1/2 days. . . . . Passengers are carried sixty miles [to Frederick] on the superb rail-road from Baltimore . . . Stockton & Stokes & Co., Baltimore to Wheeling. Neil Moore & Co., Wheeling to Maysville and to Cincinnati."[1]

So, east of the Ohio, Stockton & Stokes controlled the reins. West of there, Neil, Moore & Company dominated. Competitors still existed, of course, especially on the National Road, which in the 1830s was already crowded enough. By mid-1833, Stockton & Stokes was confronted with Horton and Beaman's Baltimore-based "People's Rail Road Line of Stages. For Wheeling and Pittsburg, Passing 60 miles on the Baltimore and Ohio Rail Road [and] running through to Wheeling in 46 hours." Regarding its ten-dollar fare, the company's ad reminded readers that "the stage fare from Baltimore to Wheeling, in Stockton & Stokes's Line of Stages was $18.75 before the People's Line of Stages was established."[2]

To those living well below Maryland, the Baltimore-based lines were of little help, but by 1832, the Metropolitan Line would carry Southerners west from the Georgia state capital at Milledgeville all the way to New Orleans, passing through "Macon, Fort Mitchell, Montgomery, Blakeley, Mobile, [and] Pascagoula." In volume three of her *Southern Tour* series, Anne Royall called this "the great travelling route from the Southern States to New Orleans ... which the people here mostly pronounce *Norlins.*" To make this "Norlins" connection, lines such as Peck & Wellford's South-western or Middle Route enterprise would bring passengers into Milledgeville from as far away as Washington, DC, coming down through the Carolinas to do so. The trip from Washington to Milledgeville took eight and a half days—a long time to bounce around inside a coach on rough roads.[3]

There was another way to make the New Orleans connection as well. Those boarding the coach in Milledgeville could travel west only as far as the Chattahoochee River, which formed the Georgia-Alabama border. Then, at newly built Columbus, Georgia, or at Fort Mitchell, Alabama, they could take passage on a steamboat south for some three hundred miles on the Chattahoochee and Apalachicola rivers to the Gulf of Mexico, and thence west by water to New Orleans.[4]

For Thomas Hamilton (who constantly found cause for complaint), a journey by coach along the National Road between Hagerstown and Wheeling was anything but pleasant. Early in March 1833, with the snow still on the ground,

> we embarked in what was called the "Accommodation Stage,"—so designated, probably, from the absence of every accommodation which travelers usually expect in such a vehicle.... With the morning of the third day our difficulties commenced. We now approached the loftier ridges of the Alleghanies; the roads became worse, and our progress slower.... On the day following our route lay over a ridge called the Savage Mountain. The snow lay deeper every mile of our advance, and at length, on reaching a miserable inn, the landlord informed us that no carriage on wheels had been able to traverse the mountain for six weeks. On enquiring for a sleigh, it then appeared that none was to be had, and the natives all assured us that proceeding with our present carriage was

impossible. The landlord dilated on the depth of snow, the dangers of the mountain, the darkness of the nights, and strongly urged our taking advantage of his hospitality till the following day. But the passengers were all anxious to push forward, and, as one of them happened to be a proprietor of the coach, the driver very unwillingly determined on making the attempt. We accordingly set forth, but had not gone above a mile when the coach stuck fast in a snow-drift, which actually buried the horses. In this predicament the whole men and horses of the little village were summoned to our assistance, and, after about two hours' delay, the vehicle was again set free.

We reached the next stage in a hollow of the mountain, without further accident, and the report as to the state of the roads yet to be travelled was very unpromising. The majority of the passengers, however, having fortified their courage with copious infusions of brandy, determined not to be delayed by peril of any sort. On we went, therefore; the night was pitchy dark; heavy rain came on, and the wind howled loudly amid the bare and bony arms of the surrounding forest. The road lay along a succession of precipitous descents, down which, by a single blunder of the driver, who was quite drunk, we might at any moment be precipitated. [But] the journey was accomplished in safety.

Hamilton's journey, however, was not quite over:

Before sunrise we were again on the road, and commenced the ascent of Laurel Mountain, which occupied several hours. The view from the summit was fine and extensive, though perhaps deficient in variety. We had now surmounted the last ridge of the Alleghanies, and calculated on making the rest of our way in comparative ease and comfort. This was a mistake. Though we found little snow to the westward of the mountains, the road was most execrable, and the jolting exceeded any thing I had yet experienced. . . . During our last day's journey we passed through a richer country, but experienced no improvement in the road, which is what is called a national one, or, in other words, constructed at the expense of the general government. If intended by Congress to act as an instrument of punishment on their sovereign constituents, it is no doubt very happily adapted for the purpose.[5]

A different–and startling–set of mishaps descended upon Carl Arfwedson and his fellow travelers a few months later:

The stage coach had shortly before broken down [just east of Cumberland], and another of a very doubtful character been substituted in its place at the first relay of horses. Every one found some fault with it, even before the animals were harnessed; but the driver assured us that there was not a better coach in the United States. In contradiction to this statement, we showed him several objectionable parts, and unanimously protested against continuing our journey in a carriage, the wheels and springs of which were in so crazy a condition. The driver, however, renewed the assurance that the coach was as strong as if it had come from the hands of the builder the day before; adding, by way of finale, that, "strong or weak, we must be satisfied with it, as no other was to be had within the distance of fifteen miles." We started accordingly, and proceeded tolerably well for a distance of about eight miles.

The travelers already began to dismiss the idea of danger, and were going to indulge in an afternoon nap, when, in the middle of a steep hill, down which the imprudent coachman drove full gallop, both hind springs gave way. The shock which the body of the coach received from the lower part of the vehicle was so violent, that the bottom broke out, and, before the travelers had had time to recover from their consternation, their feet were dangling through the opening. To call out lustily "Stop!" was infinitely more easy than for the driver to check four galloping horses. Some of the ill-fated passengers, confined in this shattered coach, had in the mean time, by the violent shaking, fallen from their seats, so that their feet trailed upon the ground. They had now no other alternative but to run as fast as the wheels rolled. Fortunately, none were hurt, although the road was full of stones and holes; a few bruises, similar to those which follow a severe boxing-match, were the only result of this catastrophe. The horses were at length stopped at the foot of the hill, and the passengers crept out one by one, some through the windows, others through the hole at the bottom. The driver, stupefied on beholding the state of the vehicle, exclaimed, "What, in the name of God, has become of the bottom?"[6]

As the building of the National Road continued across Ohio toward Indiana, the stagecoach traffic on it increased correspondingly. An Army lieutenant's comment in Columbus late in 1836 about "the vast amount of travel and emigration which follows this national thoroughfare" included newly organized coach lines that, while based in Ohio, carried their passengers to and from points as far distant as Baltimore. For example, an ad in the *Ohio State Journal* in mid-1836 for "United States' Mail Coaches" promised that the coaches leaving Columbus's Globe Inn every morning at 7 o'clock would be in Wheeling by 10 a.m. the next day, "allowing two hours for business at Zanesville. Passengers taking seats in this Line, will have preference over all others in the Coaches from Wheeling east. [These coaches] are of a superior style."[7]

By the time this ad appeared, Neil, Moore's ever-growing Ohio Stage Company had a new partner, Darius Tallmadge. Seeing opportunity in the western country, Tallmadge had moved to Maysville, Kentucky, from the east in the mid-1820s, gone into business as a horse trader, and prospered. In 1830, he moved his family to Tarlton, Ohio (a small settlement on Zane's Trace), and there assumed the management of the Ohio Stage Company's southern routes at a salary of 400 dollars a year. By 1833, he was a partner in the firm, with an annual salary of 1,200 dollars, and owned the lines he managed. It was a good example of what an enterprising individual could do in a new territory. Nor did he scrimp on expenses: his records show that he often paid between sixty and eighty dollars for a horse—a top price in the 1830s.[8]

But well managed or not, the stagecoach line, in A. A. Parker's view, was not the best way to travel. In 1834, he offered this advice: "Persons traveling to Illinois, or farther west, can take passage in a vessel or steamboat from Buffalo to Chicago. The distance by water is one thousand miles; for they must go through lake Erie, St. Clair, Huron, and lake Michigan. The distance by land is not so far by one half; but the water passage is the cheapest, attended with less hardship, and much the best way to convey goods."

Nevertheless, Parker wanted to see something of the Michigan terrain, and so took a land route across the bottom of the state.

> After spending two days at Detroit, I took the stage for the mouth of St. Joseph river, on lake Michigan–fare $9.50. . . . [T]he first forty miles is [through] a level, heavily timbered country; a deep clayey soil, and a most execrable road. Sometimes the coach became fast stuck in the deep sloughs; and we had to get out the best way we could, and help dig it out. At others, we found logs laid across the road for some distance, and the coach jolted so violently over them, that it was impossible to keep our seat.
>
> Ten miles below [Ann Arbor], on the Huron river, is situated Upsilanti, a pleasant village. The turnpike road from Detroit to Chicago passes through it; on which a stage runs, carrying the U.S. mail.

By the time he neared Kalamazoo, in the far western part of the state, "The roads had become so bad, that we left the stage coach . . . and took a wagon, without any spring seats; and I found it so fatiguing to ride, that I often preferred walking."⁹

Parker's trip could have been worse. In the summer of 1834, Baltimore papers reported a

> DARING ATTEMPT AT ROBBERY.–The U.S. Mail Stage, from Wheeling for Baltimore, was attacked near the top of a mountain, 17 miles beyond Cumberland, not far from a dismal place called the "Shades of Death," on the night of Wednesday last, at about 10 o'clock, by two highwaymen. They had cut some brush and thrown [it] across that part of the road mostly travelled, and as the Stage was ascending the mountain, one of

them sprung out from the brushes and seized one of the leaders by the bridle, and stopped the stage, and told the driver to
get down, which he refused to do, but kept whipping up his
horses; in the mean time the robber kept calling on his comrade, who was near the stage door, to fire at the driver, saying, "you damned coward, why don't you fire at him." . . .
[W]hen he found his comrade backward, [he] turned the two
leading horses square round, so that their heads were down
the mountain, and those of the wheel horses up; he then
wound the lines round his arm, and began to unhitch the
traces. The driver then summoned all his strength, and struck
his horses so fast and hard, that they broke away before he
could effect his purpose; and by keeping the stage on the full
run for three miles, finally got away. . . . Taken altogether, it
was a most daring attempt, and was near succeeding, and
should admonish those who travel to go armed. There [were]
five men and one woman in the stage, but none of them were
armed.

   Mr. Lucius W. Stockton, the spirited contractor on that line,
is, as he writes, taking such precautions as will enable his driver to '*stand*,' if hereafter demanded to do so, and *dispute the
ground* with these felons.[10]

In the 1830s, as previously, unarmed passengers–those west of
Pittsburgh, at least–were the exception rather than the rule. And
seemingly, the farther west a traveler found himself, the more
heavily armed he was apt to be. A letter sent to the *National
Intelligencer* from Texas late in 1833 included these lines: "If you
could see me mounted for the road, you would think of Don
Quixotte–a double-barrelled fowling piece hung at my saddle bow,
[f]our rifle-barrelled pistols in [saddle] holsters, and a heavy pair
of belt pistols buckled around me–to complete the whole, a large
horseman's sabre at my side."[11]
   At about the same time, on an Ohio River steamboat below
Wheeling, Thomas Hamilton made a bet and lost it:

   One day at dinner, my English fellow-traveller, who had
   resided many years in the United States, enquired whether I
   observed an ivory hilt protruded from beneath the waistcoat

of a gentleman opposite. I answered in the affirmative, and he then informed me that the whole population of the Southern and Western States are uniformly armed with daggers. On my expressing some doubt of this singular fact, he pointed to a number of [walking] sticks collected in one corner of the cabin, and offered a wager that every one of these contained either a dagger or a sword. I took the bet, and lost it; and my subsequent observations confirmed the truth of his assertion in every particular. Even in traveling in the State of New York, I afterwards observed that a great number of the passengers in stage-coaches and canal boats were armed with this unmanly and assassin-like weapon.[12]

Other educated Englishmen took the same view. A book published in London in 1835, dealing in part with self-defense for travelers, declared emphatically that "Daggers especially, or knives . . . are a disgrace to an Englishman's hand!" But Americans felt just the opposite, especially after mid-1836, when advertisements for the legendary Bowie knife and the lesser-known "Arkansas Toothpick" began appearing in numerous papers. And ironically, some of the very best knives of either kind came from English rather than American makers.

Of course, a knife or a sword cane might be of little use against a highwayman armed with a pair of pistols. In such a case, the author who regarded knives as a disgrace to an Englishman's hand was happy to recommend carrying at least one

> double-barreled pistol, not less than four inches in the barrels, up to six inches; the bore about [.56 caliber, and one barrel loaded] with six to eight buck-shot, instead of a ball; a mode that is desirable, for, by loading one barrel thus, and the other with a ball, you can show more or less mercy, as occasion may require; since you may disable a robber by wounding him with buck-shot, in some part where a ball would have proved more fatal; and it is also obvious that you are more likely to hit him with buck-shot than with a single bullet.[13]

Most Americans bound for the western country would readily agree with this philosophy. Newspaper advertisements for "a large assortment of travelling, belt, and pocket Pistols" or for "Pocket

POCKET RIFLES from 3 to 8 inches only in length, and yet warranted to shoot as far, and with the same precision as the long Rifle, for sale at a less price than the ordinary Pistol. Also, a splendid Gun, one barrel of which is rifled, the other smooth for shot; and one extra finish drilled barrel single rifle, for sale very low, by
DENNY & COLSTON,
No. 14 Main st., near Bank of Louisville.
oc 5

Advertisements for "pocket rifles," such as this one from January 1841 in the *Louisville Daily Journal*, left, became common during the 1830s and 40s when crime increased hand in hand with an increase in stagecoach, steamboat, and canal traffic. Travelers were urged to protect themselves, with the pocket rifle providing greater range and accuracy than the common smoothbore pistol–and sometimes costing less. The underhammer pocket rifle on the right was manufactured by Gibbs, Tiffany & Co. of Sturbridge, Massachusetts. It has a barrel length of six inches. (*Nick Chandler*)

Rifles" often appeared on the same page as ads for canal, steamboat, or stagecoach lines. Like most single-shot pistols, the so-called "Pocket Rifles" were usually boxed and sold in pairs, to give their owners a quick second-shot capability.[14]

While it did happen on occasion, armed robbery of a stagecoach was far less frequent than simple, sly pilferage–quiet, unobtrusive theft. A typical example was an Ohio occurrence in 1834:

> Robbery.–On the 3d inst., a tall, well dressed man entered the Steubenville stage, at Steubenville, without any baggage, and disappeared immediately after the stage had reached its destination. He had not been long gone, when it was discovered that the stage had been robbed of $4000, in bills of the Canton Bank, Ohio; $1000 in bills of the Western Reserve Bank, and a quantity of other bills, the designation of which is unknown. Cook and Cassat of Pittsburg, have offered a reward for their recovery. Mr. E.W. Cooke, who was robbed of $5,500 in the Steubenville Stage, Ohio, on the 3d inst. offers a reward of $1,000 for the recovery of the money and apprehension of the thief.[15]

No robberies occurred on Tyrone Power's 1834 trip over the Alleghenies, but he was more worried about losing his life than losing his property:

I here waited [in the rain], sheltered by a rocky projection, until the stage came up. . . . [T]he tedium of the journey, however, whilst light lasted, was greatly relieved by the constant changes of mountain scenery, as viewed through an atmosphere now wildly clear and again thick and gloomy. I found considerable amusement also in calculating the fair odds against our being pitched into one of the many deep ravines along whose edge we were, when going down hill, whirled with startling speed. It was at these descents that the driver sought to pull [make] up his lost time; and this he did with a recklessness of consequences that led me, after mature consideration, aided by the experience of much rough travel, to come to the following conclusion,–that, in crossing the Alleghany mountains, when the roads are rotten and slippery, the chances for and against a broken neck are [almost] equal. . . . We at times encountered a string of waggons at some narrow sharp turn of the corkscrew path [where one false step, at] the unguarded ledge of a precipice some four or five hundred feet deep . . . would, in all human probability, have provided the wolves and bears with a banquet, and the journalists with a neat paragraph, headed "Melancholy result of fast driving, attended with serious loss of valuable lives."

The practice is for the team to be put on a run the moment they gain the summit of the hill; and, if all things hold out, this is kept up until the bottom be reached: the horses are excellent, and rarely fail. On my asking the coachman,–by whom I rode as much as possible,–what he did in the event of a wheel-horse [falling] down in a steep pass, he replied, "Why, I keep driving ahead, and drag him along;"–an accident which he assured me had occurred more than once to himself when the roads were encrusted with ice and snow: the passengers at such times are placed in sleighs, which are perhaps less dangerous.

On the morning of Thursday we once more arrived at the frontier town of the low-lands of Pennsylvania,– Chambersburg; and here I quitted the "Good Intent" line, transferring myself, servant, and kit to the Baltimore stage; and at three o'clock A.M. on Friday, I was set down, cold and weary and wet, at the door of Barnum's hotel. A few thundering knocks brought down the porter, and I was admitted within shelter of the well-warmed hall, with: "Och murther alive! Mr. Power, is it yerself, sir? Why, thin, you're welcome!"[16]

W. M. Knight's trip through western Ohio in 1837 was across level terrain instead of the mountains, but the weather caused problems enough:

The stage left the Hotell at Dayton about a quarter before 4 o'clock with 9 passengers on the inside, one a lady, & 6 on the top with the driver, one a boy, besides the baggage and the Mail, a load too much for any stage, beside being so top heavy; we had not gone far before I saw there was great danger; we got to Harshman's Mills about dark & left one passenger; the stage proceeded on, it was soon totally dark, raining & blowing, the stage rocking from side to side in the deep ruts; after some time going on so the limbs of trees began to dash against the stage; it stopped, some of the passengers got out, & finally all; we were in the woods, lost the road in a [fallen] tree top; they hunted the road in the dark, sent for a light & with some difficulty the passengers helped the driver to get the stage out of the tree top; we walked through the woods & the rain til we came to the road again & we got in the stage; we had not gone far when the stage stopped again in mud up to the hubs; the horses could not pull it out, [so] all the folks had to get out in the rain, & it blowing hard roaring thru the woods; they went & got [fence] rails & assisted to pry out the coach. I thought we should not have got from that place all night, but after a long time we did, and after walking awhile, mud & water over shoe tops (you know how I walk) we got into the coach again; we had not gone far, rock, rock, before the stage went over with us all. I was sitting on the middle of the fore seat & had my head dashed into the mud opposite the stage door as the glass was down. . . . I waited patiently under some of [the passengers] till they all got out & then fell to hunting my hat and cane. . . . [T]here was no one seriously injured but 2 or 3 badly bruised [and] the woman seemed terrified out of her life.[17]

But at least there were no fatalities on Knight's trip. The same could not be said elsewhere. In August 1837, the *Maryland Sun* reported this mishap:

> Horrible Accident. . . . One of the Reliance line of stages, from Fredrick to the West, passed through [Clear Spring] after dark last evening, on its way to Cumberland. About ten o'clock, the ill-fated coach reached a small spur of the mountain . . . termed Millstone Point, where the driver, mistaking the track (it being a very dark night) reined his horses too near the edge of the precipice; where, in the twinkling of an eye, coach–horses–driver–and passengers–were precipitated upwards of 35 feet, on a bed of rock below–the coach was dashed to pieces, and two of the horses killed–literally smashed. A respectable elderly lady of the name of Clarke, of Louisville, Ky., and a negro child, were crushed to death. And a man was so dreadfully mangled, that life is flickering on his lips only.[18]

Accidents happened for many reasons, of course. One of the most common was when trying to pass a rival coach, which often resulted in a race. Company advertisements might say, "No racing allowed," or "All racing expressly prohibited," but drivers did not always see things that way. For instance: "Another stage accident has occurred on the Frankfort and Louisville line. The stage was upset on the 11th, near Shelbyville, by which the driver and Mr. Joseph Winter had each a leg broken. These occurrences on this road are imputed to the racing by opposition lines." Or, in 1838: "We understand that an accident occurred on the Maysville line, one day last week, by the two stages of the old and new lines coming in contact with each other. Several passengers were severely injured, some of them having bones broken." A little couplet widely repeated on the National Road at the close of the 1830s (referring to a driver for Thomas Shriver & Company) summed up the situation:

> If you take a seat in Stockton's Line,
> You are sure to be passed by Pete Burdine[19]

A lithograph of the Phoenix Line's "safety coach" of the early 1830s. The Phoenix line operated between Baltimore and Washington, DC. It was owned by George Beltzhoover & Company, rivals of Stockton & Stokes. (*Library of Congress*)

Aside from the wear and tear on existing vehicles (and the passengers inside them), the market for new stagecoaches continued to be good because of the steady march west and the consequent appearance of new stage lines. About 1834, for example, a young physician named John Temple established a line in Chicago that ran west to Ottawa, at the head of navigation on the Illinois River. By 1836, there were at least two competing lines in the field, and one of them, headed by John Frink and Martin Walker (Frink was raised in the stagecoach business), soon began edging out the others. By 1840, under the name of Frink, Walker, & Company, they were sending coaches from Chicago all the way across northern Illinois to the Mississippi—and killing a fair number of horses when crossing swollen streams while trying to maintain schedules. In mid-1842, a Milwaukee paper called them "the heaviest Stage Proprietors in the Western country." But if the paper's phrase "Western country" included everything west of Pittsburgh, then this statement was certainly open to question, with Lucius Stockton's firm (which became Stockton & Falls late in 1838), and Neil, Moore & Company doing as much business as they could handle. By 1840, even the fledgling Republic of Texas had stagecoach service, connecting Houston with Austin and Washington-on-the-Brazos.[20]

Whether in Illinois or Texas, the stagecoach of the time had to be well designed and strongly built to give its passengers a modicum of safety and comfort when bouncing over bad roads. An 1831 advertisement by Beltzhoover & Company, which operated a popular stage line between Washington and Baltimore, specifically addressed this point: "Safety Coaches!!! . . . [B]uilt on the most improved plan, combining ease, elegance, and safety. . . [the safety due] to the manner in which the Troy Built Coaches are hung, being low."[21]

In all probability, the mention of low-slung Troy coaches referred to the products of Eaton & Gilbert of Troy, New York, which during the 1830s was one of the premier coach-building firms in the country and among the best known. In the fall of 1833, a fire leveled the factory, but the partners built another, much more fire-resistant, in a matter of weeks: "Their new establishment, we are informed, measures 120 feet square, thus covering an area of about 14,000 feet. It is two stories high, besides a stone basement under the whole, the walls of which are two feet thick. The roof is covered with slate, and the walls contain between three and four hundred thousand bricks."

Apparently even this facility was too small, because by 1839, the company had expanded it appreciably.

> Some idea of the extent of the establishment may be gathered from the following dimensions of some of the apartments. The principal smith shop is a room 150 feet long by 30 in width; containing twelve forges constantly in operation, forming in the dusk of the evening as fine a panoramic view of purgatory in miniature, as can possibly be conceived. In this shop the heavy iron work of the stage coaches and carriages is prosecuted. Immediately over this, and of the same dimensions, is a shop used for making the bodies of the coaches. Communicating with this is another room, where the trimmers are at work. This room is about 75 feet by 35. Next is the painting apartment, by far the largest room in the establishment, being 200 by 35. Another apartment is appropriated to making wheels; another to sawing out the stuff;

another to steaming and bending the timber; another to turning hubs, & c., and so on throughout. . . .

The number of stage coaches and mail carriages manufactured by Messrs. Eaton & Gilbert far exceeds our former
impressions. In passing through the establishment we noticed
in one corner a cluster of seven elegant coaches, nearly finished, ordered from Virginia, and nine for Florida–in another,
a different set, destined to Georgia–others to South Carolina.
In fact, a great portion of the Southern and Western states, as
well as those near home, are furnished with stage coaches
from this Factory. . . . We cannot close this cursory notice
without referring to the great safety mail coaches . . . now
building for Messieurs Stockton, Falls & Co. of Baltimore,
[which] are designed for the national road from Baltimore to
Ohio, & c.–[22]

Presumably these coaches embodied some of the newer design
features. By the mid-1830s, the round-topped post coach so widely deployed in the 1820s was giving way to a flat-topped model
that allowed additional passengers and luggage to sit on the roof.
However, this was not always desirable, since it could throw more
of a burden onto the horses and the coach itself. More beneficial in
most respects were new spring systems, which on rough roads
lessened the shock to both vehicle and passengers. In the five years
from 1836 to 1840, the U.S. Patent Office issued at least twelve
patents for such systems, not to mention others on "running gear,"
wheel assemblies, or brakes. Several of these ideas displayed a fair
amount of ingenuity: one of them mated coil springs with rubber
buffers, while two others combined coil with flat springs. More
complex was the "Running-Gear" described in a four-page patent
of 1839, issued to Thomas Shriver of Cumberland, Maryland.
Shriver's patent did not limit itself to running gear, but included
mention of such refinements as folding seats and a ventilator in the
roof. Another feature, which by 1840 had been patented in several different forms, was a quick-release device to detach a vehicle
from a runaway team. Apparently, however, these were little used,
at least by the stagecoach lines, which tended to rely on the skill of
their drivers to deal with such mishaps.[23]

Aside from any mechanical or structural improvements, some of the coaches built by Eaton & Gilbert could be quite ornate, "having upon each panel views of various public buildings, fountains, & c." In May 1841, the *Cleveland Herald* praised the company accordingly, but added a caveat: "The Troy mechanics are the greatest coach builders in the Union. At the celebrated establishment of Messrs. Eaton & Gilbert, several new stage coaches have just been finished for routes lately established in Mexico. [But] the Buffalo Commercial states that stage coaches turned out at Raney's extensive establishment in that city compare well with the best Troy built vehicles."[24]

Indeed, in a country dotted with top-notch coachbuilders from Boston to Baltimore, and from Philadelphia to St Louis, rivals were always present. The most serious, perhaps, was Abbott & Downing of Concord, New Hampshire, which would gradually overtake Eaton & Gilbert, eventually ship its coaches all over the world, and make the term "Concord coach" a household phrase. In November 1844, a number of papers brought the company's name to public attention: "Wm. F. Paterson, of Wheeling, Va., was at Concord, N.H., last week, and contracted for as good a coach as Abbott & Downing can make, to have the likeness and name of Henry Clay painted upon it, and to be delivered to him in Wheeling on the last of December next." Henry Clay, the great statesman from Kentucky and champion of the National Road, was supposed to be thus honored when he was elected president of the United States. (Unfortunately for Paterson's plans, James K. Polk was elected instead.)[25]

As fine as the Troy and Concord coaches were, some west-bound travelers disdained stagecoach travel as too rough, too risky, or too dusty. For them, the canals offered an attractive alternative.

CANALS

WHATEVER ROUTES AN EMIGRANT'S GUIDE of 1825 to 1840 might suggest taking, one invariably included the Erie Canal. And, accordingly, westbound travelers continued to crowd onto its packet boats—or line boats, or even freight boats. Of course their experiences might vary, depending on the type of boat, or on other factors.[1]

As Carl Arfwedson said of his trip early in 1833:

> [In] Schenectady, I availed myself of a canal-boat on the point of starting for Utica. These boats are generally very long, but low, in consequence of the many bridges thrown across the canal. . . . [So] moving about upon deck was out of the question, owing to the number of bridges beneath which we had to pass; [as a result] no other alternative was left but to go down, by way of change, into the close and narrow cabin. Night made our situation still more uncomfortable. . . . [But] I already felt reconciled to my unpleasant situation, and amused myself by listening to the different sounds, from the finest tenor to the strongest bass, proceeding from the snoring gentry. A sudden thump against my side of the boat [soon] spread consternation among the travelers. The shock, occasioned by another craft coming too close to ours, was so violent that the beams cracked, and the doors flew open. About a dozen sleeping individuals were precipitated from the second and third tier [of berths onto] the unfortunate beings who were lying on

the floor. . . . [L]amentations filled the room. The ladies rushed in among us. All were running, shoving against each other, swearing, and making a noise in the dark: confusion, in short, was at its height, until the captain had made a favourable report, which restored tranquility.[2]

Tyrone Power told of a grim two days on the canal in the summer of 1834. After boarding a packet boat southwest of Lockport, he found that:

The boat for a few hours went on merrily; the eternal forest closed about us, and the sound of our horses' feet alone broke upon its silence. Towards evening the heat became great, and after sunset the southern sky began to give forth continuous sheets of flame, along whose pale surface would occasionally dart lines of red forked lightning, whilst the breeze gradually died away. My first idea was, that we were about to be favoured with a refreshing storm of rain and thunder; but vain were my hopes: I watched and listened, but no drop fell; no sound was heard.

Meantime, the heat increased as the night closed in; the little cots, however, were duly hung one below another along the sides of the cabin. I had procured an upper berth, with a window by my side; and having exhausted my patience, and wearied my sight watching the fiery sky, I at last ventured to creep below. Although a hotter atmosphere can hardly be imagined, I slept tolerably sound; but, on waking, found myself anything but refreshed. The sun was not yet above the horizon when I crept forth on to the deck; it was that hour of morning which, of all others, one expects to be invigorating and cool, as indeed it usually is in all climates; but here, enclosed within the banks of the canal, and surrounded by swamp and forest, there was no morning air for us. My mind was made up to leave the boat at the first place where a stage might be procured.

All this day the air absolutely stood still. At our places of halt we were joined by men who had left the stages in consequence of those vehicles not being able to travel. Our pace was reduced considerably; and the cattle, although in excellent condition, were terribly distressed. At Lockport we found business nearly at a stand-still; the thermometer was at 110 degrees of Fahrenheit. We passed several horses dead upon the banks of the canal, and were compelled to leave one or two of our own in a dying state. Here more persons joined than we could well accommodate, and I found positively that all movement by the stage route was at an end, forty horses having fallen on the line the day previous.[3]

Harriet Martineau disliked not only the heat:

[W]e proceeded by railroad to Schenectady [and there] stepped into a canalboat for Utica. I would never advise ladies to travel by canal, unless the boats are quite new and clean; or, at least, far better kept than any that I saw or heard of on this canal. On fine days it is pleasant enough sitting outside (except for having to duck under the bridges every quarter of an hour, under penalty of having one's head crushed to atoms), and in dark evenings the approach of the boatlights on the water is a pretty sight; but the . . . heat and noise, the known vicinity of a compressed crowd, lying packed like herrings in a barrel, the bumping against the sides of the locks, and the hissing of water therein like an inundation, startling one from sleep; these things are very disagreeable.[4]

Much more positive was a Scottish traveler's experience on the canal in 1834:

We have in the boat a family of Yankees, consisting of a father, mother, a pretty daughter, and three sons. . . . They are removing between 200 and 300 miles from their former abode, and yet they seem to think no more of it, than I would of removing from one street to another in Edinburgh; the Jews were proverbially a wandering race; but I think the Americans bid fair to match them. . . .

I have just lent my album to the Yankee's fair daughter, and she is quite delighted with it. While she is perusing it, I am jotting down her remarks as they pop out of her pretty little mouth, viz.–"It is dreadful pretty, I guess. . . . Dear ma, there, that is the prettiest of all! There, that looks just like an angel!" . . . When she ceased admiring the pictures, I requested her for a song, and she sang me a favorite Scotch song, "Ye banks and braes of bonny Doon." When I looked around, and saw the Mohawk river winding beneath, and the mountains of the Mohawk towering above, I remembered I was far from the Land of Cakes; and the words of the song recalled a thousand pleasing recollections of home.

Later, approaching Little Falls, the traveling Scot noted, "Boats are passing us on the canal every two or three minutes. I am told that not less than 3000 boats ply on this canal."[5]

So heavy did the Erie traffic become that late in 1834, Benjamin Wright, one of its more prominent engineers, said, "we see in the size of our Canal that we have made great errors, very great indeed." Two years later, construction began on a much-enlarged channel: 70 feet wide instead of 40, and 7 feet deep instead of 4, with double locks of 110 by 18 feet.[6]

Regardless of channel width, Henry Tanner's 1840 book on internal improvements printed nothing less than the truth in its summary of the enterprise:

> The completion of this magnificent work [in 1825] was cele-
> brated with great pomp and parade; [measures] fully justified
> [because the] moral effects of this herculean achievement are
> now visible in every direction. Stimulated by the complete
> success of the New York system, other states have essayed to
> imitate an example fraught with such incalculable benefits.
> Canals and rail-roads now abound every where; and every
> where may be seen preparations for augmenting the number.
> [But] the Erie Canal still maintains its supremacy: it is
> unquestionably the first in point of length, and by far the most
> important canal in the United States.[7]

Second in importance only to the Erie was the Ohio & Erie. Edward Abdy accurately called it "one of the great links of that chain of water communication which connects New York with New Orleans." Shortly after Prince Maximilian entered it from the

Ohio River side in mid-1834, he noted, "This fine canal is navigated by numerous boats, which are built in the same style as the keel-boats of the Missouri . . . seventy-seven to eighty feet in length [and] fourteen in breadth." Maximilian's passage to Lake Erie took just over five days, but this was soon to change. Early in 1837, for instance, the Ohio Canal Packet Company claimed that it could make the three-hundred-mile passage from Cleveland to Portsmouth in three days. Indeed, this was a far better option than trying to cross the same distance with a wagon and team over bad roads—a method that usually took three weeks instead of three days.[8]

For those who wanted a

A notice in the Louisville *Daily Journal* of March 1837, announcing the fast packet service along the 309-mile canal between Cleveland on Lake Erie and Portsmouth on the Ohio River.

shortcut from Lake Erie to the Ohio, the well-known Ohio & Erie route from Cleveland to Dresden, and then through the Side Cut into the Muskingum River above Zanesville, was improved when, in 1836, the state began installing a series of locks and dams on the Muskingum to ensure navigation late into the summer, when water levels would usually be low.

The Ohio & Erie could not match the Erie Canal's dramatic sites—the Genesee Aqueduct, the double locks at Lockport, or the Deep Cut through solid rock—but it did have its pleasant views, such as the Licking Narrows. Maximilian took special note of the scene: "Seven miles from Newark the canal joins Licking River, a very pretty little stream, which flows through a picturesque rocky valley, overgrown with pines and other trees. The rocks . . . have a singular stratification, with caverns in which the cattle seek the protection of the shade from the sultry sun."[9]

Political pranksters made an appearance near the spot as well. In September 1838, a paper in Newark carried this item: "[N]o democrat dare, except at the risk of his peace and his fortune, do business on the canal. An Agent on the canal somewhere in the upper part of the State, we were informed, when he saw a boat load of Democrats coming to the Newark Convention, let off the water from a short level and detained them 12 or 15 hours, and came very near depriving them of reaching the convention in time."[10]

LESS HUMOROUS WAS THE SITUATION with another canal, the Chesapeake & Ohio. From the first, this project found itself in competition with a formidable rival, the Baltimore & Ohio Railroad. Ironically, both enterprises held their groundbreaking ceremonies on the same day: July 4, 1828. The plan for the first leg of the canal was simple enough: to follow the course of the Potomac River from the nation's capital to the river's junction with Wills Creek at Cumberland, Maryland, a distance of about 185 miles.[11]

This stretch had been envisioned, and intermittently acted upon, by George Washington and others, since the 1780s. But the next leg was far more ambitious: from Cumberland the canal, by a route only vaguely specified, was to find its way over the Alleghenies to the Ohio River. And that, of course, was the real challenge. Five years before the groundbreaking, in 1823, the *Washington (DC) National Intelligencer* had commented:

> The project of connecting the waters of the Ohio and Chesapeake by a continued line of still water navigation is one of those sublime schemes, the very magnitude of which is sufficient to frighten the mind from its serious consideration. The idea of carrying a series of locks and canals over or through the immense ridge of the Alleghany, appears at first view so far removed from reality, that we are not disposed calmly to examine into its probably practicability; and it is only since the success of our northern brethren [with the Erie

Canal] that the few who have attentively considered the subject have ventured to breathe a whisper of its possibility.[12]

Cost estimates for the project were intimidating enough: more than $22 million for the whole job, with $8 million needed just for the first leg to Cumberland. Charles Fenton Mercer, an influential congressman and also the hard-driving president of the canal company, argued that these estimates were much too high; subsequent events, however, would prove otherwise. In addition to Mercer's conflict-of-interest position, a dash of irony in this mix was the fact that Congress, which had refused to allocate money for two successful enterprises–the Erie Canal and B&O Railroad–voted to contribute a million dollars of public money to the Chesapeake & Ohio venture.[13]

Construction involved the usual mishaps. Late in 1829, while working on the eastern end of the canal, an incident suggested that "Some of the workmen are a little too desirous to make rapid progress. The day before yesterday, in one of the blasts of rock in the Canal, stones of several pounds weight were thrown so far, and with such force, as to fall through the roofs of houses, and in the streets of Georgetown. One individual, riding on horseback in Bridge Street, narrowly escaped being killed by one of the pieces."[14]

In March 1830, with the work progressing and optimism increasing, the *New York Columbian* reported that:

Attracted by the interest of the scene and the beauty of the weather, a large concourse of people on horseback and on foot, went up on Sunday to that part of the Canal around the Little Falls, . . . [then] one of the largest river flour boats was filled with as many passengers as could squeeze into it; a single horse was then attached to it, which drew the whole with ease at the rate of eight miles an hour; we are assured, however, that the result of this experiment falls far short of what can be accomplished.

By October, the newspapers could

inform the friends of the Chesapeake and Ohio Canal, that it is now navigable for boats the whole distance, from Seneca down to the old locks, upwards of 20 miles. The letting in of the water was completed yesterday, and not a leak or break discovered in any part of the line. . . . We shall be happy to offer our friends from Baltimore [i.e., B&O Railroad officials], or elsewhere, an opportunity to take an excursion of pleasure, for which a boat has been already prepared.[15]

(When this notice appeared, the B&O had been carrying passengers to Ellicott's Mills for more than four months).

One advantage of a canal in a more southerly latitude was that

during the [December] cold spell we have recently had, in which the thermometer was at one time down as low as 8 degrees above zero, the navigation of the Chesapeake and Ohio Canal (as far as it extended) was not for one hour interrupted. It was, of course, plated over with ice, but so thinly that the boats easily pursued their way through it. We may presume, therefore, that our Canal will be navigable for a much larger portion of the year than the Canals north of it, which cannot fail to add greatly to the value of the stock, and to the general utility of the work.[16]

But a disadvantage of having a canal in more southerly latitudes was that a hot summer could take a greater toll of its laborers. Frances Trollope took note of this fact in 1830, while she was in Maryland:

Of the white labourers on this canal, the great majority are Irishmen; their wages are from ten to fifteen dollars a month, with a miserable lodging, and a large allowance of whiskey. It is by means of this hateful poison that they are tempted, and indeed enabled for a time to stand the broiling heat of the sun in a most noxious climate: for through such, close to the romantic but unwholesome Potomac, the line of the canal has hitherto run. The situation of these poor strangers, when they sink at last in "the fever," which sooner or later is sure to overtake them, is dreadful. There is a strong feeling against the Irish in every part of the Union, but they will do twice as much work as a Negro, and therefore they are employed. When they fall sick, they may, and must look with envy on the slaves around them; for they [the slaves] are cared for; they are watched and physicked, as a valuable horse is watched and physicked: not so with the Irishman; he is literally thrown [to] one side, and a new comer takes his place. Details of their sufferings, and unheeded death, too painful to dwell upon, often reached us.

Apparently, however, other deaths along the canal had nothing to do with overwork or heat. As Mrs. Trollope explained it:

During the summer that we passed most delightfully in Maryland, our rambles were often restrained in various directions by the advice of our kind friends, who knew the manners and morals of the country. When we asked the cause, we were told, "There is a public-house on that road, and it will not be safe to pass it." The line of the Chesapeake and Ohio Canal passed within a few miles of Mrs. S–'s residence. It twice happened during our stay with her, that dead bodies were found partially concealed near it. The circumstance was related as a sort of half-hour's wonder; and when I asked particulars of those who, on one occasion, brought the tale, the reply was "Oh, he was murdered, I expect. . . ." [But no] inquest was summoned; and certainly no more sensation was produced by the occurrence than if a sheep had been found in the same predicament.[17]

By the fall of 1831, tavern talk and newsprint were centering not on the canal's mortality rate, but on its legal problems with the railroad. The dispute arose from the question about which company had the right-of-way along the twelve-mile stretch of riverfront terrain from Point of Rocks to Harper's Ferry, a strip of land thought to be too narrow to accommodate a canal and a railroad side by side. This had been a point of contention since 1828, and now, with the railroad approaching the Monocacy River near Frederick and the canal not far behind, the issue had to be settled.

A Maryland court determined that the first choice of route would go to the company that had been organized first. The B&O's charter, granted by the state in February 1827, had stipulated that the company would be incorporated when a third of its $3 million in stock was subscribed for. That condition was met by the end of March, and the company was then organized before the end of April. A year later, in May 1828–even before the official groundbreaking–the road designated the Point of Rocks as its route.

In the canal's case, Maryland had approved its charter as early as January 1825, but the money to purchase the required one-fourth of its $6 million in stock was not fully forthcoming until May 1828, when Congress voted in favor of a $1 million subscription of public funds. The company was organized a month later and adopted its route at about the same time. Based on these dates, the railroad had its choice of routes. But there was an added complication because the canal could claim that it was the successor to the old "Potomac Company," organized by George Washington in the 1780s to improve navigation on the lower stretches of the river, and reorganized by the Virginia Legislature late in 1822.

Serious legal sparring started in October 1831, and resumed in December at the Maryland Court of Appeals in Annapolis. Arguing the railroad's case was no less a figure than Daniel Webster, who, in a four-hour speech, won praise from local attorneys and news reporters for "the masterly manner [in which] he presented the history of these two rival companies, the course of legislation pursued in relation to both of them, and the clear and manly style in which he exhibited to the court their respective legal rights." Webster believed he had won the case, but five days later, in a surprising decision, the court voted three to two in the canal's favor.

Chesapeake & Ohio President Charles Mercer then smugly deprecated the railroad and its efforts, but his victory was short-lived. Construction costs for the canal, the estimates for which he had so vigorously criticized, were coming back to bite. And Maryland legislators, who had a financial interest in the railroad as well as in the canal, let it be known that, unless the canal was more cooperative, no additional funds would be forthcoming. A compromise, finally agreed to in the spring of 1833, allowed the two to proceed side by side from Point of Rocks; the railroad would pay the canal $266,000 for grading work, and also shift its tracks to the Virginia side once above Harper's Ferry.[18]

Instead of pushing west immediately, however, the Baltimore & Ohio began building a branch line toward Washington. In the meantime, the Chesapeake & Ohio's workers kept digging, and canal boats could reach Harper's Ferry, some sixty miles above Washington, by the late autumn of 1833. But even then, railroads continued to play a part in the canal's activities; an item in the *Washington (DC) Globe* in November, headed "Chesapeake and Ohio Canal," had to include a word about the railroad as well:

> This great public work is at length completed and in full oper-ation from the District of Columbia to the head of the falls at Harper's ferry. Large quantities of merchandize and produce are afloat upon it, passing daily east and west. The Point of Rocks is now the point of attraction, and really presents as we are told an animating scene. Rail Road Cars and Canal boats [are] constantly arriving, interchanging passengers and car-goes and then departing–the bustle and confusion of a little village, suddenly arisen, as it were, out of the earth and actu-ally doing the business of a commercial emporium–its inhab-itants hardly yet acquainted with each other, and very often out numbered by the transient strangers who throng thither in pursuit of business and pleasure–the very novelty itself, of two great public enterprises so long at war with each other, just going onto harmonious operation upon the spot which may be called the battle ground.[19]

At the same time the *National Intelligencer* noted:

(Overleaf) *Maryland and Delaware [with] District of Columbia* by Samuel Breese and Sidney E. Morse (1845). This map is accurate in showing the Baltimore & Ohio tracks crossing the Potomac at Harper's Ferry and extending to Cumberland, where the first B&O train arrived in 1842. The Chesapeake & Ohio Canal, however, was bogged down cutting a tunnel to bypass the Potomac's Paw Paw Bends (approximately south of Prattsville on this map) which was begun in 1836. In 1842, the 3,100-foot tunnel was not yet half finished. It would not be until 1850, when the canal itself finally reached Cumberland. It would stop there, never to progress further as suggested by the profile at the top. (*Courtesy of the David Rumsey Map Collection, www.davidrumsey.com*)

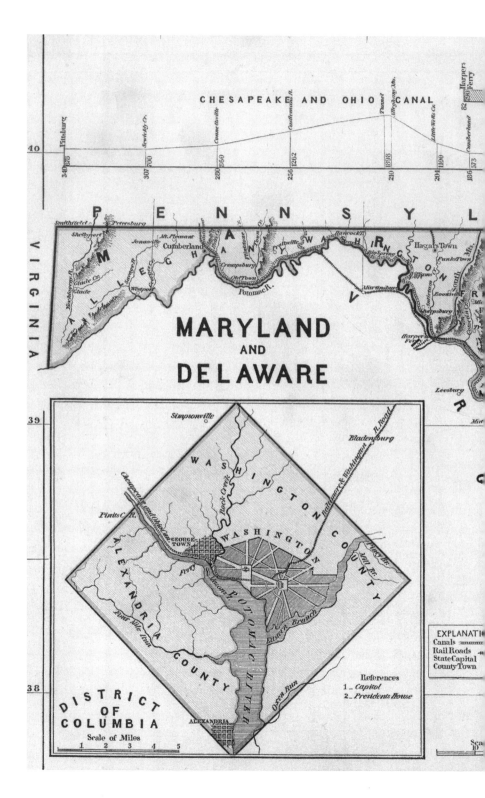

CHESAPEAKE AND OHIO CANAL

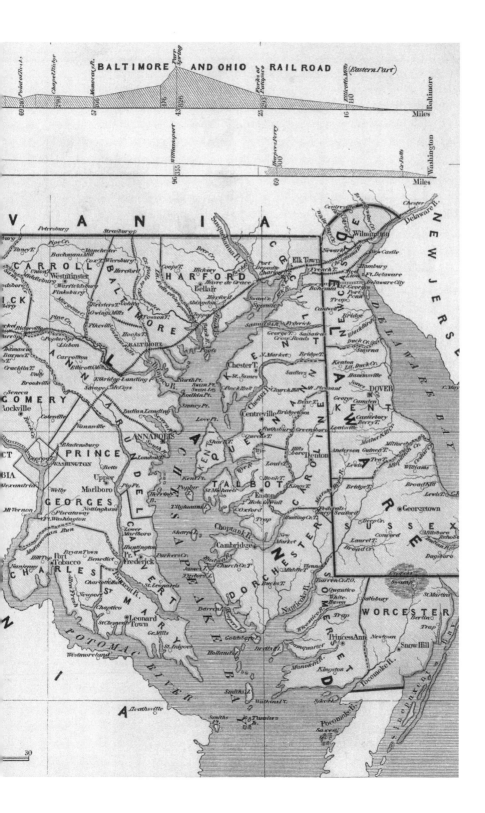

We had yesterday the pleasure of conversing with a gentleman who came down the Chesapeake and Ohio Canal from
Harper's Ferry to Georgetown on the preceding day, in a
boat, with several other gentlemen. . . . [This] important portion of the Canal, which is thus brought into use, we are glad
to learn, holds water remarkably well, and not a breach has
occurred in it; [moreover, the] portion of the Canal from the
Point of Rocks to the Falls above Harper's Ferry is said to be
a work that may challenge a comparison with any similar
structure in the world. . . . [But while] noticing the successful
prosecution thus far of our (yes, our) great public undertaking,
it is to the purpose to place before our readers the following
pregnant suggestions, which we extract from a communication published in the Baltimore Gazette:

"I am forced to become an advocate for the prosecution of
the Canal, much against my will, but situated as matters are,
it is [in] our interest to push it onward to the base of the
Alleghany, provided a Rail-Road can be made across the
mountains."[20]

In other words, a canal might be fine over level ground, but the
most practical method of crossing the mountains was with a railroad.

13

RAILROADS

In February 1832, the *Ohio State Journal* printed an advertisement by D. K. Minor of New York: "The subscriber is now publishing a weekly paper, called the AMERICAN RAIL-ROAD JOURNAL. A principal object in offering the proposed work to the Public, is to diffuse a more general knowledge of this important mode of internal communication, which, at this time, appears to engage the attention of almost every section of our country."[1]

And railroad activities had indeed engaged the country's attention, particularly the activities of the Baltimore & Ohio. For more than two years after its inaugural run in May 1830, the B&O used horses to pull its cars to their destinations. The executives there were well aware of steam locomotives, of course–and, for that matter, so were people in all walks of life, because newspapers continued to carry stories about them. For those especially interested, several books on the subject were available, including Thomas Earle's 1830 work, *Treatise on Rail-Roads,* printed in Philadelphia.[2]

Probably the most publicized event in connection with locomotive development at the time–Earle's treatise devoted more than eight pages to it–was the competitive trial held at Rainhill, England, in October 1829. Among the attendees were Nicholas Wood, author of another of the early railroad treatises, and the Stephensons, George and Robert, whose locomotive, the *Rocket,* was expected to do well. Two Americans were also there: George Brown and Ross Winans of the B&O, whose interest in the proceedings was far more than casual.

Of the five engines that actually began the tests, two quickly fell out: the *Cycloped*, which powered its wheels by means of a horse-driven treadmill, and the *Perseverance*, which, damaged en route to Rainhill, performed poorly and soon disqualified itself. Of the other three—the *Sans Pareil*, the *Rocket*, and the *Novelty*—the *Sans Pareil* and the *Rocket* were similar in general layout; both had horizontal boilers with smokestacks at the front, and separate tenders for the fuel. The *Sans Pareil*, however, had rear-mounted vertical cylinders, driving its rear wheels, while the *Rocket*'s cylinders, although also rear-mounted, lay at an angle of about thirty-five degrees from the horizontal, with long connecting rods reaching forward and downward to the front wheels. These wheels, the drivers, were about twice the diameter of those at the rear, whereas in the *Sans Pareil*, all four wheels were alike.

In contrast to the others, the *Novelty* was just that—a novel arrangement. Called a "tank engine" because it carried its own fuel and water, its features included a long, slender, horizontal boiler (only thirteen inches in diameter) mounted under the frame and hardly noticeable there, with a fat copper firebox positioned vertically and prominently at the rear. Its vertical cylinders drove a pair of four-foot wheels via bell cranks.

When the trials ended, the Stephenson *Rocket* claimed first place and the prize of five hundred pounds. Curiously, however, it was the *Novelty* that garnered the most publicity. Early in 1830, for instance, the *Baltimore Patriot* published a lengthy article on it, complete with illustrations, while the *Rocket* got barely a mention.[3]

An interested observer of these happenings was Peter Cooper, a successful inventor and wealthy businessman who in 1828 had moved to Maryland from New York to buy land adjoining the Baltimore & Ohio as an investment. With an inventor's turn of mind, he posed the question to himself about how well a locomotive would perform on the B&O's tracks. Winding through hills and valleys as it did, the road embodied elevations and radii that might prevent a locomotive from operating. At that time, a track curvature with a radius of less than four hundred feet was thought too difficult for a locomotive to handle, as was a grade steeper than a mere 1 percent (one foot in one hundred feet); whereas grades of 7 or 8 percent were common on the National Road.

George and Robert Stephenson's *Rocket*, left, participated in a locomotive trial along with *Novelty*, right, and other early engines. (*Brown, The History of the First Locomotives in America*)

Fortunately, the grade on most stretches of the B&O was about eighteen feet to the mile, or just under one-half of 1 percent. It would cause Cooper no problems, and to negotiate the sharp curves, he could design a vehicle with a short wheelbase. To get such a wheelbase (and a short overall length as well), he used a vertical boiler, with a single vertical cylinder alongside it. For the heating tubes inside the boiler, the enterprising inventor used old musket barrels.[4]

Compared to the big black-iron locomotives at the Rainhill trials, with wheel diameters of four feet or more, Cooper's design was diminutive: its wheel diameter was only thirty inches, and its total weight about one ton. The boiler, roughly five feet high, was about twenty inches in diameter, and the lone cylinder a mere three and one-quarter inches in diameter, with a fourteen-and-one-quarter-inch stroke. Like the much-discussed *Novelty*, Cooper's was a tenderless tank engine, carrying its own water and fuel. Nor was it particular about what it burned: it would take wood, coal, or coke. As the *Patriot* said proudly in August 1830:

> We are much gratified by the opportunity of furnishing another proof, that we have sufficient genius, energy, and scientific knowledge in the United States, to render it unnecessary to send to Europe for Locomotive Steam Engine Cars for our Rail Roads. . . . The locomotive engine constructed by Peter

Cooper, Esq. of New York, was put on the Baltimore and Ohio Rail Road this day, and after various trials for short distances, was finally run to the half way house, seven miles from the city, conveying from twelve to fourteen persons on the carriage of the engine. . . . [T]he average speed was from twelve to fourteen miles an hour, the engine working at not more than two thirds of its power.

Cooper's early runs were promising, even with cars attached, but the officials were having good luck with old-fashioned horsepower and continued to use it. An interesting and much-storied incident involving a race between horse and locomotive occurred on the B&O's newly laid double track, probably late in August 1830, when Cooper's little engine encountered a car pulled by a "gallant gray" from the Stockton & Stokes stables. Gradually, steadily, the locomotive pulled ahead, until a belt slipped from a pulley and the machine lost power, whereupon the horse trotted smartly past it and claimed the crown.[5]

But the victory was short-lived. In January 1831, after a continual assessment of the evidence, Philip Thomas and the railroad's board of directors announced their own version of the Rainhill Trials, inserting a notice in the Baltimore papers that called for "a supply of Locomotive Steam Engines, of American Manufacture, adapted to their road." Moreover, "they will pay the sum of Four Thousand Dollars for the best Engine which shall be delivered for trial upon the road, [and] will also pay Three Thousand five Hundred Dollars for the Engine which shall be adjudged the next best." A detailed list of requirements followed.

One engine was ready for trial almost overnight. In late February, the *Patriot* reported:

The Locomotive Steam Engine, constructed at York, Pa. by Messrs. Davis & Gartner, of that place, reached the Railroad on Thursday last. . . . Some experiments were made with it on Friday and Saturday, as indicative of its power and ultimate velocity. According to the most accurate estimate that could be made, the last trial exhibited a speed equal to from 16 to 18 miles per hour, the engine working smoothly. [And] several gentlemen, as many indeed as could find footing, were

The locomotive *Tom Thumb* pulling away from a regular horse-drawn passenger car along the B&O tracks. The locomotive soon broke down and was passed by the "gallant gray." The B&O had a gauge of 4 feet, 8 1/2 inches, which ultimately became the U.S. standard. (*Brown, The History of the First Locomotives in America*)

permitted to gratify themselves with a ride thereon. The results appeared to give general satisfaction.[6]

This engine, appropriately nicknamed the "York," met most of the company's requirements. It had a short, four-foot wheelbase supporting a vertical boiler, and it weighed no more than three and one-half tons. It also had dual cylinders, a major improvement over Peter Cooper's single cylinder. During the competitive trials in late June, only one entry, built by William T. James of New York, posed any kind of a threat to it. Nonetheless, the *York* proved itself superior, pulling a car loaded with forty passengers at an average speed of twenty miles per hour. Adjudged the winner, it was working intermittently on the line by August. (The *York*'s little Cooper-designed predecessor also turned out to be a winner, because in 1833, the company paid one thousand dollars for the rights to it.)

The *York* did have its flaws. Compared to most other locomotives, its light weight—a condition stipulated by the company—allowed its wheels to slip when climbing any kind of a grade while pulling a load. But this and some of its other faults were easily remedied, and in the fall the B&O contracted with Phineas Davis of Davis & Gartner to supply two new engines at four thousand dollars each.[7]

In the meantime, another engine was getting attention: the *DeWitt Clinton*, built by New York's West Point Foundry for the Mohawk & Hudson Railroad, which spanned the sixteen miles between Albany and Schenectady. During the first few months of its operation, the road used horse-drawn cars, but by August 1831, the engine was on the tracks, and for a special excursion in September, the usual party of dignitaries

> started with a train of ten cars, three drawn by the American locomotive "DeWitt Clinton," and seven by a single horse each. The appearance of this fine cavalcade, if it may be so called, was highly imposing. The trip was performed by the locomotive in forty-six minutes, and by the cars drawn by horses in about an hour and a quarter. . . . Among the toasts offered [later] was one which has been verified to the letter, viz.: "The Buffalo Rail Road. May we soon breakfast in Utica, dine in Rochester, and sup with our friends on Lake Erie!"

During this excursion, the engine badly frightened "the horses attached to all sorts of vehicles filled with the people from the surrounding country, or congregated all along . . . the road, to get a view of the singular-looking machine and its long train of cars . . . causing thus innumerable capsizes and smash-ups of the vehicles and the tumbling of the spectators in every direction to the right and left." The railroad passengers themselves, however, were quite happy with the trip, "and no rueful countenances were to be seen, excepting occasionally when one encountered in his walks in the city a former driver of the horse-cars, who saw that the grave had that day been dug, and the end of horsepower was at hand."[8]

With its horizontal boiler, the *DeWitt Clinton* resembled English-made locomotives of the Stephenson type. As a result, it stood in stark contrast to the first of the new B&O engines, designed jointly by Phineas Davis and the redoubtable Ross Winans, which went into service in September 1832. Dubbed the *Atlantic*, it and those immediately following were "grasshopper" engines—and despite their unconventional appearance, they worked and worked well. Like the *York*, they had vertical boilers and twin vertical cylinders; the "grasshopper" nickname was a result of the long connecting rods, which ran at a downward-and-backward angle from pivot pins on top of the boiler to the drive gears at the rear of the frame, and thus resembled a grasshopper's hind legs. A second grasshopper, the *Indian Chief*, reached the rails in 1833. (Modified shortly thereafter, it was renamed the *Traveller*.)[9]

Still, horses predominated. When Thomas Hamilton (grumbling as usual) met an acquaintance in Baltimore, likewise bound for New Orleans,

> we agreed to travel together, and on the morning of the 6th of March [1833], before daylight, stepped into the railway carriage which was to convey us ten miles on our journey. The vehicle was of a description somewhat novel. It was, in fact, a wooden house or chamber, somewhat like those used by itinerant showmen in England,

A B&O "grasshopper" engine got its name from the long connecting rods which ran from the top of the boiler to drive gears at the back of the frame. (*The Early Motive Power of the Baltimore and Ohio Railroad*)

> and was drawn by a horse at the rate of about four miles an hour. Our progress, therefore, was not rapid, and we were nearly three hours in reaching a place called Ellicot Mills, where we found a wretched breakfast awaiting our arrival.[10]

Later that year, Carl Arfwedson traveled the road from west to east:

> The great undertaking of making a railroad, for the purpose of uniting the Atlantic and Western States, had in the progress of execution reached as far as Point of Rocks, seventy miles from Baltimore. At Frederick, which is ten miles nearer to the above city, I took an opportunity of travelling this road. Six cars, each filled with sixteen persons, and drawn by horses, started from this place soon after my arrival. . . . By detention at different places, and from other causes, this journey took not less than eight hours.

Despite the length of time spent in the car, Arfwedson added that "The whole undertaking is executed by private capitalists, and holds out a prospect of becoming, in time, one of the most lucrative speculations of its kind." A book published in 1834 for travelers emphatically agreed: "The great Baltimore and Ohio Rail-road now in progress in [Maryland] is by far the most stupendous national work of the kind ever undertaken in this or any other country."[11]

Taking eight hours to cover the sixty miles to Baltimore, including stops, was not entirely unreasonable, but the company could reduce the time noticeably by using fewer horses and more engines. The third of the grasshopper locomotives, the *Arabian*, arrived in mid-1834, and the fourth, the *Mercury*, a few months later. Each incorporated various improvements on its predecessor. When the *Arabian* and the *Mercury* arrived, horses were the main prime movers, but in December 1834, the *Arabian*, unaided, managed to pull two cars over Parr's Spring Ridge, a feat that, within three years, would all but end the B&O's use of horsepower. A newspaper correspondent wrote breathlessly that the feat "never has yet been equaled; [the *Arabian*] having gained the highest summit of the Ridge with her tender, with ease, she returned to the foot of the planes, took two [loaded] wagons in tow, and conveyed them over the Ridge at the rate of ten miles an hour!"[12]

At the same time, workers finished the line to a point opposite Harper's Ferry. Sitting on the south bank of the Potomac, just above its confluence with the Shenandoah, this destination presented its own challenges. Numerous travelers commented on the spectacular scenery, but this is just what made construction there so difficult. The road leading to it through Maryland from Point of Rocks passed between swirling water on one side and high cliffs on the other; then, after crossing the Potomac to Virginia, the pathway had to skirt the National Armory and, once beyond it, again squeeze between cliffs and river. Anne Royall described the approach to the ferry from Frederick:

> The road, after reaching the [Potomac] river, is interrupted with rugged rocks, and closely hemmed in by [a] mountain, and overhung with terrific precipices of stupendous height. Those rocks, projecting over the traveller's head, seem to maintain their place by magic. The blood-chilled traveller, however, is not insensible to the deafening roar of the foaming Potomac, which is distinctly seen up to the Ferry–rolling, as it does, over huge rocks, it resounds from cliff to cliff.

Seen from Camp Hill on the Virginia side, the view was just as impressive:

> As you stand on this hill, the Potomac lies on your left, the Shenandoah on your right. The mountain to the right runs up to the junction in a bold perpendicular front of solid rock, 1200 feet high. The mountain to the left, though 1400 feet high, slopes, obliquely, down to the water's edge. The Blue Ridge, on both sides of the river, presents nothing but naked rocks. These assume every figure in nature or art; some resemble houses with chimneys [and] others, ships under sail.[13]

By 1834, of course, the B&O's engineers were well acquainted with such challenges. However, the time required to get to the Ferry–more than two years since reaching Point of Rocks, only twelve miles to the east–was due not only to the terrain, or to the legal battle with the Chesapeake & Ohio Canal, but also to the fact that in mid-1833, the company had begun a branch line to Washington, DC, forty miles to the southwest, a move urged by the *Baltimore Patriot* as early as 1826. It proved to be an expensive and trouble-filled forty miles–building the eight-arch Thomas Viaduct over the Patapsco, and dealing with two major labor riots, among other things–but the rails came into Washington in August 1835.[14]

For the company, it had been a most impressive seven years. As the *American Railroad Journal* declared late in 1835:

> It will not be saying too much, we are sure, to denominate [the Baltimore & Ohio as] the Railroad University of the United States. They have labored long, at great cost, and with a diligence which is worthy of all praise in the cause, and, what is equally to their credit, they have published annually the results of their experiments and distributed their reports with a liberal hand, that the world might be cautioned by their errors and instructed by their discoveries. Their reports

have, in truth, gone forth as a text-book and their road and work-shops have been a lecture-room to thousands who are now practicing and improving upon their experience.

John Latrobe, an accomplished B&O attorney (and son of the famous architect Benjamin), added:

> [T]he Company, stumbling along, with many a fall and many a bruise, made headway notwithstanding; and gave to the companies fast multiplying in all directions, the benefit of its experience. Nothing was more sought after by engineers than the Company's Reports. With a great deal now utterly useless, there was mixed a great deal of scientific and mathematical information. Accurate tables for the location of curves, for estimating quantities, for regulating grades, were to be found there. The Company's very errors imparted lessons of wisdom. What now seems simple was then abstruse; and it was only natural that the managers of new works should resort to the first railroad which had arrived at practical results in the United States, for information. . . . The Baltimore & Ohio Railroad set men to thinking, and gave them the benefit of its experience. But originality was everywhere aimed at; and improvement was the consequence everywhere.[15]

The company had a few more lessons yet to learn. Bridging the Potomac River to get to Harper's Ferry, on the Virginia side, was problematic enough. Then, after reaching the Virginia shore, workers had to build a 1700-foot causeway along the riverbank to stay clear of National Armory grounds. Beyond the causeway, surveys showed that the logical choice of route lay northwest, toward Martinsburg, through the relatively open country comprising the Valley of Virginia. However, this course bypassed Boonesboro and Hagerstown, the well-known stops on the Maryland Bank Road. But it was the most direct line to Cumberland, the next major goal, and in the bargain would save the company an estimated $2.5 million in construction costs.

The savings would be important, because the financial Panic of 1837 dried up the supply of ready money, and the road soon had to deal with another series of major expenses in its push west. Beyond Martinsburg, for instance, there was another expanse of mountainous country, requiring, among other things, a 1200-foot tunnel at Doe Gully, just west of Hancock, and no fewer than eleven substantial stone-and-wood viaducts over various creeks and rivers.[16]

In addition, the company was buying new equipment and refurbishing older parts of the line. In July 1837, for example, Ross Winans patented his "crab" engine, which soon became a standard on the B & O line. It differed from the grasshopper principally in that its cylinders were horizontal instead of vertical; among other things, this lowered the center of gravity, an important feature when a vertical boiler was used.[17]

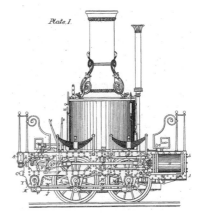

Ross Winans's 1837 patent for his "crab" engine. Unlike the "grasshopper," it has horizontal instead of vertical cylinders, and lacks the long diagonal connecting rods extending from the top of the boiler to the rear of the frame.

Refurbishing of the line included new construction at the well-known site of Parr's Spring Ridge. Late in 1838, the *Boston Morning Post* printed a letter from one David Henshaw, then traveling west. After taking the railroad from Baltimore to Frederick, Henshaw noted:

> The rail-road company [is] constructing a new road, of about six miles, around Parr's Ridge, which is to be finished in a few weeks. . . . They are also in two other places cutting off curves by new pieces of road. They are likewise laying, in place of the old plate rail, new edge rails of the T pattern, weighing 55 lbs. to the yard. . . .
>
>   It would be a great relief to travellers, crossing this formidable chain of mountains, to be able to do it by rail-road. The [Bank] road from Cumberland to this place, is a good road of the kind, but it is not in all cases well located, and no common road can ever come in competition, for convenience, comfort, and speed, with rail-roads.[18]

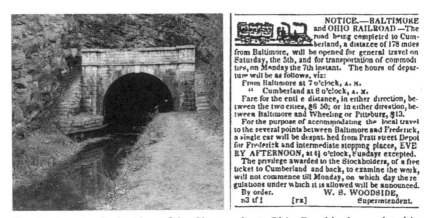

By the time the the the builders of the Chesapeake & Ohio Canal had completed its major tunnel at the Paw Paw Bends in the Potomac, left, and finally reached Cumberland, Maryland, in 1850, the B&O Railroad had already been servicing the city for eight years. A November 1842 notice in the *Baltimore Sun* announces the new Baltimore to Cumberland route. (*Historical American Building Survey/Library of Congress*)

Henshaw's last line summarized the prevailing attitude. And whatever problems the railroad had were minor compared to those faced by its long-time rival, the Chesapeake & Ohio Canal. Boats could not reach the hundred-mile mark above Washington (Williamsport, near Hagerstown) until the spring of 1835. Then, a year later, canal officials ran into real trouble when they began digging a tunnel to bypass the Potomac's repetitive Paw Paw Bends. In November 1842, when the first B&O locomotive steamed triumphantly into Cumberland, the 3,100-foot tunnel was not yet half finished. Nor would it be until 1850, when the canal itself finally reached Cumberland. And there it stopped, never to progress further. It would continue to operate at a loss, as it had previously, for another fifteen years, while the railroad made money hand over fist.[19]

CANAL AND RAILROAD
PARTNERSHIPS

Despite the situation between the Baltimore & Ohio and the Chesapeake & Ohio, railroads and canals were not always competitive with one another. Nor did they need to be. Canal boats, wider and much longer than the typical railroad car, were better suited to carrying large, bulky loads. Railroads, traveling much faster than canal boats, were well suited to carrying passengers or lighter goods. Regarding passenger cars, some roads continued using horses to draw them well into the 1830s, while using locomotives to pull freight cars. After all, freight would not complain when showered by sparks or shrouded in smoke.

One example of the cooperation between railroad and canal on the Erie line appeared in the *New York Spectator* in June 1833:

> Canal Packet Boats and Rail Road Arrangement. A Packet Boat will leave Schenectady daily for Utica, at 11 o'clock, A.M., at 2 o'clock, P.M., and at half past 6 o'clock, P.M. Passengers for the Packets will leave Albany by the Cars that leave at 10 A.M., at 11 A.M., and 5 P.M. These are the only Cars that meet the Packets. By this arrangement there is no delay, as the Packets will leave Schenectady immediately on the arrival of the Cars.[1]

The "Cars" were part of the Mohawk & Hudson operation, which was doing very well indeed. In 1834, Carl Arfwedson wrote that "Although the Erie Canal goes as far as the Hudson, with which it forms a junction at Albany, still the communication by the railroad between this city and Schenectady is so active, that the cars, generally loaded, run almost every hour of the day."[2]

The Erie Canal, in fact, was about to be flanked by railroads for its entire 360-mile length. The seventy-seven-mile Utica & Schenectady, begun in 1834 and completed two years later at a cost of $20,000 per mile, was soon joined by the fifty-three-mile Syracuse & Utica and the twenty-six-mile Syracuse & Auburn. And by 1840, an Auburn & Rochester was under contract, with the grading in progress.[3]

To some observers this may have seemed excessive, but, as Arfwedson noted, the money to build them was readily available:

> In no country in the world are there so many railroads as in America; their number is daily increasing to such a degree that, within the ordinary period of a man's life, they will be more numerous than in all other parts of the globe put togeth-er. Since my arrival in the country [in 1832], I have counted at least a dozen which have been partly begun, partly opened for conveyance, not one less than fifteen miles in length, and the greater part exceeding fifty miles. Large sums have thus been invested by private capitalists for promoting the public good; and although here, as in other places, the expences generally exceed the original estimate by fifty per cent, yet speculators are always ready to take shares. It seldom happens that a com-pany cannot be formed for want of subscribers: I found that, in most cases, shares were taken in a shorter period than we in Europe take to consider, or to sign our names. This does not exclusively apply to railroads, but also to banks, canals, and all possible undertakings. . . . In this manner have the United States, within a few years, derived more internal improve-ments from the speculations of private individuals, than if the whole had been left to Government.[4]

From his canal boat in the summer of 1834, Tyrone Power watched the work with approval:

> We frequently ran along the line of cuttings for the railroad now in progress between Utica and Schenectady. The rocky

nature of the ridge whose line they pursue, offers formidable impediments: but the work was proceeding with great rapidity notwithstanding. This railway, when complete, together with the canal by whose side it runs, will afford a facility of communication between New York and Utica, which, for speed and convenience, can have no rival.[5]

But Joshua Toulmin Smith and his wife, riding the Utica & Schenectady in 1837, were not quite so pleased:

> Arrived at Utica 27th [of September] by Railroad from Albany distance about 100 miles, 6 hours & 1/2 on Journey–that is 15 miles an hour while the Liverpool & Birmingham performs the same distance in 4-1/2 hours. Railroad laid on wood–very shaky–dreadfully noisy & very unpleasant on account of sparks from engine–this arises from the fuel being wood instead of coal & must be remedied with all its inconveniences–[yet the] railway is preferable to common stage [and the] country of the Mohawk Valley is very beautiful.

After a grim experience or two in bouncing stagecoaches on "horrid" roads, the couple again opted for the rails, whereon Mrs. Smith found a comparison with a famous literary character:

> We took a railroad [from Rochester west] to Batavia; the road lay through much forest & land undergoing the process of clearing. . . . Remarked that the poor wood cutters whom we passed on our route looked somewhat like what Frankenstein must have done, when his monster first arose: they stared with visible emotion at the monster (our train) they had made . . . . [Then I] consider when passing along the way in the railway carriages, that here we are thus in active employment of that which may be considered as the very highest exponent of what is called civilization–i.e. locomotive steam carriages–in the very midst & surrounded close on all sides . . . by the mighty boundless forest, planted by the hand of nature only and which the foot of man has never traversed–Here is the most striking antithesis of Art & Nature which can perhaps be witnessed.[6]

Perhaps the best example of a partnership between a canal and a railroad was the Pennsylvania plan. Pennsylvanians had committed to a canal system by 1826, but, realistically, soon decided that the only practical way over the Allegheny ridges was by railroad, and acted accordingly. As finalized, the system, called the Main Line of Public Works, fell into four divisions: a railroad west from Philadelphia to Columbia, on the Susquehanna River; a canal from Columbia along the Susquehanna and the Juniata to Holidaysburg; a portage railroad over the Allegheny summit to Johnstown; and a canal along tributaries of the Allegheny River to the Allegheny itself, and then south along the Allegheny to Pittsburgh.

Digging of the canals started in 1826–some of the contractors even advertised in Ireland to get laborers–and railroad construction began in 1829. The shorter of the two canals, the western branch, was navigable for its entire 104-mile length by January 1831, and went into full usage with the spring thaw. The 172-mile eastern branch was not finished until late in 1832, and then the system had to wait for completion of the railroad, which took eighteen months more.[7]

Tyrone Power had a chance to ride on part of it in 1833:

> At Philadelphia I took my place for Pittsburg, in the "Good Intent [stage] line," professing to carry only six inside; but . . . [w]e commenced our journey with seven; the bookkeeper making it a favour that we should take in one gentleman who was greatly pressed for time. I perceived, as we started, another person get outside, which made us eight. We were very soon transferred to the Columbia rail-road, which was in progress and now travelled upon for about twenty-one miles, [and] I was very sorry when we were once again to be re-packed in our stage.[8]

Robert Baird, readying the second edition of his *View of the Valley of the Mississippi* for the press, had nothing but praise for the project:

> One of the most important of the lines of communication between the eastern and western parts of our country is the Pennsylvania Canal and Rail Road, extending from

Philadelphia to Pittsburg. . . . A vast amount of business is now doing (1833) on this canal, although the Rail Road is not completed across the mountain. It is calculated that the tolls will this year be $200,000 on this canal. In the course of a few months that road will be finished, and also the Rail road from Philadelphia to Columbia, on the Susquehanna. . . . [T]he amount of business on this great channel of trade and intercourse will be immense.[9]

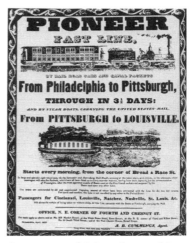

A poster explaining the combination railroad and canal service between Philadelphia and Pittsburgh, and on to Louisville. In Pennsylvania, passengers had to switch from train cars to canal boats and then back again. (*Carnegie Library, Pittsburgh*)

By mid-1834, both the thirty-seven-mile portage railway over the Allegheny summit and the eighty-one-mile Philadelphia & Columbia were open for business. As had happened with the Baltimore & Ohio, the stagecoach lines altered their routes and schedules to meet the railroad:

Philadelphia and Columbia Rail Road.–The opening of this Rail-road for travel, has produced some change in the route of the principal thoroughfare between Philadelphia and Pittsburg. Hitherto, and since the removal of the [state capital] to Harrisburg, that town and Carlisle have been principal points on this route. But the Rail-road has worked a change. The course of travel is about to be turned back into its original channel, by way of York and Gettysburg. Already, as we learn from the York Gazette, the fast line of stages from Philadelphia to Pittsburg, have commenced running through that place [York], daily.[10]

For more than a year after its opening, the Philadelphia & Columbia used horses to draw its cars. An unusual feature of its operation was that it allowed privately owned, horse-drawn cars to use its tracks also—for a fee, of course—but, not surprisingly, this practice led to problems and was eventually outlawed.

One of the early travelers on Pennsylvania's Main Line was English sportsman Charles Augustus Murray, then on his way to the Kansas prairies:

> I went on to Philadelphia, where I remained twenty-four hours, and took my place in the canal and railroad line from thence to Pittsburgh. . . . The opening of this great railroad, after passing the celebrated waterworks of Fairmount, mounts the range of hills which overlook the city to the westward by an inclined plane, the [pulling]-power being placed in a steam-engine worked at the summit. . . . Thence the rail-road carried us through one of the richest and most pleasant valleys in America, called Lancaster Vale, from the town situated in its bosom. . . . After travelling seventy-two miles on this railroad, we arrived at Columbia, a village that seems to possess a brisk trade in lumber, judging from the vast piles collected on each side of the road. [There] my eye was regaled by the first view of the sweet and now classic Susquehanna. . . . Here we left the railroad and took to the canal-boat, which, to my great delight, followed the course of the river, and gave us an opportunity of enjoying, for many miles, the view of its picturesque and woodland banks.
>
> After passing Harrisburgh, the canal leaves the Susquehanna at Petersburgh, and courts her rival and younger sister the Juniata. . . . The packets, or track-boats as they are here called, are tolerably comfortable; and their rate of going is about four miles an hour; which I preferred to greater speed, as it enabled me in the evening and morning, when the heat was not intense, to walk many miles in the enjoyment of the fresh hill breeze and the lovely ever-changing scenery.
>
> The company on board these boats is very mixed, including every grade, from the operative to the highest class in Philadelphia. I was very fortunate in meeting with an elderly gentleman well known as one of the most eminent and accurate reporters in this country, [whose] abilities are employed

Top, a period engraving of passengers disembarking canal boats, seen in the lower left, at Holidaysburg, Pennsylvania, to waiting cars that would carry them along the Portage Railroad across the Alleghenies. Later on, canal boats were built in two sections, below, which could be transported by rail, so that passengers would no longer have to switch service while traveling across the state. (*Pennsylvania Railroad Company*)

in the service of the National Intelligencer. . . . [But] I found an amusing contrast in the manners of some western travelers, who were cast in a rougher mould: they were not satisfied till they had found out who I was, where I came from, why I came, where I was going to, how long I meant to stay, and, in addition to these particulars, how much my umbrella cost, and what was the price of my hat. This last inquiry was followed by the party taking it up from the bench, and putting it on his head, which was not very cool; neither did it appear to have suffered much annoyance from water or from comb; luckily the hat did not fit, and after giving it two or three stout pulls in a vain attempt to draw it over his scalp, he returned it to me. . . .

On the eve of the 25th [of May, 1834] we arrived, about four, at a place where one of the locks was undergoing some repairs, and consequently the boat could proceed no further until they were completed; an operation which was expected to last some three or four hours. I was informed that it was only twelve or fourteen miles to Holydaysburgh, where the canal terminates, and the journey is resumed the following morning on a railroad across the Alleghanies. I accordingly left the boat, and with my stout stick in my hand . . . I set off on foot over the hills.

The recently completed Portage Railroad over the summit incorporated five inclined planes on each side of the ridge line, each with its own stationary steam engine to pull the cars uphill.

On Monday morning I entered the railroad-car that was to convey me across the Alleghanies. We had to go up many inclined planes before we could reach the summit. Some passengers are much alarmed at that part of the journey, because all the cars are attached by one rope, which hauls them up the hill by the power of a steam-engine; and if that were to break, the cars and all their contents would probably be dashed to pieces. . . . The passage over the mountain is one continued scene of rough wild woodland. The railroad is carried along the sides of ridges of considerable height, and almost precipitous; where I should think that persons troubled with nerves might be now and then annoyed and alarmed. . . . However, we arrived in safety at Johnstown, where we were transferred again to the canal. . . .

. . . [T]he canal [now] follows the course of the river Conemaugh, and we felt that the journey was drawing to a close, as the waters now ran to the west—all of them following their multitudinous channels to swell the mighty tide of the Mississippi. After travelling some distance along the banks of the Conemaugh, its name, probably from some intermediate tributary stream, is changed to the Kiskiminitas; the pronunciation of which among a party of strangers gives rise to much merriment and laughter. On both sides of its channel are extensive salt-works, and coal and lime abound. . . . At Freeport we joined the course of the Alleghany River, and mingled our muddy Kis-kiminatian waters with its clear and transparent stream. The country now assumed a more tame and settled appearance, while the continual recurrence of coal-smoke and steam-engines reminded us of our return to civilization [at] Pittsburg.

Impressed by his rail-and-canal trip, Murray concluded:

The whole line reflects the highest credit both on the engineers and on the State [especially] when we consider the difficulties that have been overcome, the wonderful facilities of transportation that have been acquired, and the mingled courage and perseverance with which the rugged chain of the Alleghanies have been obliged to "bend their stiff necks," and lend their rough backs, to carry the comforts and luxuries of life between the Atlantic cities and the "Great Valley."[11]

While visiting Pennsylvania in 1834, David Crockett, the congressman from Tennessee, mentioned two incidents of note, one of them involving the railroad:

Mr. James M. Sanderson informed me that the young whigs of Philadelphia had a desire to present me with a fine rifle, and had chosen him to have her made agreeably to my wishes. I told him that was an article I knew somewhat about, and gave him the size, weight, & c. . . . Next morning the land admiral, Col. Reeside, asked me to call on him, and take a ride. I did so; and he carried me out to the rail-road and Schuylkill bridge. I found that the rail-road was finished near a hundred miles into the interior of the state, and is only one out of many; yet they make no fuss about it.

Elsewhere Crockett, with his customary humor, described his first trip on a railroad, a description that presumably applied to almost any locomotive-drawn train of the time:

This was a clean new sight to me; about a dozen big stages hung on to one machine, and to start up hill. After a good deal of fuss we all got seated, and moved slowly off; the engine wheezing as if she had the tizzick. By-and-by she began to take short breaths, and away we went with a blue streak after us. The whole distance is seventeen miles, and it was run in fifty-five minutes.

While I was whizzing along, I burst out laughing. One of the passengers asked me what it was at. "Why," says I, "it's no wonder the fellow's horses run off."

[Then I told him the story.] A Carolina waggoner had just crossed the rail-road, from Charleston to Augusta, when the engine hove in sight with the cars attached. It was growing dark, and the sparks were flying in all directions. His horses ran off, broke his wagon, and smashed his combustibles into items. He run to a house for help, and when they asked him what scared his horses, he said he did not jist know, but it must be hell in harness.[12]

(Crockett's "rail-road, from Charleston to Augusta" was the then-famous Charleston & Hamburg, running from Charleston more than 130 miles across South Carolina to Hamburg, on the Savannah River opposite Augusta, Georgia. At its completion in 1833, it was the longest railroad in the world. Its first locomotive, the American-built *Best Friend of Charleston*, went into service late in 1830.)[13]

The flying sparks that Crockett mentioned could do more than frighten horses. Harriet Martineau pointed out this fact after a rail trip in 1836:

One great inconvenience of the American railroads is that, from wood being used for fuel, there is an incessant shower of large sparks, destructive to dress and comfort, unless all the windows are shut; which is impossible in warm weather. Some serious accidents from fire have happened in this way; and, during my last trip on the Columbia and Philadelphia rail road, a lady in the car had a shawl burned to destruction on her shoulders; and I found that my own gown had thirteen holes in it.[14]

Even then, inventors were patenting "spark-catchers" or "spark arresters," and the engines themselves were continually improving. By 1836, the Philadelphia & Columbia was using locomotives built by soon-to-be-renowned makers Richard Norris and Matthias Baldwin, both of Philadelphia. And the road itself was increasingly prominent. In 1840, Henry Tanner said, "The Columbia and Philadelphia Rail-Road [is] the first link in the great western chain. . . . [It] forms a part of the great thoroughfare to Pittsburg and the western states, and is the most important outlet of the city of Philadelphia, toward the valley of the Mississippi."[15]

WITHIN PENNSYLVANIA, THE Philadelphia & Columbia could indeed be called a "first link in the great western chain." But by the close of 1834, another "first link," or pair of links, had fallen into place east of it: the Delaware & Raritan Canal, and the Camden & Amboy Railroad, both of which ran generally southwest across New Jersey from points just below New York City to the broad waters of the Delaware River near Philadelphia. With the New Jersey system in operation, European emigrants landing in New York City could follow a complete canal-and-rail connection all the way through Pennsylvania to the Ohio River at Pittsburgh.

The Camden & Amboy was a story unto itself. Its prime mover was none other than John Stevens, whose 1812 booklet on the "superior advantages of railways and steam carriages" had predicted that locomotives would one day travel at speeds of one hundred miles per hour. Appropriately, Stevens (or one of his sons—the news account doesn't specify which) was a witness to the inaugural run of the Baltimore & Ohio in May 1830. A year later he went to England and, among other things, purchased for his line a Stephenson-built ten-ton locomotive, soon to be famous as the John Bull.[16]

Pennsylvanians, meanwhile, continued to lay track westward, and by 1838, two new lines were completed. One of them, the Harrisburg, Portsmouth, Mountjoy, & Lancaster, ran from Lancaster some thirty-five miles west-northwest to Harrisburg; from that point, the Cumberland Valley Railroad wound its way

nearly fifty miles west-southwest through Carlisle and
Shippensburg to Chambersburg.¹⁷ Partly because of the expense of
operating the canal-and-rail "Main Line of Public Works," railroads
in Pennsylvania were steadily gaining the ascendancy over canals.

As in Pennsylvania and New Jersey, there was another partnership—at least in theory—between canal and railroad, this one farther
south, in Virginia. Although a canal along the James River from
Richmond toward western waters had been the subject of serious
discussion since the 1780s, with George Washington himself an
interested participant, little had been done about it. As Henry
Tanner stated in 1830, "This highly important improvement has
for a long time remained stationary, notwithstanding [that] the
interests of the country through which it is to pass, would seem to
require its early completion." Things were still dormant when
George Mitchell published his *Accompaniment* to his reference map
in 1834: "James river admits vessels of 125 tons [from the Atlantic,
through Hampton Roads] to Rockett's, the port of Richmond. At
that city commence the falls or rapids, to pass which a series of
short canals have been constructed. . . . These canals and locks,
with other slight improvements, [have] opened a navigation at all
seasons of 12 inches water to Lynchburg."

Another short canal far upriver, between Lynchburg and the old
Philadelphia Wagon Road, had been cut "through the Gap of the
Blue Ridge, [near] Balcony Falls." Even with this canal in place, the
twelve-inch depth of water Mitchell referred to was not always
enough to assure navigation, and he explained that "The above
works may be considered as [only] the commencement of a series
of improvements for the purpose of connecting the waters of James
river with those of the Great Kanawha, and when completed will
afford the shortest and most direct line of communication from the
Ohio river to the Atlantic Ocean." One of the delays in commencing these improvements resulted from disagreement about
whether to build a canal at all. In 1830, Claudius Crozet, the well-
known state engineer, had recommended scrapping the canal system entirely and replacing it with a railroad, running all the way
from Richmond to Covington, west of the Wagon Road. For most
of those involved, the idea was too radical, but they were willing
to consider building a railroad for at least part of the distance to
western waters.

The Kanawha Canal along the James River at Richmond, Virginia, in 1834. The canal did not reach Lynchburg until late in 1840, and eventually got to Buchanan, on the old Philadelphia Wagon Road, in 1851. (*Library of Congress*)

In 1832, a new company took shape under the leadership of Joseph C. Cabell, a political force in Virginia. Urging subscriptions to the company's stock, Cabell declared, "Subscribe, else your commerce will be diverted to other states, [and] Virginia will decline in power and influence." His ally in this effort was no less a figure than U.S. Chief Justice John Marshall, who, with his usual eloquence, said: "It is with you, fellow-citizens, whether this great work shall succeed or totally fail. You are now to decide whether it shall raise us to our former rank among our sister states, or add one to the examples already given of the ruinous apathy with which we neglect the natural advantages which Providence has bestowed upon our country." The money soon came in, and other key figures joined the enterprise, including Benjamin Wright of New York and Charles Ellet of Pennsylvania. The plan finally agreed upon was to carry the canal west to Lynchburg, or to a location somewhat beyond, and from there build a railroad "to some convenient point on the Great Kanawha river, below the falls thereof." Again, some of the stockholders argued for abandoning a waterway altogether and substituting a railroad, but a majority favored the canal.

By October 1835, most of the route had been surveyed, and a year later some 1,300 men and 350 horses were working on it. In the fall of 1837, company officials reported that "The valley of the river has exhibited a vast scene of activity and animation . . . the contractors with their throngs of laborers and teams, forming a line almost unbroken of the most lively and cheerful industry for 120 miles." As it turned out, the industry was not always cheerful: in May 1838, the Irish workers struck for higher pay, finally returning to work on a promise of a 20 percent increase once they finished the canal. The 1840 edition of Tanner's *Canals and Rail Roads* noted, "This work is nearly completed . . . with some slack-water navigation, between Richmond and Lynchburg, and is under contract between Lynchburg and the mouth of the North River, in Rockbridge county." And so it was. In December 1840, two freight boats traveled the 146 miles from Richmond to Lynchburg without incident, stopping amidst "cheers and acclamations by the inhabitants of the town, who had assembled to witness their arrival."[18]

By that time there was little if any resistance to continuing west by rail, but now financial problems intervened, and the projected railroad did not materialize for years.

A RAILROAD THAT DID MATERIALIZE, and not very far away, was the Winchester & Potomac. It was only thirty miles long, running southwest from Harper's Ferry to Winchester, but it turned out to be an important thirty miles. For one thing, its completion carried some very real benefits for the Baltimore & Ohio, as the *Baltimore Patriot* explained in October 1834:

> The advantages thus to be anticipated, when the main stem
> of the Baltimore and Ohio Rail Road shall be extended to
> Harper's Ferry [which it was two months later], will be great-
> ly increased upon the completion of the Winchester and
> Potomac Rail Road. This, it is understood, may be confident-

ly expected within the year 1835 [it was 1836], when the great stream of western travel will, it is believed, be diverted into this course, aiming for the Ohio river, either at Parkersburg, by crossing the mountains from Winchester, or at Guyandotte [later Huntington], by ascending the valley of the Shenandoah to Staunton, and then turning to the West through Jenning's Gap, and by the White Sulphur Springs of Virginia. Indeed, the Board of Directors feel more and more confident that the Winchester and Potomac Rail Road is but the commencement of a chain of Rail Roads by which the Western waters and the cotton growing districts of the south west will become connected with the Atlantic sea board.[19]

Winchester, of course, was on the old Philadelphia Wagon Road trending southwest through Staunton, and was also astride Virginia's Northwestern Turnpike leading west through Romney and Clarksburg to the Ohio River at Parkersburg.

The Erie Railroad steams across the Starrucca Viaduct. By 1848, when this bridge was completed, trains were the dominant means of westward migration to the Missouri River. (*Library of Congress*)

RAILROADS WEST OF THE MOUNTAINS

By 1830, THANKS LARGELY TO THE B&O's success, a charter had been issued to a railroad west of the Alleghenies: Kentucky's Lexington & Ohio. Although it extended about the same distance as the Winchester & Potomac, this road did not fare as well–not initially, at least. It was supposed to reach from Lexington to the Ohio River at Louisville, but was unable to go into full operation until January 1835, and then ran only to Frankfort, twenty-nine miles away.[1]

More important, and more heavily traveled, was Ohio's Mad River & Lake Erie Railroad, planned (like the Ohio & Erie Canal) to link Lake Erie with the Ohio River. Even the Eastern papers waxed enthusiastic over this project. The *New York Spectator* said, "When presented upon the map, it becomes obvious that no other route has been, or can be, so direct as this in the line of conveyance between our great commercial emporium [New York City] and the waters of the Mississippi."[2]

(An interesting tale about this project involved certain citizens of Sandusky, the road's northern terminus; bypassed by all of Ohio's major canals, they retaliated by working vigorously for development of a railroad.)

Groundbreaking ceremonies took place in September 1835, with the usual fanfare, and with war hero and future U.S. president William Henry Harrison in attendance. The *Spectator* cheerfully took note of the occasion:

We are happy to perceive that this long projected enterprise has at length been commenced, under auspices which give a guaranty of its early completion.–The vast commercial importance of this road is every day more clearly developed. ... [It] will be but a link in the great chain of communication between New-York and the south, and when this, together with those [railroads] projected from the Hudson to [Buffalo] shall have been completed, the travel from New-Orleans to the Atlantic cities of the north, will seek an inland route, as being more expeditious than that which is now resorted to.[3]

The *New Orleans Commerical Bulletin* agreed with this assessment–but added a touch of humor to its comments on the Mad River's name:

A western paper says [that] 35 miles of the "Mud River and Lake Erie Rail Road" were to have been put under contract for clearing and grading, on the 30th ult. at Sandusky City, Ohio. As to the name of the river, it is not quite so bad as that. It is mad river–that is, a little foamy and fractious occasionally, not mud river. The Mad River Rail Road, which is thus in a fair way of being completed at an early period, promises to be one of great importance.[4]

As this road was to be powered by locomotives from the first, an order went to Rogers, Ketchum, & Grosvenor of Paterson, New Jersey, for an engine. By October 1837, it was nearly finished, and when delivered in December, it was named, appropriately, the *Sandusky*. It was a big one: nine and one-half tons, with driving wheels very nearly five feet in diameter. Moreover, it featured a steam whistle.[5]

With the engine on the tracks, events moved rapidly, and by May 1838, the Ohio papers could report that "business has fairly commenced on 15 miles of this road. The locomotive has been put on, and a train of freight and passenger cars are now making regular trips between Sandusky city and Bellevue. The first run from Bellevue to Sandusky was made in 40 minutes, to the great enjoyment of passengers and spectators, and [the] fright of cattle and dogs, who had no ear for the music of the shrill steam-whistle."[6]

By late October 1841, the road had come more than thirty miles and was "very near its completion from Sandusky City to Tiffin. The new locomotive Wyandott, has already made several trips from Scipio to the immediate vicinity of Tiffin, and last Thursday came as far as the bridge across the Sandusky, (a part of the distance on the wooden rails) with several cars attached." The railroad reached Tiffin in December, and later the *Cleveland Herald* noted that it had carried more than 6,700 passengers in 1841, a respectable start.[7]

Two years before that, the *Herald* had mentioned that "The Mad River Rail Road, it is well known, is to be extended to Cincinnati." But things did not work out quite that way. Instead, the Little Miami Railroad, chartered early in 1836, started construction northward from Cincinnati in 1841; it was to meet the Mad River & Lake Erie at Springfield, where, fittingly enough, the National Road would intersect the railway.

In November 1841, the *Herald* reported:

> The Cincinnatians anticipate travelling from that city to Lake Erie by Rail Road in two or three years from this. A few miles of their end of the Little Miami Rail are completed, and the locomotive "Gov. Morrow" is puffing away upon it. The Chronicle says the road will be ready for use to Milford, 15 miles, in about two weeks. The road to Xenia, 60 miles, will be finished in about a year. Thence to Sandusky city, in connection with the Mad River Rail Road, the work is in progress, and a portion completed.[8]

By 1844, the railroad situation in Ohio could be summarized this way:

> To the north and east [Cincinnati] is stretching her colossal arms of iron in search of new conquests. The Little Miami rail-road is already under contract to Xenia, and will be continued thence, to connect with the Mad River rail-road, terminating at Sandusky on the Lake. When this is completed, we shall have a continuous chain of steam communication with the cities on the sea-board by way of Lake Erie and Buffalo. The Baltimore and Ohio rail-road is already complet-

ed to Cumberland, Md., and active preparations are making to extend it on to the Ohio at some point below Wheeling that can be reached by steam-boat in twenty-four hours. Soon, therefore, may we expect to see "the horse of iron, with ribs of steel and sinews of brass" scale the mountain barrier– descend into the broad Western valley, and drink for the first time of the waters of the Ohio.[9]

The Baltimore and Ohio's iron horse did indeed drink of the waters of the Ohio, but not until the close of 1852, ten years after reaching Cumberland, and only after chipping and blasting its way through obstacles more formidable than any faced in Maryland. Ohio's iron horses drank of the waters four year earlier, in 1848, when the Little Miami met the Mad River & Lake Erie near Springfield, just as planned.[10]

CONCLUSION

IT HAD BEEN AN AMAZING FORTY YEARS, beginning with horse-drawn wagons bumping slowly over rough, rutted roads, and ending with canal boats and locomotives gliding or rolling to the banks of the Ohio, where steamboats took over and pushed their way into the Mississippi and then up the Missouri–westward, always westward.

One illustration of the technological leap occurred between 1829 and 1843. Late in 1829, a Stockton & Stokes express rider, carrying a copy of a presidential message,

> left Washington precisely at twenty five minutes before one o'clock P.M. . . . and at five minutes after two o'clock the same rider was before the City Hotel in Baltimore, having performed the distance, over a heavy road, in the incredibly short period of ONLY ONE HOUR AND A HALF, or at the rate of Twenty Four Miles an Hour!!! In order to accomplish this most extraordinary speed, eight horses were stationed at intervals along the road, and successively used as the rider came to them.[1]

This was indeed fast traveling–carrying a message nearly forty miles by horseback in an hour and a half. Fifteen years later, however, it was possible to transmit a message the same distance not in hours but in mere seconds. Early in 1843 a brief article appeared in a newspaper in far-off Texas: "The Electro-Magnetic Telegraph.–the utility of the plan of Professor Morse to convey intelligence by means of electricity is so plain, that we wonder why it is not put in immediate use."[2]

As Timothy Flint had written in 1826, only the Pacific Ocean stopped the westward march. An emigrant might move west, be content for a time, then move west again–and again. In 1841, a wagon train from Missouri journeyed all the way to California, and in his later years John Bidwell, one of its leaders, told how it all started: "In the spring of 1839,–living at the time in the western part of Ohio,–being then in my twentieth year, I conceived a desire to see the great prairies of the West, especially those most frequently spoken of, in Illinois, Iowa, and Missouri." Two years later he was in California–never having planned things that way.[3]

NOTES

PART 1, 1803–1819
1 Alexis de Tocqueville, *Democracy in America*, ed. Richard D. Heffner (New York, 1956), 130–31.
2 John Bradbury, *Travels in the Interior of America . . .*2nd ed. (1819), in Reuben Gold Thwaites, ed., *Early Western Travels, 1748–1846*, vol. 5 (Cleveland, 1904–07), 296.
3 Columbus *Ohio Monitor*, Nov. 21 and 28, 1816.
4 Henry Schoolcraft, *A View of the Lead Mines of Missouri* (New York, 1819), 244.
5 *Mississippi Herald and Natchez Gazette*, Aug. 18, 1807. Fortescue Cuming, *Sketches of a Tour to the Western Country . . .* (1810), in Thwaites, *Early Western Travels*, 231.

CHAPTER 1: WATERWAYS, 1803–1819
1 Albert Gallatin, "Roads and Canals," April 4, 1808, in *American State Papers, Miscellaneous*, vol. 1, 724.
2 Ibid, 733.
3 A version of the Lewis and Clark journals can be found at http://lewisand-clarkjournals.unl.edu/.
4 Zadok Cramer, *The Navigator*, 6th ed. (Pittsburgh, 1808), 40–83. The 3rd edition (titled the *Ohio and Mississippi Navigator*) was published in 1802, and the 8th in 1814. Note: the page numbers cited here cover Cramer's description of the Ohio all the way to its mouth.
5 Thomas Ashe, *Travels in America, Performed in 1806 . . .* (London, 1808), vol. 1, 40–42.
6 Cuming, *Sketches*, 77, 246–47.
7 Ibid., 104.
8 Christian Schultz, *Travels on an Inland Voyage . . .* (New York, 1810), vol. 1, 137.
9 Ashe, *Travels*, vol. 2, 110.
10 An account of an 1807 voyage down the Kanhawa and up the Scioto in a large batteau is in "Leaves from an Autobiography," *The Ladies' Repository*, Aug. 1852, 297–98.
11 Schultz, *Travels*, vol. 1, 176–77, 182, 189, 191–93, 200–201.
12 "Letter from a Traveller to the West," *Alexandria (VA) Herald*, Aug. 9, 1819.

Daniel Hewett's *American Traveller, or National Directory* of 1825 gives the Ohio's length as 949 miles.

13 Schultz, *Travels,* vol. 1, 205–6.

14 John Woods, *Two Years' Residence in the Settlement on the English Prairie* (1822), in Thwaites, *Early Western Travels,* 228.

15 Major Amos Stoddard, *Sketches, Historical and Descriptive, of Louisiana* (Philadelphia, 1812), 303–4, 371–75.

16 Timothy Flint, *Recollections of the Last Ten Years* (Boston, 1826), 86–87, 91, 103–4.

17 Judge James Hall, *Letters from the West . . .* (London, 1828), 324.

18 Schultz, *Travels,* vol. 2, 200–201.

19 Flint, *Recollections,* 15–16.

20 Gallatin, "Roads and Canals," 735–36.

CHAPTER 2: ROADWAYS, 1803–1819

1 Gallatin, "Roads and Canals," p. 739.

2 "Cumberland Road," *American State Papers, Misc.,* vol. 1, 432–34, 474–77, 714–15, 718, 940–41, 947; Merritt Ierley, *Traveling the National Road* (Woodstock, NY, 1990), 31–48. Thomas B. Searight, *The Old Pike* (Uniontown, PA, 1894), 20–43.

3 Ierley, *National Road,* 38–48. The commissioners' report of 1806 is in *American State Papers, Misc.,* vol. 1, 474–77; the reports of 1808 are on 714–15 and 940–41; *Washington (DC) National Intelligencer,* Nov. 20, 1810.

4 Abraham Bradley Map, 1804 edition. Various editions of Bradley's maps can be viewed on the Library of Congress and the David Rumsey Web sites. *Charleston (SC) City Gazette,* Aug. 7, 1797.

5 Gallatin, "Roads and Canals," 873–75.

6 Ibid., 883, 893. Timothy Flint, *Recollections,* 8.

7 Parke Rouse Jr., *The Great Wagon Road* (Petersburg, VA, 1992).

8 Abraham Bradley Maps, 1809 and 1812.

9 *Philadelphia Gazette,* May 24, 1794; "Ferries in the Northwestern Territory," *American State Papers, Misc.,* vol. 1, 145; *Chillicothe (OH) Gazette,* Nov. 7, 1805; Cramer, *The Navigator,* 8th ed. (1814), 94, 110.

10 Cuming, *Sketches,* 213.

11 Ashe, *Travels,* vol. 2, 130.

12 Ibid., vol. 1, 240.

13 Abraham Bradley Map, 1812.

14 Ibid.

15 Ibid.

16 Philip H. Nicklin [Peregrine Prolix, pseud.], *Letters Descriptive of the Virginia Spring . . .* 2nd ed. (Philadelphia, 1837), 20.

17 Abraham Bradley Maps, 1804 and 1809.

18 *United States Gazette* (Philadelphia), March 5, 1805.

19 Abraham Bradley Maps, 1804–1812.

20 *Washington (DC) National Intelligencer,* Nov. 12, 1806.

21 William N. Blane [An English Gentleman, pseud.], *An Excursion through the United States and Canada* (London, 1824), 124.

22 Gallatin, "Roads and Canals," 739, 883.

23 U.S. Census, 1810, Manufactures; George Shumway et al, *The Conestoga Wagon, 1750–1850* (York, PA, 1964); Bernhard, Duke of Saxe-Weimar, *Travels through North America, 1825–1826,* vol. 1, 185.

24 David Thomas, *Travels through the Western Country in the Summer of 1816* (Auburn, NY, 1819), 75.

25 *Richmond (VA) Enquirer,* Nov. 20, 1810; Gallatin, "Roads and Canals," 883.

26 *Richmond (VA) Enquirer,* Nov. 20, 1810.

27 Schultz, *Travels,* vol. 1, 110–11.

28 Samuel Williams, "Leaves from an Autobiography," *Ladies' Repository,* Sept. 1854, 421–23.

29 Columbus *Ohio Monitor,* Nov. 28, 1816.

30 *Farnsworth's Cincinnati Directory,* 1819.

31 James Hall, *Letters from the West,* 346–48.

32 E[manuel] Howitt, *Selections from Letters Written During a Tour through the United States* (Nottingham, England, 1820), 24–25.

33 William Amphlett, *The Emigrant's Directory to the Western States of North America* (London, 1819), 70–71.

34 "Cumberland Road," *American State Papers, Misc.,* vol. 2, 175–76.

35 Gallatin, "Roads and Canals," 738, 883.

36 John Melish Map of the National Road, 1822; Ierley, *Traveling the National Road, passim*; Searight, *The Old Pike, passim*; Bradley Maps of 1809 and 1812; *American State Papers, Misc.,* vol. 2, 175, 177, 182. For a contemporary reference to the hard pulls, see W. M. Gillespie, *A Manual of the Principles and Practice of Road-Making,* 2nd ed. (New York, 1848), 42. Today, the original route is closely (but not always) followed by U.S. Route 40.

37 *American State Papers, Misc.,* vol. 2, 177, 182.

38 *Alexandria (VA) Gazette,* Sept. 17, 1818.

39 *American State Papers, Misc.,* vol. 2, 205, 226, 263, 297–98.

40 Cuming, *Sketches,* 241.

41 *Brownsville (PA) American Telegraph,* Dec. 7, 1814. Additional requests for proposals for the "United States Western Road" are in the *Washington (DC) National Intelligencer,* June 22, 1815, and the *Baltimore Mechanics' Gazette and Merchants' Daily Advertiser,* July 20, 1815. See also *American State Papers, Finance,* vol. 3, 137.

42 *American State Papers, Misc.,* vol. 2, 263; Ibid, vol. 1, 477. As early as 1806 the Cumberland Road commissioners had alluded to the difficult topography, report-

ing that, "The face of the country within the limits prescribed is generally very uneven, and in many places broken by a succession of high mountains and deep hollows, too formidable to be reduced within five degrees of the horizon [except]by crossing them obliquely, a mode which, although it imposes a heavy task of hill-side digging, obviates generally the necessity of reducing hills and filling hollows, which, on these grounds, would be an attempt truly Quixotic."

43 *American State Papers, Misc.,* vol. 2, 301–2.

44 Ibid, 467. Based on the mile markers, this would put the completed roadway a few miles west of the Youghiogheny.

45 Ibid., 526.

46 *Baltimore Patriot,* Dec. 10, 1818; *Albany (N.Y) Argus,* Jan. 1. 1819.

47 James Flint, *Letters from America* (Edinburgh, 1822), in Thwaites, *Early Western Travels,* 105.

48 *Washington (DC) National Intelligencer,* Feb. 23, 1818.

49 *Uniontown (PA) Genius of Liberty,* June 1, 1819; *American State Papers, Misc.,* vol. 2, 585.

50 Woods, *Two Years' Residence,* 207–15.

51 Thomas Hulme, *A Journal Made During a Tour in the Western Countries of America,* in Thwaites, *Early Western Travels,* 77.

52 "Letter from a Traveller to the West," July 1819, *Alexandria (VA) Herald,* Aug. 25, 1819.

53 *Franklin (PA) Gazette,* April 29, 1819.

54 Hulme, *Journal,* 35–36.

55 *Philadelphia Weekly Aurora,* Jan. 26, 1818. Today, the old Pennsylvania State road is generally followed by U.S. Route 30.

56 Samuel Breck, *Sketch of the Internal Improvements Already Made by Pennsylvania,* 2nd ed. (Philadelphia, 1818), 12–13. See also the *Franklin Gazette,* March 20, 1818.

57 Adlard Welby, *A Visit to North America and the English Settlements in Illinois* (London, 1821), in Thwaites, *Early Western Travels,* 192–95.

58 Woods, *Two Years' Residence,* 221.

59 Hulme, *Journal,* 76. Thomas, *Travels,* 90. See also the *Chillicothe (OH) Scioto Gazette,* Aug. 9, 1808.

60 Blane, *An Excursion,* 184–85.

61 *Easton (MD) Gazette,* May 10, 1819.

62 *Edwardsville (IL) Spectator,* Dec. 4, 1819, citing only the *Centinel.*

63 Hulme, *Journal,* 46.

64 *American State Papers, Misc.,* vol. 2, 227; Ierley, *Traveling the National Road,* 46–47.

65 *American State Papers, Misc.,* vol. 1, 145.

66 Cramer, *The Navigator,* 6th ed. (1808), 50.

67 "Letter from a Traveller to the West," Aug. 25, 1819.

68 *Wheeling (VA) Gazette,* Jan. 1, 1824.

69 Schultz, *Travels,* vol. 1, 160–64. Welby, *Visit to North America,* 227.

70 Woods, *Two Years' Residence,* 232.

71 W. Faux, *Memorable Days in America; Being a Journal of a Tour to the United States* (London, 1823), in Thwaites, *Early Western Travels,* 185.

CHAPTER 3: STAGECOACH LINES, 1803–1819

1 *American State Papers, Post Office,* 21–22, 28–30, 119–20. Interesting background material on coaching in England can be found in Samuel Smiles, *Lives of the Engineers . . . History of Roads* (London, 1904).

2 Poulson's *American Advertiser* (Philadelphia), July 10, 1804; *Pennsylvania Correspondent,* July 25, 1804; *Aurora General Advertiser* (Philadelphia), Jan. 25, 1805; *Washington (DC) National Intelligencer,* Oct. 1, 1804; *New York Daily Advertiser,* Sept. 28, 1804; *United States Gazette* (Philadelphia), Aug. 31, 1804.

3 *New York Commercial Advertiser,* Dec. 19, 1806; Poulson's *American Advertiser,* Dec. 26, 1806; *United States Gazette,* Dec. 29, 1806.

4 Quotation in Oliver W. Holmes and Peter T. Rohrbach, *Stagecoach East* (Washington, DC, 1983), 172; also in the files of the Ohio Historical Society, Columbus, OH. #VFM 606.

5 Chillicothe *(OH) Scioto Gazette,* Oct. 9, 1806; see also *United States Gazette* (Philadelphia), Aug. 11, 1806.

6 Cuming, *Sketches,* 211, 222, 225.

7 Cramer, *The Navigator,* 6th ed. (1808), 47.

8 *Columbus (OH) Gazette,* April 23, 1818; *Chillicothe (OH) Scioto Gazette,* Aug. 27, 1819.

9 "Letter from Traveller to the West," *Alexandria (VA) Herald,* Aug. 25, 1819.

10 Woods, *Two Years' Residence,* 218–20.

11 Faux, *Memorable Days,* 164.

12 *Baltimore Patriot,* July 25, 1820.

13 *Albany (NY) Advertiser,* Oct. 28, 1815.

14 *Albany (NY) Gazette,* Sept. 19, 1796; *Utica (NY) Patriot,* July 23, 1804; *Washington (DC) National Intelligencer,* July 2, 1811.

15 John M. Duncan, *Travels through Part of the United States and Canada in 1818 and 1819,* (Glasgow, 1823), vol. 2, 6–14, 316.

16 *Lexington (KY) Western Monitor,* June 13, 1817.

17 *New York Herald,* April 16, 1808; *Washington (DC) National Intelligencer,* July 23, 1816; *Charleston (SC) City Gazette,* Sept. 20, 1805. In Virginia, a Richmond to Lynchburg stagecoach line was in place by 1814; see the *Richmond* (VA) *Enquirer,* Jan. 18, 1814.

18 Breck, *Internal Improvements,* 70.

19 *Washington (DC) National Intelligencer,* May 12 and Sept. 5, 1818.

PART 2, 1819–1832

1 *Vincennes (IN) Western Sun,* Oct. 8, 1825.

2 Timothy Flint, *Recollection of the Last Ten Years* (Boston, 1826), 201–3.

CHAPTER 4: WATERWAYS, 1819–1832

1 *Charlestown (VA) Farmer's Repository,* Dec. 13, 1811. *Washington (DC) National Intelligencer,* Oct. 26, Nov. 2, and Dec. 12, 1811.

2 Edmund Burke, comp., *List of Patents for Inventions and Designs . . .* (Washington, DC, 1847), 151–66.

3 Morris Birkbeck, *Notes on a Journey in America,* 4th ed. (London, 1818), 146. The early prevalence of man-powered craft was due in part to the supposed monopoly on steam travel that Fulton and Livingston thought they enjoyed because of their patent. Long's expedition is detailed in Edwin James, *Account of an Expedition from Pittsburgh to the Rocky Mountains,* 3 vols. (London, 1823), in Thwaites, *Early Western Travels. New York Columbian,* July 12, 1819, citing a Boon's Lick item of May 23.

4 Amphlett, *Emigrant's Directory,* 149, 161.

5 Lewis C. Beck, *A Gazetteer of the States of Illinois and Missouri* (Albany, NY, 1823), 337–341; Franklin *Missouri Intelligencer,* July 25, 1828; Philip St. George Cooke, *Scenes and Adventures in the Army* (Philadelphia, 1859), 38.

6 Samuel Cumings, *The Western Pilot . . .* (Cincinnati, 1829), 89.

7 James Hall, *Letters from the West,* 91–94, 322–23.

8 Cumings, *Western Pilot,* 51.

9 Mrs. Anne Royall, *Mrs. Royall's Southern Tour* (Washington, DC, 1830), vol. 3, 78.

10 *Vincennes (IN) Western Sun,* March 27, 1830, citing the *Illinois Gazette.*

11 Charleston *Virginia Free Press & Farmer's Repository,* Nov. 10, 1830, citing the *Baltimore Patriot.* See also the *Chillicothe (OH) Scioto Gazette,* Nov. 24, 1830.

12 Cramer, *The Navigator,* 8th ed. (1814), 164.

13 *Pensacola (FL) Gazette,* March 11, 1837.

14 Frances Trollope, *Domestic Manners of the Americans* (New York/London, 1832), 152. See also Carl Arfwedson, *The United States and Canada in 1832, 1833, and 1834* (London, 1834), vol. 2, 110.

15 Royall, *Southern Tour,* vol. 3, 80–81.

16 *Richmond (VA) Inquirer,* Nov. 26, 1836, citing the *Cincinnati Register,* 1833.

CHAPTER 5: ROADWAYS, 1819–1832

1 *Lancaster (PA) Journal,* Jan. 3, 1823.

2 *Baltimore Patriot,* Dec. 12, 1821

3 Blane, *An Excursion,* 82.

4 *North American Review,* Jan. 1825; Mrs. Anne Royall, *The Black Book* (Washington, DC, 1828), vol. 1, 296.

5 *Baltimore Patriot,* Sept. 6, 1822; John Loudon MacAdam, *Remarks on the Present System of Road Making,* 4th ed. (London, 1821), 35, 41, 47–48.

6 Gallatin, "Roads and Canals," 883.

7 *American State Papers, Misc., vol. 2, 798.*

8 *Washington (DC) National Intelligencer,* Aug. 10, 1822.

9 James Hall, *Letters from the West,* 55.

10 *Baltimore Patriot,* Feb. 6, 1819.

11 Blane, *An Excursion,* 86–87.

12 *American State Papers, Military Affairs,* vol. 3, 109, 139, 361–62.

13 *Washington (DC) National Intelligencer,* March 26, 1823.

14 Blane, *An Excursion,* 90–91, 104.

15 Franklin *Missouri Intelligencer,* Sept. 16, 1825.

16 Abraham Bradley Map, 1825 edition; Stoddard, *Sketches,* 192–197; William Darby, *The Emigrant's Guide to the Western and Southwestern States and Territories. . .* (New York, 1818), 44–45.

17 David Vance Map, 1825; George Douglas Brewerton, *Overland with Kit Carson* (Lincoln, NE, 1993), 183.

18 Daniel Hewett, *The American Traveller, or National Directory* . . . (Washington, DC, 1825), 60–64.

19 Duke Bernhard, *Travels, vol. 2, 156–57; American State Papers, Mil. Aff., vol. 3,* 630–31.

20 Trollope, *Domestic Manners,* 157–64.

21 Mrs. Anne Royall, *Mrs. Royall's Pennsylvania* (Washington, DC, 1829), vol. 2, 180.

22 *Vincennes (IN) Western Sun,* July 31, 1830; *American State Papers, Mil. Aff.,* vol. 4, 168, 595, 732; vol. 5, 48.

23 *American State Papers, PO,* 217–19; *Vincennes (IN) Western Sun,* Jan. 3, 1830.

24 Register of Debates, House of Representatives, 21st Cong., 1st sess. (1830), 820.

25 Much has been published about the Maysville Road. A good summary is in Daniel Walker Howe, *What Hath God Wrought* (New York: Oxford University Press, 2007), 357–59.

26 Simon A, Ferrall, *A Ramble of Six Thousand Miles through the United States* . . . (London, 1832), 232.

CHAPTER 6: STAGECOACH LINES, 1819–1832

1 *Wheeling (VA) Gazette,* Dec. 25, 1824.

2 *Washington (DC) National Intelligencer,* Sept. 5, 1818; *City of Washington Gazette,* Sept. 16, 1818.

3 *Washington (DC) National Intelligencer,* Sept. 21, 1815; *Baltimore Patriot,* May 4, 1816; June 18, 1817; Aug. 12, 1818; Sept. 14, 1819.

4 Wheeling *Virginia North-Western Gazette,* Aug. 18, 1821. *Alexandria (VA) Herald,* April 11, 1823.

5 Nicklin, *Virginia Springs,* 17–20.

6 *Hampden (MA) Patriot,* Sept. 25, 1822, citing the *Pittsburgh Mercury.*

7 Royall, *The Black Book,* vol. 1, 295–97.

8 *St. Louis Enquirer,* Sept. 19, 1820; see also the *Edwardsville (IL) Spectator,* Sept. 12, 1820.

9 Franklin *Missouri Intelligencer,* June 25, 1821, and Dec. 30, 1823.

10 Carrie M. Zimmerman, "Through Ohio in Old Tavern and Stagecoach Days," unpublished manuscript, in Tallmadge Stagecoach Records, MSS 124, Ohio Historical Society, Columbus, OH; Columbus *Ohio State Journal,* May 11, 1826.

11 Columbus *Ohio State Journal,* Dec. 6 and 19, 1827.

12 Duncan, *Travels,* vol. 2, 6–8. Coach and coach-spring advertisements are in the *New York Gazette and General Advertiser,* May 29, 1813, and March 9, 1818; the *New York Daily Advertiser,* Aug. 11, 1818; and the *City of Washington Gazette,* Nov. 29, 1819.

13 *Cincinnati Annual Advertiser,* Cincinnati, 1829.

14 *Vincennes (IN) Western Sun,* July 1, 1826. See also the coaching ads in the St. Louis *Missouri Republican,* July 18, 1825; Aug. 31, 1826; and June 3, 1828.

15 *American State Papers, PO,* 218–19.

16 *Baltimore Patriot,* July 1, 1831.

CHAPTER 7: CANALS, 1819–1832

1 *Newark (NJ) Centinel of Freedom,* Nov. 19, 1819, citing the *Utica (NY) Gazette.*

2 The literature on the Erie Canal is abundant. A readable and well-documented account is Ronald E. Shaw, *Erie Water West* (Lexington, KY, 1990). A much-quoted source is Noble E. Whitford, *History of the Canal System of the State of New York* (Albany, NY, 1906). Much of what follows is based on these two sources. Shaw gives the citations for the annual reports of the canal commissioners.

3 Jedidiah Morse, *American Gazetteer* (Boston, 1797), n.p.

4 Schultz, *Travels,* vol. 1, 10–11.

5 Gallatin, "Roads and Canals," 734–35.

6 Shaw, *Erie Water West, passim.*

7 Gallatin, "Roads and Canals," 918.

8 *Washington (DC) National Intelligencer,* Feb. 16, 1810.

9 Ibid., Dec. 12, 1811.

10 *Cooperstown (NY) Federalist,* June 27, 1812.

11 *Chillicothe (OH) Supporter,* March 12 and Dec. 24, 1816.

12 Charles G. Haines, *Considerations on the Great Western Canal,* 2nd ed. (Brooklyn, NY, 1818), 42, 46.

13 Shaw, *Erie Water West,* 91–2.

14 Duncan, *Travels,* vol. 1, 324–28; vol. 2, 11. The simple machines developed for quick removal of trees and stumps along the canal's route are described in Shaw, *Erie Water West,* 93–94.

15 John Howison, *Sketches of Upper Canada . . .* 2nd ed. (London and Edinburgh, 1822), 314-15.

16 *Cincinnati Western Spy,* Dec. 1, 1821, citing the *Utica (NY) Gazette.*

17 St. Louis *Missouri Gazette,* Jan. 9, 1822.

18 Capt. Basil Hall, *Travels in North America in the Years 1827 and 1828,* (London and Edinburgh, 1830), vol. 1, 158–59.

19 Franklin *Missouri Intelligencer,* Dec. 16 and 23, 1823. See also the Wheeling *Virginia North Western Gazette.* Oct. 24 and 31, 1823.

20 Blane, *An Excursion,* 387–94.

21 *Poughkeepsie (NY) Journal,* May 12 and June 2, 1824.

22 A. Levasseur, *Lafayette in America in 1824 and 1825* . . . (Philadelphia, 1829), vol. 2, 191–94.

23 Duke Bernhard, *Travels,* vol. 1, 61–65, 71–74.

24 Broadside, Library of Congress Collection.

25 Blane, *An Excursion,* 387.

26 Royall, *The Black Book,* vol. 1, 32–37.

27 Basil Hall, *Travels,* vol. 1, 118–20, 126–27.

28 Royall, *The Black Book,* vol. 1, 57–59.

29 Basil Hall, *Travels,* 172–74. See also, Shaw, *Erie Water West,* 124–25.

30 William Bullock, *Sketch of a Journey through the Western States of North America* (London, 1827), xxviii–xxix.

31 *American State Papers, Mil. Aff.,* vol. 2, 700. See also *North American Review,* Jan. 1827.

32 Haines, *Great Western Canal,* 13–14. See also Gallatin, "Roads and Canals," 735.

33 Cramer, *The Navigator,* 6th ed. (1808), 50.

34 See, for example, J. E. Hagerty *et al., History of the Ohio Canals* . . . (Columbus, OH, 1905). The annual reports of the canal commissioners were published separately, and often reprinted in Ohio newspapers; for example, the Ninth Annual Report is in the Chillicothe *Scioto Gazette,* Jan. 26, 1831; the Tenth Annual Report is in the Columbus *Ohio Monitor,* Jan. 16, 1832. A lengthy extract from the Eleventh Annual Report is in the *Scioto Gazette,* Feb. 6, 1833.

35 Columbus *Ohio Monitor,* Nov. 12, 1825.

36 *Vincennes (IN) Western Sun,* Aug. 6, 1825, citing the *Lancaster (PA) Eagle; Vincennes (IN) Western Sun,* Sept. 17, 1825.

37 Columbus *Ohio Monitor,* Nov. 12, 1828.

38 *Washington (DC) National Journal,* Oct. 12, 1829.

39 Joseph Suppiger Journal, in Emily Foster, ed., *The Ohio Frontier: An Anthology of Early Writings* (Lexington, KY, 1996), 171–74.

40 Columbus *Ohio Monitor,* July 5 and Sept. 3, 1828; *Chillicothe (OH) Scioto Gazette,* Jan. 26, 1831. Suppiger Journal.

41 Cramer, *The Navigator,* 8th ed. (1814), 237; *Chillicothe (OH) Scioto Gazette,* Oct. 26, Nov. 2, and Nov. 9, 1831.

42 *Chillicothe (OH) Scioto Gazette,* April 25, 1832.

43 Ibid., Aug. 22, Sept. 19, and Oct. 3, 1832; Henry S. Tanner, *A Brief Description of the Canals and Railroads of the United States* (Philadelphia, 1834), 59–60.

44 *Washington (DC) National Intelligencer,* April 16, 1835, citing the *Williamsport (MD) Banner.*

45 Duke Bernhard, *Travels,* vol. 2, 130.

46 Quotation in Shaw, *Erie Water West,* 273.

CHAPTER 8: RAILROADS, 1819–1832

1 Gallatin, "Roads and Canals," 916.

2 Charles E. Lee, "Early North-East Coast Railways," *Colliery Engineering,* June 1939.

3 Background information on Trevithick is in Walter H. Tregellas, *Cornish Worthies,* vol. 2 (London, 1884), 305–42; Samuel Smiles, *The Life of George Stephenson, Railway Engineer,* 3rd ed. (London, 1857), 58–80. See also Robert H. Thurston, *A History of the Growth of the Steam Engine,* 4th ed. (New York, 1897).

4 Gallatin, "Roads and Canals," 916.

5 John Stevens, *Documents Tending to Prove the Superior Advantages of Rail-Ways and Steam-Carriages Over Canal Navigation* (1812; repr., Tarrytown, NY, 1917).

6 Quotation in James D. Dilts, *The Great Road: The Building of the Baltimore & Ohio, the Nation's First Railroad, 1828–1853* (Stanford, CA, 1993), 83. This well-documented and well-written work is the most detailed study of the Baltimore & Ohio, and, except where noted, has provided most of the information on that railroad in the chapters that follow.

7 *North American Review,* Jan. 1827.

8 *Vincennes (IN) Western Sun,* Feb. 12, 1825.

9 *Baltimore Patriot,* Feb. 22 and May 8, 1826.

10 Dilts, *Great Road,* 36–46.

11 Blane, *An Excursion,* 375.

12 Dilts, *Great Road,* 52–54.

13 *North American Review,* July 1827.

14 *First Annual Report of the Acting Committee of the Society for the Promotion of Internal Improvement in the Commonwealth of Pennsylvania* (Philadelphia, 1826).

15 Smiles, *George Stephenson,* 182–207.

16 *Lancaster (PA) Journal,* Nov. 18 and Dec. 9, 1825; March 10, 1826; Dilts, *Great Road,* 36, 83–84.

17 Dilts, *Great Road,* 56–60.

18 *Baltimore Patriot,* Jan. 2, 1828. The advertisement itself is dated Nov. 9, 1827.

19 Dilts, *Great Road,* 58, and B&O 1831 map following 158. For more on the surveys, see *Report of the Engineers on the Reconnaissance and Surveys* (Baltimore, 1828; cited in Dilts), and Stephen H. Long, *Rail Road Manual* (Baltimore, 1829).

20 Franklin *Missouri Intelligencer,* April 18, 1828.

21 Dilts, *Great Road,* 10–11.

22 *Baltimore Patriot,* July 25 and 29, 1828; William Prescott Smith [A Citizen of Baltimore, pseud.], *A History and Description of the Baltimore and Ohio Rail Road* (Baltimore, 1853), 20–21.

23 Dilts, *Great Road,* 73–78; *Baltimore Patriot,* June 16, 1829.

24 *Baltimore Patriot,* Nov. 20, 1828.

25 Dilts, *Great Road,* 73–78. For the Long and McNeill point of view on the controversy, see Lt. Col. Stephen H. Long and Capt. William Gibbs McNeill, *Narrative of the Proceedings of the Board of Engineers of the Baltimore & Ohio Rail Road Company* . . . (Baltimore, 1830).

26 Dilts, *Great Road,* 122–28.

27 Ibid., 84–86.

28 *Baltimore Patriot,* June 16, Sept. 8, and 30, Oct. 5, 1829; Jan. 23, 1830. See also the Columbus *Ohio Monitor,* April 8, 1829; Dilts, *Great Road,* 72–73.

29 Dilts, *Great Road,* 127–29.

30 Ibid., 80.

31 James Boardman [A Citizen of the World, pseud.], *America, and the Americans* (London, 1833), 261–62.

32 Dilts, *Great Road,* 73; B&O Third Annual Report, in the *Baltimore Patriot,* Oct. 12, 1829. The company's annual reports (or substantial extracts thereof) were sometimes published in local papers. For example, the Eighth Annual Report is in the *Baltimore Patriot,* Oct. 13, 1834; the Ninth is in the *Washington (DC) United States Telegraph,* Oct. 16, 1835; and the Tenth is in the *Washington (DC) National Intelligencer,* Oct. 11, 1836.

33 *Baltimore Patriot,* Jul. 6 and Oct. 12, 1830; *Louisville Public Advertiser,* Jan. 20, 1830, citing the *Cincinnati Advertiser.*

34 *Baltimore Patriot,* Feb. 13, 1830.

35 Ibid., May 20, 24, and 27, 1830.

36 Ibid., June 17 and 30, 1830; quotation from the B&O Fourth Annual Report, Appendix, in J. Snowden Bell, *The Early Motive Power of the Baltimore & Ohio Railroad* (New York, 1912), 5.

37 Some of the English patents are shown in the *London Journal of Arts and Sciences,* 1822–1827. Winans's Patent X5247 of Oct. 11, 1828; Finlay's Patent X5691 of Oct. 27, 1829. Other patents in the field, some of which preceded (and did not survive) the Patent Office fire of 1836, are given in Burke, *List of Patents for Inventions,* 212–15; Dilts, *Great Road,* 70–71. *Baltimore Patriot,* Jan. 23, 1830; Columbus *Ohio Monitor,* April 28, May 12 and 26, 1830.

38 *Baltimore Patriot,* Sept. 3, 1830.

39 Ibid., Dec. 17, 1830. See also the *Louisville Advertiser,* Dec. 11, 1830.

40 *Baltimore Patriot,* Feb. 22, 1826.

41 Ibid., Oct. 28 and Nov. 15, 1830.

42 Ibid., Feb. 8 and May 10, 1831.

43 Ibid., March 14 and 21, 1831.

44 Dilts, *Great Road,* 137–39. *Baltimore Patriot,* July 2, 1831.

45 Dilts, *Great Road,* 146–48.

46 Charleston *Virginia Free Press and Farmer's Repository,* Dec. 8, 1831.

47 B&O Fifth Annual Report, in the *Washington (DC) Globe,* Oct. 12, 1831.

48 John B. Wyeth, *Oregon; or a Short History of a Long Journey* . . . (Cambridge, 1833), in Thwaites, *Early Western Travels,* 35.

PART 3, 1832–1843

1 A. A. Parker, *Trip to the West and Texas* . . . , 2nd ed. (Boston, 1836), 28–31.

2 Quotation in Dilts, *Great Road,* 282–83.

3 John Mason Peck, *A New Guide for Emigrants to the West* . . . (Boston, 1836), v.

CHAPTER 9: WATERWAYS, 1832–1843

1 Abraham Lincoln speech, *Sangamo (IL) Journal,* March 9, 1832.

2 *American State Papers, Mil. Aff.,* vol. 3, 631; vol. 4, 167–68, 595, 731, 735–36.

3 Margaret Jean Furrh, "Henry Miller Shreve: His Contributions to Navigation on the Western Rivers of the United States" (master's thesis, Texas Tech University, Lubbock, TX, 1971), 12–22.

4 Shreve's Patent 913 of Sept. 12, 1838. *American State Papers, Mil. Aff.,* vol. 5, 47, 187; vol. 6, 888–90; vol. 7, 683–84.

5 Thomas Hamilton, *Men and Manners in America,* (London and Edinburgh, 1833), vol. 2, 167.

6 *Charleston (SC) Southern Patriot,* May 2, 1843, citing the *Cincinnati Gazette.*

7 *Baltimore Patriot,* Sept. 1, 1834, citing the *Wheeling (VA) Times.*

8 Indianapolis *Indiana Journal,* Oct. 17, 1834, citing the *Lawrenceburg (IN) Palladium.*

9 Charles Augustus Murray, *Travels in North America During the Years 1834, 1835 & 1836* . . . , vol. 2, 96.

10 Baltimore *Maryland Sun,* Nov. 4, 1839, citing the *Wheeling (VA) Times.* Another keelboat reference is in the issue of Sept. 23, 1840.

11 *Houston Telegraph,* March 10 and April 7, 1838; *Sing-Sing (NY) Hudson River Chronicle,* April 7, 1840.

12 [Robert Baird], *View of the Valley of the Mississippi* . . . 2nd ed. (Philadelphia, 1834), 349-66; Peck, *New Guide for Emigrants,* 364–74.

CHAPTER 10: ROADWAYS, 1832–1843

1 Henry S. Tanner Map, 1829. See also the David Vance Map of 1825.

2 *American State Papers, Public Lands,* vol. 6, 253–58. Indianapolis *Indiana Journal,* March 17, 1832.

3 See, for example, Robert F. Hunter, "Turnpike Construction in Western Virginia," *Technology and Culture,* Spring, 1963. An interesting sidelight is Douglas Young, *A Brief History of the Staunton and James River Turnpike* (Charlottesville, VA, 1975; rev. 2003).

4 Tyrone Power, *Impressions of America; During the Years 1833, 1834, and 1835* (London, 1836), 331–32.

5 Prince Maximilian, *Travels in the Interior of North America,* pt. 3, in Thwaites, *Early Western Travels,* 152.

6 *American State Papers, Mil. Aff.,* vol. 4, 168, 595, 732; vol. 5, 188–89, 391, 415–18, 699–703; vol. 6, 896–900. The size of the stone continued to be a matter of debate; Gillespie's *Manual of the Principles and Practice of Road-Making* (2nd ed., 1848, and 3rd ed., 1850), after quoting MacAdam at length, said: "The stone should be broken into pieces, which are as nearly cubical as possible, (rejecting splinters and slices) and the largest of which, in its longest dimensions, can pass through a ring two and a half inches in diameter. In reducing them to this size, there will of course be many smaller stones in the mass. These are the proper dimensions, according to Telford and Parnell. Edgeworth prefers 1-1/2 inches. Penfold names two inches for brittle materials. If smaller they would crush too easily; but on the other hand, the less the size of the fragments, the smaller are the interstices exposed to be filled with water and mud. The tougher the stone, the smaller it may be broken. The less its size, the sooner will it make a hard road; and for roads little travelled, and over which only light weights pass, the stones may be reduced to the size of one inch."

7 *A Narrative of the Life of David Crockett . . . Written by Himself* (Philadelphia and Boston, 1834); pt. 2: *Col. Crockett's Exploits and Adventures in Texas . . . Written by Himself* (Philadelphia, 1837), 85–88. While the specifics of the quotation may be open to question, Crockett definitely disliked Van Buren.

8 Mary Reed Eastman Diary, in Ierley, *Traveling the National Road,* 115–20.

9 *American State Papers, Mil. Aff.,* 700–701.

10 [Edmund Flagg], *The Far West, or a Tour Beyond the Mountains,* 2 vols. (New York, 1838), vol. 1, in Thwaites, *Early Western Travels,* 359–60.

11 *American State Papers, Mil. Aff.,* vol. 6, 898.

12 Frederick Hall, *Letters from the East and from the West* (Washington and Baltimore, 1840), 55–58.

13 *American State Papers, Mil. Aff.,* vol. 7, 701–9. Interesting items on the National Road are in the *St. Louis Commercial Bulletin,* Feb. 1, 1838, and in the Indianapolis *Indiana Journal,* May 12, 1838; June 29, 1839; and June 20, 1840.

14 Quotation in Searight, *The Old Pike,* 142.

15 *American State Papers, Mil. Aff.,* vol. 6, 899–900, vol. 7, 698–99; Ierley, *Traveling the National Road* 46–47, 105; David Henshaw, *Letters on the Internal Improvements and Commerce of the West* (Boston, 1839), 8–9.

Chapter 11: Stagecoach Lines, 1832–1843

1 *Washington (DC) National Intelligencer,* Jan. 21, 1832.

2 *Washington (DC) Globe,* July 26, 1833.

3 *Washington (DC) National Intelligencer,* Aug. 24, 1832; *Washington (DC) Globe,* Aug. 30, 1832; Royall, *Southern Tour,* vol. 3, 1, 12.

4 Dozens upon dozens of stagecoach routes are listed in *An Accompaniment to Mitchell's Reference and Distance Map of the United States* (Philadelphia, 1834 and 1835). See also Mitchell's *Principal Stage, Steam-Boat, and Canal Routes in the United States* (Philadelphia, 1834).

5 Hamilton, *Men and Manners,* vol. 2, 161–64.

6 Arfwedson, *United States and Canada,* vol. 2, 145–46.

7 Columbus *Ohio State Journal,* Sept. 17, 1836.

8 Tallmadge Stagecoach Records, MSS 124, Ohio Historical Society, Columbus, OH.

9 Parker, *Trip to the West,* 35–39.

10 *Baltimore Patriot,* Aug. 9, 1834.

11 *Washington (DC) National Intelligencer,* Feb. 7, 1834. An interesting letter on a fight between Comanches and a party of Texans that included James and Rezin Bowie is in the Sept. 26, 1833 issue.

12 Hamilton, *Men and Manners, vol.* 2, 175–76.

13 Baron de Berenger, *Helps and Hints: How to Protect Life and Property* (London, 1835), 126–28; Norm Flayderman, *The Bowie Knife: Unsheathing an American Legend* (Lincoln, RI, 2004), *passim.*

14 *Washington (DC) National Intelligencer,* Feb. 3, 1824; March 31, 1832; and June 16, 1836; *New York Herald,* Feb. 16 and May 21, 1836; *Baltimore Patriot,* April 21, 1834; *Louisville Daily Journal,* Jan. 15, 1841.

15 *Baltimore Patriot,* May 17, 1834. See also the *Uniontown (PA) Genius of Liberty,* Sept. 1, 1842.

16 Power, *Impressions of America,* 334–36.

17 W. M. Knight letter, VFM 2265, Ohio Historical Society, Columbus, OH.

18 Baltimore *Maryland Sun,* August 10, 1837.

19 *Louisville Daily Journal,* Jan. 15, 1841; Philadelphia *Pennsylvania Inquirer and Courier,* Oct. 20, 1837, and Sept. 26, 1838. See also the Baltimore *Maryland Sun,* Aug. 13, 1840; quotation in Searight, *The Old Pike,* 149, 181.

20 *Journal of the Illinois State Historical Society,* Summer, 2002; *Milwaukie Journal,* Feb. 2, 1842; *Milwaukie Sentinel,* July 2, 1842.

21 *Washington (DC) Globe,* July 16, 1831.

22 *Washington (DC) National Intelligencer,* Oct. 25, 1833; *Philadelphia North American,* April 13, 1839; *New York Spectator,* April 15 and Sept. 9, 1839; *Cleveland Herald.* May 26, 1841; *New York Herald,* Aug. 7, 1842.

23 See, for example, the following U.S. patents: Melish's X9315 of 1836; Croasdale's 116 of 1837; Patton's 569 of 1838; Shriver's 1399 of 1839. Others are given in Burke, *List of Patents for Inventions,* 208, 210–11. See also the illustrations in Holmes and Rohrbach, *Stagecoach East.*

24 *Cleveland Herald,* May 26, 1841.

25 *New York Herald,* July 23, 1842, and Nov. 22, 1844.

CHAPTER 12: CANALS, 1832–1843

1 Baird, *Valley of the Mississippi,* 349–57; Peck, *New Guide for Emigrants,* 364–72.

2 Arfwedson, *United States and Canada,* vol. 2, 277–307. See also Parker, *Trip to the West,* 16–25.

3 Power, *Impressions of America,* 411–17.

4 Harriet Martineau, *Retrospect of Western Travel* (New York, 1838), vol. 1, 62–63.

5 A Citizen of Edinburgh, *Journal of an Excursion to the United States and Canada in the Year 1834* (Edinburgh, 1835), 70–86.

6 Quotation in Shaw, *Erie Water West,* 241.

7 Henry S. Tanner, *A Description of the Canals and Railroads of the United States* (New York, 1840), 51–52.

8 Edward Abdy, *Journal of a Residence and Tour in the United States . . .* (London, 1835), vol. 3, 85–86; Prince Maximilian, *Travels in the Interior,* vol. 3, 146–58; *Louisville Daily Journal,* March 22, 1837.

9 Prince Maximilian, *Travels in the Interior,* vol. 3, 146–58.

10 *Newark (OH) Advocate,* Sept. 29, 1838, and April 13, 1839.

11 Tanner, *A Description of the Canals and Railroads* (1840), 158–59; Dilts, *Great Road,* 29–34.

12 *Washington (DC) National Intelligencer,* June 21, 1823, citing the *Baltimore American.*

13 Dilts, *Great Road,* 33.

14 *Washington (DC) National Intelligencer,* Nov. 7, 1829.

15 Ibid., March 5 and Oct. 4, 1830.

16 Ibid., Dec. 28, 1830.

17 Trollope, *Domestic Manners,* 137, 233.

18 Dilts, *Great Road,* 100–21.

19 *Washington (DC) Globe,* Nov. 19, 1833, citing the *Frederick (MD) Times.*

20 *Washington (DC) National Intelligencer,* Nov. 7, 1833.

CHAPTER 13: RAILROADS, 1832–1843

1 Columbus *Ohio State Journal,* Feb. 8, 1832.

2 Dilts, *Great Road,* 196–97, 201; Thomas Earle, *A Treatise on Rail-Roads and Internal Communications* (Philadelphia, 1830).

3 Earle, *Treatise on Rail-Roads,* 62–68; London *Mechanics' Magazine,* issues of Oct. 10, 17, 24, and 31, 1829; Dilts, *Great Road,* 87–90; *Baltimore Patriot,* Feb. 13, 1830.

4 Dilts, *Great Road,* 90–97. The Baltimore & Ohio experimented briefly with a wind-powered "sail car" in 1830.

5 *Baltimore Patriot,* Aug. 26, 1830; Bell, *Early Motive Power,* 5–8; William H. Brown, *History of the First Locomotives in America* (New York, 1871), 107–122; Dilts, *Great Road,* 94. Cooper's relevant patents are X5086 of April 28, 1828, and X6796 of Oct. 13, 1831.

6 *Baltimore Patriot,* Jan. 10 and Feb. 21, 1831; Bell, *Early Motive Power,* 13–15; Brown, *First Locomotives,* 137–140.

7 Dilts, *Great Road,* 97–99.

8 *New York Herald,* Aug. 4, 1830; *Cooperstown (NY) Watchtower,* Aug. 1, 1831; *Ithaca (NY) Journal,* Aug. 17, 1831; *Albany Argus,* quoted in Brown, *First Locomotives,* 176–187.

9 Dilts, *Great Road*, 99; Bell, *Early Motive Power*, 17–20.

10 Hamilton, *Men and Manners*, vol. 2, 157.

11 Arfwedson, *United States and Canada*, vol. 2, 147–48; *Accompaniment to Mitchell's Reference Map* (1834), 251.

12 Bell, *Early Motive Power* 17–20; Dilts, *Great Road*, 196; B&O Eighth Annual Report, in the *Baltimore Patriot*, Oct. 13, 1834. The Arabian's ascent of the ridge is in the *Patriot*, Dec. 3, 1834.

13 Royall, *The Black Book*, vol. 1, 281–82.

14 Dilts, *Great Road*, 159–84; *Baltimore Patriot*, Feb. 22, 1826.

15 The *American Railroad Journal* and Latrobe quotations are in Bell, *Early Motive Power*, 2–3.

16 Smith, *History and Description of the Baltimore and Ohio*, 47, 55–63; Dilts, *Great Road*, 259–64.

17 Dilts, *Great Road*, 237–38; Winans's Patent 305 of July 29, 1837; Bell, *Early Motive Power*, 22–30.

18 Henshaw, *Letters*, 6.

19 *Washington (DC) National Intelligencer*, April 8, 16, and 21, 1835; Dilts, *Great Road*, 265–68, 277–78, 354–55, 443.

CHAPTER 14: CANAL AND RAILROAD PARTNERSHIPS, 1832–1843

1 *New York Spectator*, June 10, 1833.

2 Arfwedson, *United States and Canada*, vol. 2, 261.

3 Tanner, *A Description of the Canals and Railroads* (1840), 70–80.

4 Arfwedson, *United States and Canada*, vol. 2, 262–63.

5 Power, *Impressions of America*, 421.

6 Joshua Toulmin Smith, *Journal in America, 1837–38,* ed. Floyd B. Streeter (Metuchen, NJ, 1925), 11–15.

7 *Lancaster (PA) Journal,* Jan. 7 and 14, 1831; Dec. 7 and 21, 1832; Oct. 10, 1834; Tanner, *A Brief Description of the Canals and Railroads* (1834), 21–26; Tanner, *A Description of the Canals and Railroads* (1840), 95–98, 113–124; Dilts, *Great Road*, 26–28.

8 Power, *Impressions of America*, 291.

9 Baird, *Valley of the Mississippi*, 353–55.

10 *Baltimore Patriot*, May 21, 1834.

11 Murray, *Travels in North America*, vol. 1, 186–94. See also Harriet Martineau, *Society in America* (New York and London, 1837), vol. 2, 15–20.

12 [David Crockett], *An Account of Col. Crockett's Tour to the North and Down East . . . Written by Himself* (Philadelphia, 1835), 15–16, 35–36.

13 Brown, *History of the First Locomotives,* 141–58.

14 Martineau, *Society in America*, vol. 2, 8.

15 Patents for spark arresters are in Burke, *List of Patents for Inventions*, 154–55; Tanner, *A Description of the Canals and Railroads* (1840), 113–14, 124–25.

16 Tanner, *A Brief Description of the Canals and Railroads* (1834), 17, 19–20; Tanner, *A Description of the Canals and Railroads* (1840), 85–90.

17 Tanner, *A Description of the Canals and Railroads* (1840), 132–46.

18 Henry S. Tanner, *Memoir on the Recent Surveys, Observations, and Internal Improvements in the United States* (Philadelphia, 1830), 51–52; *Accompaniment to Mitchell's Reference Map* (1834), 259–60; Tanner, *A Description of the Canals and Railroads* (1840), 160–61; Wayland Fuller Dunaway, *History of the James River and Kanawha Company* (New York, 1922), 92–132.

19 Dilts, *Great Road,* 190–91; *Baltimore Patriot,* Oct. 13, 1834; *Charleston (VA) Free Press,* Nov. 26, 1835; March 3 and April 7, 1836; *American State Papers, Mil. Aff.,* vol. 5, 345.

CHAPTER 15: RAILROADS WEST OF THE MOUNTAINS, 1832–1843

1 Tanner, *A Description of the Canals and Railroads* (1840), 193.

2 *New York Spectator,* Oct. 17, 1833. Some of the information that follows is based on Edward Eyre Hunt, "The Story of a Pioneer Railroad (the Mad River & Lake Erie, 1832-1857)," unpublished manuscript, Ohio Historical Society, Columbus, OH.

3 *New York Spectator,* Oct. 8, 1835, citing the *Buffalo Commercial Advertiser; Cleveland Herald,* Sept. 25, 1835.

4 *New Orleans Commercial Bulletin,* Oct. 29, 1835.

5 *New York Spectator.* Oct. 26, 1837; Hunt, "Pioneer Railroad."

6 *Cleveland Daily Herald & Gazette,* May 22, 1838. See also the April 9, 1839 issue.

7 *Sandusky (OH) Clarion,* April 30 and Oct. 16, 1841; *Cleveland Herald,* May 4, 1841, and Feb. 7, 1845; Columbus *Ohio State Journal,* Oct. 27, 1841; *Tiffin (OH) Gazette,* Dec. 30, 1841.

8 *Cleveland Herald,* Nov. 12, 1841; *New York Spectator,* Dec. 25, 1841.

9 *Cleveland Herald,* Aug. 21, 1844.

10 *Chillicothe (OH) Scioto Gazette,* Aug. 30, 1848; *Washington (DC) National Intelligencer,* Sept. 7, 1848, and Dec. 20, 1852.

CONCLUSION

1 *Washington (DC) National Journal,* Dec. 10, 1829. See also the *United States Telegraph,* Dec. 10, 1829, and, for an earlier ride, the *Baltimore Patriot,* Dec. 8, 1821.

2 *Galveston (TX) Civilian & City Gazette,* Feb. 8, 1843.

3 "First Emigrant Train to California," *Century Magazine,* Nov. 1890.

BIBLIOGRAPHY

PRIMARY SOURCES

Abdy, Edward. *Journal of a Residence and Tour in the United States* . . . 3 vols. London: 1835.

An Accompaniment to Mitchell's Reference and Distance Map of the United States. Philadelphia: 1834 and 1835.

American State Papers, Military Affairs. 7 vols. Washington, DC: 1832–61.

American State Papers, Miscellaneous. 2 vols. Washington, DC: 1834.

American State Papers, Post Office. Washington, DC: 1834.

Amphlett, William. *The Emigrant's Directory to the Western States of North America.* London: 1819.

Arfwedson, Carl D. *The United States and Canada in 1832, 1833, and 1834.* 2 vols. London: 1834.

Ashe, Thomas. *Travels in America, Performed in 1806* . . . 3 vols. London: 1808.

[Baird, Robert]. *View of the Valley of the Mississippi* . . . 2nd ed. Philadelphia: 1834.

Beck, Lewis C. *A Gazetteer of the States of Illinois and Missouri.* Albany, NY: 1823.

Berenger, Baron de. *Helps and Hints: How to Protect Life and Property.* London: 1835.

Bernhard, Duke, of Saxe-Weimar. *Travels through North America, During the Years 1825 and 1826.* 2 vols. Philadelphia: 1828.

Birkbeck, Morris. *Notes on a Journey in America.* 4th ed. London: 1818.

[Blane, William N.] *An Excursion through the United States and Canada* . . . . London: 1824.

Breck, Samuel. *Sketch of the Internal Improvements Already Made by Pennsylvania.* 2nd ed. Philadelphia: 1818.

Bullock, William. *Sketch of a Journey through the Western States of North America.* London: 1827.

Burke, Edmund, comp. *List of Patents for Inventions and Designs . . . from 1790 to 1847*. Washington, DC: 1847.

A Citizen of Baltimore [William Prescott Smith]. *A History and Description of the Baltimore and Ohio Rail Road*. Baltimore: 1853.

A Citizen of Edinburgh. *Journal of an Excursion to the United States and Canada in the Year 1834*. Edinburgh: 1835.

A Citizen of the World [James Boardman]. *America, and the Americans*. London: 1833.

Cramer, Zadok. *The Navigator*. 6th ed. Pittsburgh: 1808; 8th ed. Pittsburgh: 1814.

[Crockett, David]. *An Account of Col. Crockett's Tour to the North and Down East . . . Written by Himself*. Philadelphia: 1835.

———. *A Narrative of the Life of David Crockett . . . Written by Himself*. Philadelphia and Boston: 1834.

Cumings, Samuel. *The Western Pilot . . .* Cincinnati: 1829.

Darby, William. *The Emigrant's Guide to the Western and Southwestern States and Territories . . .* New York: 1818.

Duncan, John M. *Travels through Part of the United States and Canada in 1818 and 1819*. 2 vols. Glasgow: 1823.

Earle, Thomas. *A Treatise on Rail-Roads and Internal Communications*. Philadelphia: 1830.

Fairbairn, Henry. *A Treatise on the Political Economy of Railroads*. London: 1836.

Fearon, Henry Bradshaw. *Sketches of America: Narrative of a Journey of Five Thousand Miles . . .* 3rd ed. London: 1819.

Felton, William. *A Treatise on Carriages . . .* London: 1794.

Ferrall, Simon A. *A Ramble of Six Thousand Miles through the United States . . .* London: 1832.

First Annual Report of the Acting Committee of the Society for the Promotion of Internal Improvement in the Commonwealth of Pennsylvania. Philadelphia: 1826.

Flint, Timothy. *Recollections of the Last Ten Years*. Boston: 1826.

Fordham, Elias P. *Personal Narrative of Travels . . .* Edited by Frederic Austin Ogg. Cleveland: 1906.

Gillespie, William M. *A Manual of the Principles and Practice of Road-Making . . .* 2nd ed. New York: 1848; 3rd ed. New York: 1850.

Haines, Charles G. *Considerations on the Great Western Canal . . .* 2nd ed. Brooklyn, NY: 1818.

Hall, Capt. Basil. *Travels in North America in the Years 1827 and 1828*. 2nd ed., 3 vols. London and Edinburgh: 1830.

Hall, Frederick. *Letters from the East and from the West.* Washington and Baltimore: 1840.

Hall, Judge James. *Letters from the West* . . . London: 1828.

Hamilton, Thomas. *Men and Manners in America.* 2 vols. London and Edinburgh: 1833.

Harris, William Tell. *Remarks Made During a Tour through the United States* . . . London: 1821.

Hebert, Luke. *A Practical Treatise on Rail-Roads and Locomotive Engines* . . . London: 1837.

Hewett, Daniel. *The American Traveller, or National Directory* . . . Washington, DC: 1825.

Howison, John. *Sketches of Upper Canada, Domestic, Local, and Characteristic* . . . 2nd ed. London and Edinburgh: 1822.

Howitt, E[manuel]. *Selections from Letters Written During a Tour through the United States.* Nottingham, England: 1820.

Kilbourn, John. *The Ohio Gazetteer, or Topographical Dictionary,* 6th ed. Columbus: 1819.

LeCount, Lt. Peter. *A Practical Treatise on Railways* . . . Edinburgh, 1839.

Levasseur, A. *Lafayette in America in 1824 and 1825* . . . Translated by John D. Godman, M.D. 2 vols. Philadelphia: 1829.

Long, Lt. Col. Stephen H., and Capt. William Gibbs McNeill. *Narrative of the Proceedings of the Board of Engineers of the Baltimore and Ohio Rail Road Company* . . . Baltimore: 1830.

Martineau, Harriet. *Retrospect of Western Travel.* 2 vols. New York: 1838.

——. *Society in America.* 2 vols. New York and London: 1837.

Morse, Jedidiah. *American Gazetteer.* Boston: 1797.

Murray, Charles Augustus. *Travels in North America During the Years 1834, 1835, & 1836* . . . 2 vols. London: 1839.

Nicklin, Philip H. [Peregrine Prolix, pseud.]. *Letters Descriptive of the Virginia Springs* . . . 2nd ed. Philadelphia: 1837.

Pambour, Comte F[rancois] M. G. de, *A Practical Treatise on Locomotive Engines* . . . 2nd ed. London: 1840).

Parker, A. A. *Trip to the West and Texas* . . . 2nd ed. Boston: 1836.

Peck, John Mason. *A New Guide for Emigrants to the West* . . . Boston: 1836.

Power, Tyrone. *Impressions of America; During the Years 1833, 1834, and 1835.* London: 1836.

The Principal Stage, Steam-Boat, and Canal Routes in the United States, Philadelphia: 1834.

Royall, Mrs. Anne. *The Black Book.* 2 vols. Washington, DC: 1828.

——. *Mrs. Royall's Pennsylvania.* 2 vols. Washington, DC: 1829.

——. *Mrs. Royall's Southern Tour.* 3 vols. Washington, DC: 1830–31.

Schoolcraft, Henry. A *View of the Lead Mines of Missouri.* New York: 1819.

Schultz, Christian, Jr. *Travels on an Inland Voyage* . . . 2 vols. New York: 1810.

Smith, Joshua Toulmin. *Journal in America, 1837–38.* Edited by Floyd B. Streeter. Metuchen, NJ: 1925.

Stevens, John. *Documents Tending to Prove the Superior Advantages of Rail-Ways and Steam-Carriages Over Canal Navigation.* New York: 1812.

Stoddard, Major Amos. *Sketches, Historical and Descriptive, of Louisiana.* Philadelphia: 1812.

Tanner, Henry Schenck. *A Brief Description of the Canals and Railroads of the United States.* Philadelphia: 1834.

——. *A Description of the Canals and Railroads of the United States.* New York: 1840.

——. *Memoir on the Recent Surveys, Observations, and Internal Improvements in the United States.* Philadelphia: 1829 and 1830.

Thomas, David. *Travels through the Western Country in the Summer of 1816.* Auburn, NY: 1819.

Thwaites, Reuben Gold, ed. *Early Western Travels, 1748–1846.* 32 vols. Cleveland: 1904–07.

Tocqueville, Alexis de. *Democracy in America.* Edited by Richard D. Heffner. New York: 1956.

Tredgold, Thomas. *A Practical Treatise on Rail-Roads and Carriages* . . . London and New York: 1825.

Trollope, Frances. *Domestic Manners of the Americans.* New York and London: 1832.

Wood, Nicholas. *A Practical Treatise on Rail-Roads and Interior Communication in General.* London: 1825.

SECONDARY SOURCES

Bell, J. Snowden. *The Early Motive Power of the Baltimore and Ohio Railroad.* New York: 1912.

Brown, William H. *History of the First Locomotives in America.* New York: 1871.

Dilts, James D. *The Great Road: The Building of the Baltimore & Ohio, the Nation's First Railroad, 1828–1853.* Stanford, CA: 1993.

Dunaway, Wayland Fuller. *History of the James River and Kanawha Company.* New York: 1922.

Dunbar, Seymour. *A History of Travel in America.* 4 vols. Indianapolis: 1915.

Flayderman, Norm. *Flayderman's Guide to Antique American Firearms.* 8th ed. Iola, WI: 2001.

——. *The Bowie Knife: Unsheathing an American Legend.* Lincoln, RI: 2004.

Hicks, John D. *The Federal Union,* 4th ed. Cambridge, MA: 1964.

Holmes, Oliver W., and Peter T. Rohrbach. *Stagecoach East.* Washington, DC: 1983.

[Huntington, C. C., and C. P. McClelland,] *A History of the Ohio Canals . . .* Columbus: 1905.

Ierley, Merritt: *Traveling the National Road.* Woodstock, NY: 1990.

Rouse, Parke, Jr. *The Great Wagon Road.* Petersburg, VA: 1992.

Searight, Thomas B. *The Old Pike.* Uniontown, PA: 1894.

Shaw, Ronald E. *Erie Water West.* Lexington, KY: 1990.

Shumway, George, et al. *The Conestoga Wagon, 1750–1850.* York, PA: 1964.

Smiles, Samuel. *The Life of George Stephenson, Railway Engineer.* 3rd ed. London: 1857.

Smiles, Samuel. *Lives of the Engineers . . . History of Roads.* London: 1904.

Thurston, Robert H. *A History of the Growth of the Steam Engine,* 4th ed. New York: 1897.

Whitford, Noble E. *History of the Canal System of the State of New York.* Albany, NY: 1906.

NEWSPAPERS

Among the more important newspapers used for this book were:

National Intelligencer. Washington, DC, 1804–1844

Baltimore Patriot. Baltimore, MD, 1812–1834

Scioto Gazette. Chillicothe, OH, 1806–1840

Ohio Monitor. Columbus, OH, 1816–1832

Western Sun. Vincennes, IN, 1824–1832

INDEX

Acknowledgments

Among those who rendered signal assistance in the completion of this work are Dr. William F. Deverell Jr., James D. Dilts, Karen Saxen Garavaglia, Michael J. Garavaglia Jr. (C.E.), Pat Medert, Earleena Tressler, Donna Wasileski, and Chuck Worman.

To Mike and Mary Anne Garavaglia, Carol Hoey Pritchard, and Randy Martin, who gave me quiet places to write when I most needed them, my sincere thanks.

Repeated thanks to Sam Bardwell, my long-time friend and business associate, for favors and accommodations beyond measure.